D0906476

German Nationalism and the European Response 1890–1945

German Nationalism

and the European Response, 1890–1945

Edited by

Carole Fink, Isabel V. Hull, and MacGregor Knox

279171

CONNETQUOT PUBLIC LIBRARY
760 OCEAN AVENUE
BOHEMIA, NEW YORK 11716

University of Oklahoma Press : Norman and London

Library of Congress Cataloging in Publication Data

Main entry under title:

German nationalism and the European response, 1890-1945.

Includes bibliographical references and index.
1. Germany—Politics and government—1871-1933—Addresses, essays, lectures. 2. Germany—Politics and government—1933-1945—Addresses, essays, lectures. 3. Nationalism—Germany—Addresses, essays, lectures. 4. Germany—Foreign relations—Europe—Addresses, essays, lectures. 5. Europe—Foreign relations—Germany—Addresses, essays, lectures. I. Fink, Carole. II. Hull, Isabel V. III. Knox, MacGregor.
DD221.G39   1985   943.08   85-1201
ISBN 0-8061-1946-2 (alk. paper)

The paper in this book meets the guidelines for permanence and durability of the Committee on Production Guidelines for Book Longevity of the Council on Library Resources, Inc.

Copyright © 1985 by the University of Oklahoma Press, Norman, Publishing Division of the University. Manufactured in the U.S.A. First edition.

To Hans W. Gatzke
Scholar, Teacher, and Friend

Contents

Maps

Editors' Preface

This collection of articles analyzes Germany's difficult relations with its neighbors during the violent half century between 1890 and 1945. Germany's internal conflicts and its intolerant, expansionist nationalism ultimately destroyed Bismarck's Reich and reduced to the plaything of the superpowers the continent it sought to dominate. Until recently work in German history has concentrated on the captured German documents and, using traditional methods, has focused almost exclusively on Germany itself. This book seeks to broaden the analysis of German nationalism by employing new historical approaches, examining the records of Germany's neighbors, and probing how the Reich's grasp for hegemony affected the other European powers.

The first three articles present three manifestations of German nationalism: in the Wilhelmian Reich, the unloved Weimar Republic, and the ascendant Nazi state. Subsequent articles consider the international context: thorny Russo-German dynastic relations before 1914, the Allies' failure to establish a postwar security system and the Russo-German Entente of 1922, French appeasement policies during the 1920s, German Jewish reactions to Nazi racism, the class ramifications of British policies toward Hitler, and the reasons why, despite the German example, Mussolini's "parallel war" of 1940 was a dismal failure. The concluding article honors Hans W. Gatzke, of Yale University, to whom this book is dedicated. Gatzke's career epitomizes the links between Germany and the United States and the development of a critical historical scholarship on the German question. Treating new subjects, such as monarchical ritual and France's economic diplomacy, and examining in a new light familiar ones such as German rearmament and British appeasement, this book aims at a broad and penetrating study of Germany's nationalism and its neighbors' responses.

We thank the contributors for their dedication and patience; Doris Radford Morris, of the University of Oklahoma Press, for her skillful editing; William Harris, Professor of Earth Sciences in the University of North Carolina at Wilmington, for drafting the maps; and the University of North Carolina at Wilmington for its assistance.

Wilmington, North Carolina   CAROLE FINK
Ithaca, New York   ISABEL V. HULL
Rochester, New York   MACGREGOR KNOX

Abbreviations Used in the Footnotes

ACS	Archivio Centrale dello Stato, Rome
ADAP	*Akten zur deutschen auswärtigen Politik, 1918-1945* (Baden Baden and Göttingen, 1950–)
Adm	Great Britain, Admiralty, Public Record Office, London
AHR	*American Historical Review*
AN	Archives Nationales, Paris
BA	Bundesarchiv, Koblenz
BA/MA	Bundesarchiv-Militärarchiv, Freiburg im Breisgau
BGSA	Bayerisches Geheimes Staatsarchiv, Munich
Cab	Great Britain, Cabinet Papers, Public Record Office, London
CAE 13	France, Chambre des Deputés, Commission des Affaires Étrangères, 13e Législature
CEH	*Central European History*
CID	Great Britain, Committee of Imperial Defence, Public Record Office, London
CSDN	France, Conseil Supérieur de la Defénse Nationale
DBFP	*Documents on British Foreign Policy, 1919-1939* (London, 1947–)
DDF	*Documents diplomatiques français, 1871-1914,* 40 vols. (Paris, 1929-59) *Documents diplomatiques français, 1932-1939,* (Paris, 1963–)
DDI	*I documenti diplomatici italiani* (Rome, 1952–)
DRC	Great Britain, Defence Requirements Committee, Public Record Office, London

DZA	Deutsches Zentralarchiv, Potsdam
EHR	*English Historical Review*
FO	Great Britain, Foreign Office, Public Record Office, London
FRUS	*Foreign Relations of the United States* (Washington, D.C., 1861–)
FzBPG	*Forschungen zur Brandenburg-Preussischen Geschichte*
GFM	German Foreign Ministry, Microfilmed Records Series T-120
GP	*Die Grosse Politik der Europäischen Kabinette, 1871–1914,* 40 vols. (Berlin, 1922–27)
GWU	*Geschichte in Wissenschaft und Unterricht*
HHStA	Haus- Hof- und Staatsarchiv, Vienna
HJ	*Historical Journal*
HP	*The Holstein Papers,* 4 vols. (Cambridge, 1955–63)
HZ	*Historische Zeitschrift*
IMT, *TMWC*	International Military Tribunal, *Trial of the Major War Criminals* 42 vols. (Nuremberg, 1947–49)
IZ	Institut für Zeitgeschichte, Munich
JCEA	*Journal of Central European Affairs*
JCH	*Journal of Contemporary History*
JMH	*Journal of Modern History*
LGP	Lloyd George Papers, Archives of the British House of Lords, London
MAE(B)	Ministère des Affaires Étrangères et du Commerce Extérieur, Brussels
MAE(F)	Ministère des Affaires Étrangères, Paris
MAE(I)	Ministero degli Affari Esteri, Rome
NARS	National Archives and Records Service, Washington, D.C., German Military and Government Records cited by microcopy, roll, and frame numbers
OKH	Oberkommando des Heeres (German High Command)
ÖKra	Österreichisches Kriegsarchiv, Vienna
PA	Politisches Archiv des Auswärtigen Amts, Bonn

PAM	France, Corporate Archive of Saint Gobain-Pont-à-Mousson
PSQ	*Political Science Quarterly*
RA	Royal Archives, Windsor
VfZG	*Vierteljahrshefte für Zeitgeschichte*
YV	Yad Vashem, Jerusalem

German Nationalism and
the European Response
1890-1945

Introduction

MACGREGOR KNOX

"Germany has nine neighbors, and that is Germany's greatest problem." These words of wisdom from a postwar German language primer well summarize a certain German middle opinion that has survived two catastrophic wars and national socialism: Germany's "encirclement" by envious and vengeful neighbors has been the source of most of its woes. If only Germany were not locked between indefensible borders in the center of the Continent. If only it had achieved unity in the sixteenth rather than the nineteenth century. If only its history had made it a leader in the race for empire, not a follower unjustly condemned to suffer the stigma of illegitimacy. If only, if only . . .[1]

Understandably, Germany's neighbors have tended to see things differently. Proximity to Germany has tended to be *their* greatest problem. For Otto von Bismarck's Prussia-Germany, despite its initial claims to be a "satiated" power, proved anything but satiated. Even if it had been, its large and rapidly growing population, its immense economic strength, its central location, and the military traditions of the Prussian monarchy ensured that it would dominate the Continent. And if German borders (except the Alps) were indefensible, so were those of Germany's neighbors, as they discovered in 1866, 1870, 1914, and 1939–41. The events of those years have understandably caused Germany's neighbors to greet with relief the post-1945 creation of several Germanies.

---

[1]This weltanschauung has not lacked foreign converts; for an example see David P. Calleo, *The German Problem Reconsidered* (New York, 1978).

The force that three times turned Europe upside down was German nationalism. In 1866–71 that nationalism was the junior partner of Bismarck and the Prussian army in crushing Austria and France and establishing the Reich. In Europe this meant the destruction of the preexisting balance of power and the achievement of a "semi-hegemonial position" for the new Germany; as one power-crazed Prussian put it in the summer of 1870, "We ourselves with a million soldiers are the equilibrium of the future."[2]

But German nationalism was Bismarck's servant, not his master. He curbed and stunted its principal political expression, the National Liberal party. He designed the new Germany to leave out Roman Catholic German Austria, pursuant to the Prussian maxim that "the limit of our power is where we no longer have Junkers to fill our commissions in the army."[3] One result, as Isabel Hull emphasizes in her article on Prussian dynastic ritual, was that in the new Reich Prussian dynastic loyalty and rituals vied with German national ones. Bismarck lovingly preserved Germany's particularisms and religious divisions in the interests of Prussian domination. His king, William I, resolutely refused the slightest concession to "Germany." But with the coming of a new generation in the 1890s, the Prussian dynastic element of Bismarck's Germany began to lose ground, and with it the monarchy itself, unless it could transform itself into a German, bourgeois, and popular *"Volkskaisertum."* That was a purpose of the battle fleet that William II and Alfred von Tirpitz built against England and the purpose of the "bombast and ludicrous fantasy" that has moved contemporaries and historians to levity or despair but concealed a serious political and ideological intention.

Unfortunately for the kaiser and his entourage, both the inherited social rigidity that petrified most Prussian court rituals and the

---

[2]For "semi-hegemonial" see Ludwig Dehio, *Deutschland und die Weltpolitik im 20. Jahrhundert* (Munich, 1955), p. 15; quotation: Wimpffen to Beust, 13 August 1870, in Helmut Böhme, *The Foundation of the German Empire* (Oxford, 1971), p. 16.

[3]Gen. Lothar von Schweinitz, one of Bismarck's ambassadors, quoted in Erich Eyck, *Bismarck and the German Empire* (New York, 1964), p. 151.

nobility's own "control mania" made it almost impossible to accomplish that purpose. The increasing distance of the dynastic ritual from the realities of even nineteenth-century Germany led to the decline in court morale that Hull analyzes. Despite William II's sporadic attempts to enlarge the scope of ritual and the circle of its participants, its reception increasingly foreshadowed the end of the monarchy itself.

Nevertheless, it required the great war that William helped summon up to create a new German unity centered not on the monarchy but on the army, the institution that, as Hull points out, was most successful as a purveyor of ritual before 1914. The storm of steel that welded "Prussians and Bavarians, officers and men" together in "an overpowering desire to kill"[4] also made possible the political breakthrough of the most radical wing of the nationalism that Bismarck had sought to cage. On the eve of war Heinrich Class, of the Pan-German League, had called for a "führer" to reform the state and hack through Germany's ring of enemies.[5] In war Class and like-minded figures in the military increasingly ignored the monarchy; the Erich Ludendorff–Paul von Hindenburg combine was a national dictatorship in all but name.

It did not last. Defeat destroyed first dictatorship, then monarchy, while leaving the forces of radical nationalism in too much disarray to fill William's shoes—yet. But defeat did not create as "open" a situation as some commentators have discerned.[6] The second article in this collection, Erich Hahn's discussion of the German Foreign Ministry's handling of the "war-guilt" issue, shows why. The failure of the revolution's often unwilling leaders to disband or purge the old bureaucracies ultimately obliged the new German regime to endorse the bureaucrats' vociferous denials of German responsibility for the war, however embarrassing the

[4]Ernest Jünger, *In Stahlgewittern* (*Werke,* [Stuttgart, 1960], vol. 1), pp. 247, 250.

[5]Daniel Frymann [pseud. Heinrich Class], *Wenn ich der Kaiser wär'* (Leipzig, 1913, pp. 242, 263 ("In Erwartung des Führers").

[6]For the phrase and the argument see Reinhard Rürup, "Problems of the German Revolution 1918-19," *JCH* 3, no. 4 (1968): 113.

evidence of that responsibility. Friedrich Ebert hailed the "unconquered" army at the Brandenburg Gate in December 1918 and thus accredited the nationalist myth that revolution had stabbed Germany's victorious heroes in the back; Hermann Müller conveniently ascribed the war to international economic rivalries; Philipp Scheidemann denounced the Versailles Treaty in terms worthy of the Right ("What hand would not wither which placed this chain upon itself and upon us?").[7] The new rulers lacked the courage and the backing of enough members of the German elite to make the necessary break with imperial Germany.

The "preemptive historiography" of Bernhard Wilhelm von Bülow at the Foreign Ministry that Hahn describes also throws an interesting light not only on 1918–19 but also on Bülow's later career as a formulator of German foreign policy in the last years of Weimar and the first years of the Third Reich. Respectable nationalists and Nazis united in attack on the "war-guilt lie" and in simultaneous insistence on "one last partition of Poland."[8] From the Foreign Ministry's penchant for recasting the origins of the war in accordance with national "*gesunden Verstand*" to the Nazis' efforts to impose "healthy *Volk* consciousness" as the standard for everything from sex to jurisprudence was a relatively short step.

Shorn of its monarchical trappings and restraints, respectable nationalism ultimately coalesced with radical *völkisch* nationalism in putting Hitler into power on 30 January 1933. As the torchlight parade that wound past the Reich Chancellory that evening demonstrated, Germany had at last acquired a truly national ritual. Nevertheless, success in "carrying through in Europe that selfsame revolution we have carried through on a smaller scale in Germany," as Goebbels elegantly put it in April 1940, depended not on German rituals but on the German army. That army, as

---

[7]Quoted in Erich Eyck, *A History of the Weimar Republic* (Cambridge, Mass., 1967), 1:98.

[8]See the Stahlhelm resolution of September 1928, quoted in Eyck, *Weimar Republic,* 2:167–68; "Nur noch *eine* Teilung Polens": Günter Wollstein, "Eine Denkschrift des Staatssekretärs Bernhard von Bülow vom März 1933," *Militärgeschichtliche Mitteilungen* 13 (1973): 80.

Williamson Murray points out in his article, was unfortunately the most innovative, open-minded, and learned of the armies that had fought the Great War. Its officers studied and thought about war. They found *Kriegsspiele* more enticing than polo. In defeat they preserved and strengthened the tradition of tactical and operational originality ("Operation ist Bewegung") that had almost brought victory in 1914–18.

After 1933, when Hitler opened the budgetary floodgates, the army gave its motorization and mechanization pioneers the freedom to create the armored instrument that proved itself in Poland, knifed through France, and nearly destroyed the Soviet Union. As Murray demonstrates, those who have seen in this outcome a deep-laid Hitlerian "blitzkrieg strategy" have—for once in dealing with Hitler—overrationalized events. The führer indeed wanted a great war and racist world revolution, but he had help: until 1938 the generals took care of the details of rearmament. It was they, following their professional noses and without regard for megalomaniacal strategic requirements the dictator was careful to conceal, who created the instrument that crushed Germany's immediate neighbors and almost won the war.

The response to German nationalism, whether in its Wilhelmian or radical form, has inevitably taken a wide variety of shapes, as the remaining articles in this collection suggest. Lamar Cecil has traced the bad-tempered Russian reaction to William II's malapropisms and to his attempts to establish by diplomacy the "Napoleonic supremacy"[9] he saw as Germany's rightful place in Europe. The indifferent success of the "All-Highest" testifies to his talent for "oratorical derailments" both public and private. It also illuminates the decreasing strength of dynastic ties in an age of national antagonisms. Neither German nor Russian nationalism could tolerate William's abortive 1905 Treaty with Nicholas II at Björkö. The culmination of this development came in 1914–18, when the good monarchists—and nationalists—of the Foreign

[9]John C. G. Röhl, "A Document of 1892 on Germany, Prussia, and Poland," *HJ* 7, no. 1 (1964): 144.

Ministry and the general staff gleefully violated all concepts of monarchical and social solidarity through their massive and ultimately successful aid to Russia's revolutionaries. It remained for Hitler to bring the development full circle with a racist nationalism so extreme that it rejected even temporary use of disaffected elements within Russia to help bring Stalin down.

In the West, as Carole Fink's article on the Genoa Conference of 1922 suggests, post-1918 Germany could at least count on a measure of British goodwill. But Lloyd George's attempts to reconcile Germany to its new status foundered both on French refusal to abandon Versailles and on German insistence on making obscure threats of Russo-German alliance against the West. German actions at Genoa and Rapallo and the murder of Walther Rathenau shortly thereafter showed once more how grudgingly Germany had accepted Versailles and how unlikely it was to acquiesce in anything less than the overthrow of the postwar settlement.

Once the French had tried, in the wake of Genoa, to enforce Versailles by mining Ruhr coal with bayonets and had found themselves isolated and financially besieged, the way was open for a more ductile French policy, the limited appeasement of Aristide Briand that is the subject of Edward Keeton's article. As Briand learned (or may always have known), the price the Germans asked for the rapprochement he sought rose with each new French concession: Gustav Stresemann, that moderate, sought to drive the French back "from trench to trench."[10] Briand and his backers, too impressed by Germany's potential industrial and military strength—as opposed to its current vulnerability—gave ground warily. Soon it was too late. Stresemann's death in 1929 and, above all, the withdrawal of the last French troops from the Rhineland in 1930 removed any incentive for the Germans to bargain with Briand at the expense of Germany's future greatness. Time was on Germany's side.

---

[10]Stresemann to General von Scheüch, 27 July 1925, quoted in Annelise Thimme, "Stresemann and Locarno," in Hans W. Gatzke, ed., *European Diplomacy Between Two Wars* (Chicago, 1972), p. 84.

Hitler's coming in January 1933 realized the worst fears of the French, but their reaction, in the absence of British willingness to take any position whatsoever,[11] was paralytic. Others did no better. As Herbert Levine reminds us, among the very first victims of triumphant German radical nationalism were the German Jews, that "never precisely foreign, never entirely integrated" community that had existed in Germany since the Romans. As Levine suggests, their incomprehension of the nature of the threat, their attempts to negotiate a modus vivendi that would ensure survival as a community, resembles the incomprehension of the foreign leaders whose lack of resolve Hitler mocked. All hoped for the best and aspired to be devoured last.

After the initial shock of the boycott of April 1933 and the removal of Jews from the professions and the civil service came a period of relative calm in which Nazi attention to the Jewish community was sporadic and for the most part routinely administrative. Like their counterparts in foreign chancellories, the German Jewish organizations tended to mistake routine for Nazi policy. Administrative historians have placed wholly disproportionate emphasis on that routine and on the vagaries of the various Nazi bureaucracies concerned with the "Jewish question."[12] As Hitler once remarked, he had three levels of secrecy: things talked about "with one other person," things "kept back for myself," and a third level, "which is problems for the future, which I have not [yet] begun to think about."[13] That the "final solution of the Jewish question," until 1938 or so, in general belonged to the third category is scarcely evidence of indecision about final goals. Hitler proclaimed wrathfully the day after the Reichskristallnacht ("night of shattered glass") pogrom that "cir-

---

[11]See especially Nicholas Rostow, *Anglo-French Relations, 1934–36* (London, 1984).

[12]See particularly Uwe Dietrich Adam, *Judenpolitik im Dritten Reich* (Düsseldorf, 1972); and Martin Broszat, "Hitler und die Genesis der 'Endlösung,' " *VfZG* 25, no. 4 (1977): 739–75; for a rebuttal of Broszat see Christopher S. Browning, "Zur Genesis der 'Endlösung,' " *VfZG* 29, no. 1 (1981):97–109.

[13]Admiral Erich Schulte-Mönting (Admiral Erich Raeder's chief assistant), quoted in Jochen Thies, *Architekt der Weltherrschaft* (Düsseldorf, 1976), p. 18.

cumstances have forced me *for decades* to speak almost exclusively of peace. . . . Hard necessity [*Der Zwang*] was the reason that year after year I spoke only of peace."[14] Once he began to speak of war, the Jews of Germany and Europe were doomed.

Paralysis in the face of this challenge had a wide variety of causes, not least in the British case that Charles Bright dissects. British inaction stemmed not merely from Stanley Baldwin's lethargy and from "the heavy and ominous breathing of a parsimonious and pacific electorate." Within the charmed circle of Britain's rulers the most important considerations were the empire's defense requirements against Japan and the smug doctrinairism of the Treasury, whose experts predicted national bankruptcy from "great armaments" which in fact did not break a pathetic 6 percent of national income until 1938.[15] These pressures, not a predilection for Hitler's putative anti-Bolshevism, were what impelled Neville Chamberlain, after the sham and fiasco of Baldwin's League of Nations policy in 1935–36, to seek accommodation with the dictators in the name of "realism."

These forces do not account for Chamberlain's failure to appreciate the revolutionary magnitude of Nazi aspirations, or his messianic fervor in pursuing the führer to Munich in 1938. Those aberrations sprang from Chamberlain's lack of imagination and of understanding of national socialism and Germany, and from his related conviction that *nothing* could be worse than a new world war. But the pressures Bright carefully analyzes did create a situation in which Chamberlain's solution to Britain's security dilemma, his thrusting, preemptive brand of appeasement, found not only public support but the spaniel loyalty of the overwhelming majority of the Conservative party. Not until September 1939 did that loyalty begin to crack, in the face of events that mocked Chamberlain's claim to realism and

[14]Hildegard von Kotze and Helmut Krausnick, eds., "*Es Spricht der Führer*" (Gütersloh, 1966), pp. 269, 270.

[15]British defense expenditure as a percentage of national income was as follows: 1935, 3.3 percent; 1936, 4.2 percent; 1937, 5.6 percent; 1938, 8.3 percent. Even the French did better. For sources, and comparison with the other powers, see MacGregor Knox, *Mussolini Unleashed, 1939–1941* (Cambridge, 1982), app. 2.

made a shambles of British policy. By then it was almost too late.

For at least one European leader those events nevertheless came too soon. The fall of 1939 was unsuitable for the "inevitable war" between the "plutocratic nations . . . and the populous and poor ones"[16] that Mussolini had long hoped for. Italy was in no condition to fight, and Mussolini lacked the leverage to move military and monarchy to battle. Then Hitler's crushing victory in the West in May–June 1940 rescued the duce from grave embarrassment and "unleashed" him against the British in the Mediterranean. But for reasons I attempt to analyze in my own article on Italy's defeat in 1940, Mussolini lacked Hitler's good fortune in military establishments. Opportunity produced not victory, as it initially did for the Wehrmacht, but the fiascos in Albania, at Taranto, and in the desert.

The concluding article, by Annelise Thimme and Carole Fink, deals with the consequences of German nationalism for an individual, Hans W. Gatzke. It suggests, among other things, that the field of choice for individuals, as for nations, was wider than many would willingly concede. Hans Gatzke grew up as a German nationalist, yet by 1937 he had concluded that the new Germany was going places he had no desire to go. He therefore left. When he returned, much later, in the uniform of the U.S. Army, it was to a land he had long ceased to regard as his own. His subsequent scholarly work has distinguished itself by its uncompromising analysis of the political and diplomatic consequences of the German nationalism he rejected in 1937. Unfortunately for Germany and for Europe, all but a tiny minority of Germans chose another path, and the consequence was the final destruction not only of Bismarck's Germany but of Europe's position in the world.

Forty years after the collapse of the Third Reich and of Prussia-Germany, some of the ghosts of German radical nationalism have been laid. The Federal Republic of Germany has proved a stable

---

[16]Mussolini to Hitler, 30 May 1939, *DDI,* 8th ser., vol. 12, doc. 59.

democracy. Its eastern counterpart, as long as the Group of Soviet Forces Germany remains, should prove a stable despotism. But some old sentiments linger in new forms. While German historians have sifted the past with unparalleled diligence and considerable moral courage, their fellow citizens have often preferred the illusion that Auschwitz and Dresden, the *Einsatzgruppen* (extermination teams) and Hiroshima were historically and morally equivalent. Contemporaries of the Third Reich have suffered an epidemic of selective amnesia. Many of those born after 1945, to judge from the words of their self-appointed spokesmen, are in bad-tempered and uncomprehending revolt against the consequences of the German past: Germany's division first of all, and economic, military, and cultural dependence upon the respective superpowers. Some observers believe that a new German nationalism, cloaked in woolly ethnic sentimentality, pacifist slogans, or (in the East) Prussian revivalism, is taking the place of the old *völkisch* militance that Hitler's failure discredited. Will this new nationalism, if that is what it is, be as great a threat to the balance of power as was its predecessor? Germany's neighbors, especially the French, are anxiously waiting to find out.

1

Prussian Dynastic Ritual and the End of Monarchy

ISABEL V. HULL

When Wilhelmians reflected upon the characteristics of their age, they never failed to mention its pomp and ceremony. They remembered the huge parades, the balls, the monuments, the medals. If they enjoyed display, they called it "brilliant." If they suspected that the "brilliance" actually marked a kind of emptiness, they complained of a typically Wilhelmian fixation on "superficiality" (*Ausserlichkeit*) or "luxury." In the past twenty years modern German historians have begun to take public ceremony as seriously as contemporaries did.[1] The historical literature has so far concentrated upon national rites and symbols: the flag, the national anthem, holidays, and monuments. Dynastic rites, those pertaining to a particular state (in this case Prussia) or to its ruling family, have excited little historical interest.

In the following pages I examine Prussian dynastic ceremonies during the reign of Germany's last monarch, Kaiser William II (1888–1918), to see what they can tell us about the adaptability of the Wilhelmian system. The discussion revolves around change: changes in the dynastic ceremonies and changes in the way the participants and observers responded to the ceremonies. These changes mark the skirmishes in a larger, protracted struggle. On

[1]Medievalists have long used ritual and symbol as important historical sources. See, for example, Percy Ernst Schramm, *Herrschaftszeichen und Staatssymbolik: Beiträge zu ihrer Geschichte vom dritten bis zum sechzehnten Jahrhundert,* 3 vols. (Stuttgart, 1954–56).

13

the one hand, the dynasty tried to ensure that its rites and symbols would continue to appeal to the generation which had lived through German unification and then the quickening pace of economic and social change. On the other hand, limitations internal to the Prussian dynasty undercut and disfigured this attempt. All the while the Prussian nobles, the most unquestioning monarchical supporters and, at once, the audience for and the actors in the dynastic rites, observed the process of ritual change and drew conclusions from it. The present discussion focuses upon that process and those conclusions.

To some extent the knotty and paradoxical problems that the dynasty encountered in its ritual endeavors are inherent in ritual per se, which unites in itself opposing tendencies. The first is its integrating and legitimating function. Under this aspect rituals interpret the social order in a stabilizing way. They make abstractions like "hierarchy" or "prestige" concrete. They prescribe what ought to be and then create models of that perfection through ordered, repetitive performance. Rituals beguile with pageantry, bewitch with interwoven symbols, and then seduce the individual into affirming his or her role in the social contract, either through participation or simply by providing the audience for a periodic renewal of social bonds. The magical multiplicity of symbolism enables ritual to knit together the various spheres of life, the economic, the social, the political, the religious, the moral, into a single, self-sustaining, mutually reinforcing whole.[2] In this guise, then, ritual seems the perfect establishment instrument, and that, indeed, was how the Prussian dynasty and the nobility chiefly regarded it. Although they were not indifferent to its aesthetic charms, both the dynasty and the nobility had a largely functionalist understanding of ritual. They measured its success or failure by the degree to which it helped support their status quo.

However, Wilhelmian functionalism tended to overlook a second aspect of symbolic ritual, one that produces its characteristic tension. By its very mediation ritual acknowledges divisions in

[2]Roy A. Rappoport, "The Obvious Aspects of Ritual" (manuscript in the possession of the author), p. 27.

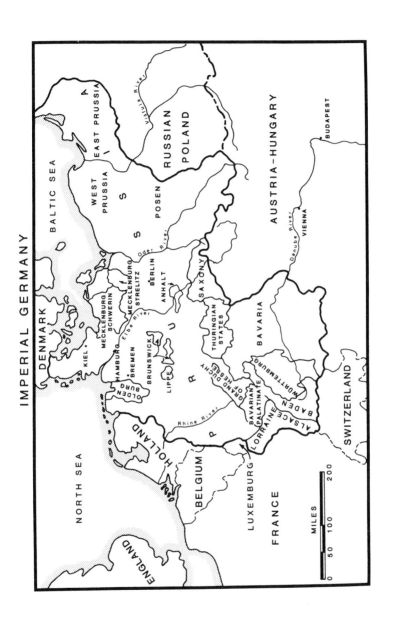

IMPERIAL GERMANY

society and juxtaposes cultural, social, and other elements that are at base mutually irreconcilable. One might even say that ritual is one record of past and ongoing social struggles among groups and among their various interpretations of society. That clash of interpretations is never resolved in a monolithic manner. The power of symbols lies precisely in their ability to evoke several interpretations simultaneously. Even the clarity produced by ritual performance is spurious, because who can tell whether the performers believe in the performance or understand it?[3] The ritual process is very complex and often contradictory. Nonetheless, it is clear that ritual, if it stays vital, is as intimately concerned with expressing conflict and difference as it is with promoting harmony.[4] Thus, on a less abstract level, the Prussian dynastic and noble interest in manipulating other social strata through ritual obscured the extent to which these strata themselves determined the success of a ritual. The Prussian monarchical establishment thus overestimated its own manipulative abilities at the same time that it ignored the effects which manipulation has upon the manipulators. The story of Prussian dynastic rites at the turn of the century pivots around the monarchy's failure to use ritual as it wanted or needed to do and around the way the nobility interpreted that failure.

Dynastic ceremonies date back to the times when the nobility was the "nation." Prussian dynastic ritual, especially court as opposed to military rites, retained that audience into the twentieth century. Accordingly, the *Hofgesellschaft* (court society) was limited to some nobles and to a few assimilated hauts bourgeois, usually ministers, state secretaries, and other high government officials. Court functions renewed the bonds between the king and his loyal nobles and state servants and reemphasized the exclusivity and, by implication, the excellence of the leading strata, which were heavily Junker and military. Military rites

---

[3]Ibid., p. 41.

[4]Clifford Geertz, "Ritual and Social Change: A Javanese Example," in Clifford Geertz, *The Interpretation of Cultures* (New York, 1973), pp. 142–45; Victor Turner, cited in Raymond Firth, *Symbols Public and Private* (Ithaca, N.Y., 1973), p. 191.

(parades, reviews, swearings-in) did much the same thing for the officer corps, though in addition they touched other social strata represented in the ranks or among public onlookers. The focus of both kinds of ritual was the dynasty and the virtues peculiar to Prussia, in a word, dynastic particularism.

In the seventeenth and eighteenth centuries the rites and symbols of the various German dynasties stood relatively unchallenged as the legitimate expressions of German political life. Of course, dynastic rituals were not the only ones current in society. Both religion and the Holy Roman Empire made ritual claims to greater universality, but since 1648 few Germans would have denied the concrete political supremacy of the dynasties and hence of their symbols. At the same time innumerable popular festivals and ritual customs played an important role in people's daily lives and had political meaning on the local level, but they never inhabited the same sphere as dynastic ritual, nor did they aspire to. The middle plane of political ritual belonged securely to the dynasties.

That security ended in 1789. Thereafter the dynasties themselves faced a twofold attack. Nationalism threatened to dissolve them altogether in favor of a higher, German unity, while the reform movements sought to open them to social influences beyond, or rather below, that of the nobility. During the nineteenth century these expansionary tendencies had two analogous consequences for dynastic ritual. First, by exalting the nation, they undermined the particularist content of the rituals. Second, by widening the social base of politics, they implicitly challenged the nobility's right to be the exclusive participant-audience for these rituals. Thus the nineteenth century witnessed a crisis in dynastic ritual which was intimately connected with the formation of the German nation-state and with the rites and symbols appropriate to it. That crisis formed the framework within which contemporaries interpreted and judged dynastic ritual, and for that reason we must now examine this framework in greater detail.

At first glance it is surprising that there should have been a struggle between dynastic and national ritual after 1871. Although German nationalism in the early part of the century was a largely bourgeois and liberal effort directed against the Prussian particularist, noble, and military traditions which stood in its way, things had changed by the 1860s and 1870s. Otto von Bismarck redirected nationalist momentum into channels less dangerous to Prussia by putting Prussia, its army, and its noble officer corps at the head of actual unification and by securing Prussian predominance in the new German government. Under the circumstances one might expect Prussia's dynastic rites and symbols to have become German national ones. This did not happen, however. Instead the conflict between both kinds of political ritual continued unabated.

Germany's first emperor, William I (1861–88), wanted this state of affairs. Both he and his nobles had acquiesced in German unity to save Prussia's essence, not to merge it into something else (Germany) or to lend its prestige to nationalism that might overrun Prussia and change it forever. Precisely because rituals interpret the political and social order, they were especially dangerous to the new Prusso-German state. Bismarck had done his best to cloak iron Prussian autocracy and social reaction with constitutional and progressive lace. He retained and even exacerbated social, religious, political, and other internal divisions so that he could manipulate them in the interests of the Prussian monarchy and the Junkers.[5] Interpretative confusion about the actual nature of the new Reich was a boon to these efforts. For all these reasons William I steadfastly thwarted both the establishment of real national symbols or rituals and the transformation of Prussian symbols for national use.[6] The new state, for example, had no national anthem,[7] no official national holi-

---

[5]This is the theme of Hans-Ulrich Wehler, *Das deutsche Kaiserreich 1871–1918* (Göttingen, 1973).

[6]Theodor Schieder, *Das Deutsche Kaiserreich von 1871 als Nationalstaat* (Cologne and Opladen, 1961), p. 82. Chapter 5 of this book and the three appendices remain the only extended discussions of political symbolism in the Kaiserreich. Elizabeth Fehrenbach, "Über die Bedeutung der Politischen Symbole im Nationalstaat," *HZ* 213 (1971): 296–357, is a most intelligent comparative exploration of the subject.

[7]Fehrenbach, "Symbole," pp. 318–19; Schieder, *Nationalstaat*, p. 75.

day,[8] and a flag which the government did not designate "national" until 1892.[9]

This is not to say that the monarchy made no effort to exploit nationalism for its own benefit. It assiduously tried to imprint upon nationalism the Prussian military stamp, and its success in permeating the German polity and society in this manner represents its greatest ritual triumph on the national level.[10] Its success not only was displayed on the surface of "obvious" rituals, such as parades and oath takings, but, more important, shaped the very ways in which many strata of society defined national problems and solutions.[11] With the exception of those rituals concerning the German navy, a truly national institution, the "obvious" military rituals were mostly dynastic and are discussed below. But the real importance of the military to German life lies outside the confines of dynastic ritual and therefore of this article. It should be noted, however, that, despite the triumph of military values, the monarchy and its noble supporters were ultimately unable to control either the symbol of the military or nationalism. The former escaped them in two ways. First, they were more the prisoners than the masters of the military mentality, whose iron

[8]Schieder, *Nationalstaat,* pp. 76-77, 125-53; Hartmut Lehmann, "Friedrich von Bodelschwingh und das Sedanfeier," *HZ* 212 (1966): 542-73; Georg Müller, "Friedrich von Bodelschwingh und das Sedanfest," *GWU* 14 (1963): 77-90; George L. Mosse, *The Nationalization of the Masses: Political Symbolism and Mass Movements in Germany from the Napoleonic Wars Through the Third Reich* (New York, 1975), pp. 91-92.

[9]Fehrenbach, "Symbole," pp. 345-48.

[10]The problem of the Prussian military and German society is well researched. For an introduction see the section "Militarismus," by Werner Conze, Michael Geyer, and Reinhard Stumpf, in Otto Brunner et al., eds., *Geschichtliche Grundbegriffe: Historisches Lexikon zur politisch-sozialen Sprache in Deutschland,* vol. 4 (Stuttgart, 1978), pp. 1-48; Manfred Messerschmidt, "Die Armee in Staat und Gesellschaft—Die Bismarckzeit," and the companion essay by Wilhelm Deist, "Die Armee in Staat und Gesellschaft 1890-1914," in Michael Stürmer, ed., *Das kaiserliche Deutschland. Politik und Gesellschaft 1870-1918* (Düsseldorf, 1970), pp. 89-118, 312-39.

[11]See Manfred Messerschmidt's very intelligent essay, *Militär und Politik in der Bismarckzeit und im Wilhelminischen Deutschland,* vol. 43 of *Erträge der Forschung* (Darmstadt, 1975), especially pp. 55-74.

grip prevented them from handling problems flexibly.[12] Second, in the public mind the military increasingly seemed independent of and superior to the monarchy itself until World War I, when the Germans sooner entrusted their fate to Generals Ludendorff and Hindenburg than to the emperor. Nationalism, too, frustrated the government's attempts to tame it. It soon spilled into radical channels that challenged the Wilhelmian status quo as much as social democracy did.[13]

The dynasty's failure to control national ritual became apparent only gradually. Where William I, aside from his enthuastic forays into military ritual, had rigorously upheld dynastic ritual at the expense of national ritual, William II had more dynamic ideas. Unlike his grandfather he positively reveled in ceremony. A brilliant orator and tireless traveler, he crisscrossed Germany (not merely Prussia) to dedicate monuments, consecrate churches, lead parades, review troops, judge song fests, tour factories, inspect restorations, open art galleries, bestow orders, dine with dignitaries, and address multitudes. William possessed a thoroughly modern appreciation of propaganda and a love of technology, scientific invention, and fiery rhetoric that jostled somewhat disconcertingly against his conviction of the divine right of kings, his ignorance of the constitution, and his utter belief in the historic Hohenzollern mission. This odd mixture of qualities made William himself a particularly fitting symbol of the old-new Prussia-Germany,[14] and he conscientiously inundated Germany with a flood of rituals, symbols, and ceremonies designed to equate, in the eyes of the average German, the Hohenzollern monarchy with Germany's glorious future. He wanted dynastic symbolism to win non-Prussian, non-Protestant, nonnoble Germany for the dynasty. To this end

[12]Isabel V. Hull, *The Entourage of Kaiser Wilhelm II, 1888–1918* (London and New York, 1982), chapters 7–9.

[13]See Geoff Eley, *Reshaping the German Right: Radical Nationalism and Political Change After Bismarck* (New Haven, Conn., and London, 1980).

[14]William tried to capitalize on his own symbolic possibilities and succeeded in becoming both a positive and a negative symbol for a variety of qualities. Elizabeth Fehrenbach's excellent *Wandlungen des Kaisergedankens 1871–1918* (Munich and Vienna, 1969) explores some of the aspects of William as symbol, but a truly comprehensive study would be most worthwhile.

he propagated the Hohenzollern memory in the entire land through monuments, speeches, orders, and other symbolic events. His most famous campaign, and one which is typical of all his symbolic efforts, was the creation of the legend of "William the Great."

In life William I was modest, sober, and hard-working. In death he became associated with bombast and ludicrous fantasy, because it was his misfortune to become the centerpiece for his grandson's ritualistic designs. William II was determined to make the first emperor into the national hero of Germany. This was a poor choice, for, as everyone knew, the two real heroes of unification were Field Marshal Helmuth von Moltke and Chancellor Bismarck. But William I was at least unequivocally dynastic, and besides, after 1890, William II and Bismarck were mortal enemies. So the old emperor became for his grandson, if for no one else, "William the Great."[15] Across Germany William II encouraged and sometimes directly interceded in the erection of statues of the old man. At final count there were close to four hundred of them,[16] but this wave of statuary could not erode those particular promontories it was designed to engulf. Very few statues were in the Hanse areas, or in south Germany, particularly in Bavaria. In Prussia itself Protestant areas subscribed to the new cult with much more alacrity than did Catholic ones.[17]

To the flood of monuments William added a veritable deluge of medallions commemorating the one hundredth anniversary of his grandfather's birth. In good dynastic-national fashion they bore on the front William I's likeness with the inscription "William the Great, German Kaiser, King of Prussia." Everyone who had served under the old kaiser was to receive one. In the navy alone

---

[15]Baroness Hildegard von Spitzemberg, *Das Tagebuch der Baronin Spitzemberg geb. Freiin v. Varnbüler: Aufzeichnungen aus der Hofgesellschaft des Hohenzollernreiches,* ed. Rudolf Vierhaus, 4th ed. (Göttingen, 1976), pp. 352-53 (3 March 1897).

[16]Thomas Nipperdey, "Nationalidee und Nationaldenkmal in Deutschland im 19. Jahrhundert," in Thomas Nipperdey, *Gesellschaft, Kultur, Theorie. Gesammelte Aufsätze zur neueren Geschichte* (Göttingen, 1976), p. 142.

[17]Ibid.

that amounted to 23,812 men.[18] Of course, the enormous number of medals cheapened even their sentimental value and eroded entirely any propaganda effect William II had intended to achieve. They quickly became known as the "contemporaries' medals," with the suggestion that anyone who had been alive between 1870 and 1888 would receive one. Furthermore, the German public was not much taken with the statues. The official national monument to Kaiser William I, designed by Reinhold Begas and erected in Berlin in 1897, was an out-and-out failure.[19] Much larger than any previous German monument, it was an equestrian statue whose base depicted allegorically the efforts of the other German states and of the bourgeoisie to unify the Reich. These figures, lost in detail, were completely dwarfed by the monarch, however, and the whole gave the impression of baroque gigantism. The critics and public reacted negatively to its blustering preoccupation with might. They interpreted it and the sheer number of the other statues not as signs of the dynasty's greatness but as products of dynastic nervousness or insecurity.[20]

Worse than the monuments and medallions were William II's speeches on the subject of William the Great. The most famous of these and the one that exemplifies William's speeches in general was his address at the festival dinner of the Brandenburg Provincial Landtag on 26 February 1897. William's advisers dreaded this annual event, hallowed in Hohenzollern history, because it led to so many hair-raising imperial speeches, whose damage they could never contain.[21] On this particular night William affirmed that "the memory of Kaiser William the Great" bound true sons of the Brandenburg Mark to fight "with all means against revolution. . . . That party which dares to attack the foundations of

---

[18]Naval Cabinet Chief Gustav Baron von Senden-Bibran to Prussian War Minister Heinrich von Gossler, 5 January 1897, BA/MA, Kaiserliches Marinekabinett, RM 2, vol. 80, "Bestimmungen über Jubiläumsfeiern, Fahnen- und Kirchenweihen (1897–1915)" (hereafter RM 2/80).

[19]My description follows Nipperdey, "Nationaldenkmal," pp. 142–43.

[20]Ibid., p. 142.

[21]Friedrich von Holstein to Philipp zu Eulenburg, 27 February 1893, John Röhl, ed., *Philipp Eulenburgs Politische Korrespondenz*, vol. 2 (1892–95), (Boppard am Rhein, 1979), no. 775, p. 1031.

state, which raises itself against religion and does not even stop at the person of the all-highest lord [a formula meaning the kaiser] must be vanquished." Having thus disposed of the party of Germany's workers, Wilhelm went on to say that the struggle could be successful only if the fighters remembered

> the man whom we all have to thank for our Fatherland, the German Empire, [the man] in whose presence, through God's grace, there were so many fine, capable advisers, who had the honor to carry out his ideas, who were all, however, tools [*Werkzeuge,* or handymen (*Handlanger*), or pygmies (*Pygmäen*)] of his lofty desire, filled with the spirit of this excellent Kaiser.[22]

We do not know whether William said both "handymen" and "pygmies" or just "handymen."[23] He did not say "tools." Embarrassed cabinet officials substituted that word in the printed version to lessen the disaster (a vain effort, since Progressives present at the dinner took care to circulate William's actual words).[24] The effect was immediate, electric, and wholly negative.[25] William's bombast annihilated what little credibility the William the Great cult may still have had.

The William the Great episode illustrates why William II's direct manipulation of dynastic symbols on the national level was so seldom effective. The dynasty's functionalist purposes were too transparent and too willful. They ignored the reciprocal nature of ritual and symbol. They aimed instead to graft the other German states onto Prussia without relinquishing any of Prussia's fundamental characteristics and without accommodating symbolically the independent religious, political, class, and local traditions of the rest of the country. Because the challenge to the dynasty and its nobility had first come from the bourgeois strata,

---

[22]Official toast reported in E. Schröder, ed., *Zwanzig Jahre Regierungszeit: Ein Tagebuch Kaiser Wilhelms II: Vom Antritt der Regierung, 15. Juni 1888 bis zum 15. Juni 1908 nach Hof- und anderen Berichten* (Berlin, 1909), pp. 265–68.

[23]See Vierhaus's note, Spitzemberg, *Tagebuch,* p. 352 n. 43.

[24]BGSA 1068 (Politische Berichte und Instruktionen, teilweise Politische Akten, besonders Berichte), no. 125 (5 March 1897).

[25]Ibid.; see also Anton Monts to Bernhard Bülow, 2 March 1897, BA, Nachlass Bülow, 106:195–98.

they remained the primary audience whom the dynasty tried to seduce.[26] For the dynasty the bourgeoisie was the measuring rod which determined whether its own seductive efforts had succeeded or failed. The decline of liberalism, the spread of militarism, and the withering of rival particularist sentiments among the bourgeois strata should have heartened the dynasty. Instead, these practical successes paled next to the dynasty's failure to shape national ritual in the way it wanted to. Despite William II's noisy efforts, and partly because of them, there remained as large a national symbolic vacuum at the end of the monarchy as in the beginning. The situation was only worsened because the dynasty had tried to fill the vacuum and failed.

The patriotic bourgeoisie finally felt compelled to invent its own cult: the Bismarck statues and towers[27] which dotted the German landscape after 1898.[28] The students who called for them directed that "our national hero [should be] celebrated not in pomp, but rather simply and with dignity."[29] The towers were "a political protest against *'Wilhelminismus,'* against pathos and prestige, superficiality and vainglory" [*Veräusserlichung und*

[26]Although Mosse hesitates to admit it, his material shows that the nationalist movement in Germany began with the intellectuals and students in the Napoleonic period and slowly spread through the *Bildungsbürgertum* and into the old *Mittelstand* (artisan and shopkeeper stratum, or lower middle class) by about 1870; Mosse, *Masses*, pp. 129–30, 137–38, 141, 149–51. Later on the working class added to the dynasty's list of alienated classes, but the dynasty used only military pomp to try to win the workers' loyalty; it never attempted to integrate workers into other rituals. Despite Mosse's assertions, the workers seem to have remained indifferent or hostile to military-national blandishments, but much more work needs to be done on this subject. For a beginning see Werner K. Blessing, "The Cult of Monarchy, Political Loyalty and the Workers' Movement in Imperial Germany," *JCH* 13 (1978): 357–75; Gerhard A. Ritter, "Workers' Culture in Imperial Germany: Problems and Points of Departure for Research," *JCH* 13 (1978): 165–89.

[27]See Nipperdey, "Nationaldenkmal," pp. 166–70; Mosse, *Masses*, pp. 36–38; Volker Plagemann, "Bismarck-Denkmäler," in Hans-Ernst Mittig and Volker Plagemann, eds., *Denkmäler im 19. Jahrhundert, Deutung und Kritik* (Munich, 1972), pp. 217–52.

[28]Mosse claims that one architect built five hundred of these in ten years; Mosse, *Masses*, p. 36, no source given. See also Plagemann, "Bismarck-Denkmäler," p. 219.

[29]Nipperdey, "Nationaldenkmal," p. 167.

Renommiersucht].[30] These were the qualities which people associated with the empire, largely in reaction to the monarchy's misuse of ritual and ceremony. As Theodor Mommsen remarked, "Neither gun salutes nor rockets [were] necessary" to prod German national spirit,[31] and in any case the dynastic symbols peddled by the monarch were not a viable substitute for that spirit. Contemporaries therefore found the dynasty's obsession with symbolic display unsettling. William II's efforts tended to discredit obvious ritual altogether in their eyes. Years of whistling in the dark made the Wilhelmians long for silence.

In the end the struggle between national and dynastic ritual had two structural consequences for the latter. First, the monarch and his noble supporters judged dynastic ritual according to new functionalist criteria appropriate to the national level. Exercising the privilege of personal contact with the king (kaiser), basking in noble exclusivity, even the aesthetic charms of dynastic ritual no longer satisfied. New expectations saddled dynastic ritual with the burden of appealing to the bourgeoisie as well. Second, this burden coincided with a growing widespread disdain for obvious ritual. Together these two constraints formed the new context for Prussian dynastic ritual at the turn of the century.

The Prussian court's ritual year began with its most active month. New Year's Day preceded a hectic round of events, including the annual dinner for the commanding generals (2 January), the kaiser's birthday, the investiture of the new knights of the Johanniterorden, the investiture of the recent recipients of the Schwarzer Adler Orden (Prussia's highest nonmilitary medal), and the various formal dinners and court balls which marked Berlin's season until it ended at the beginning of Lent. The Prussian Landtag and the Bandenburg Provincial Landtag dinners occurred in February. The rest of that month elapsed, along with March and April, undistinguished by rituals other than an occasional court hunt and the obligatory swearing-in of recruits. By contrast, May and

---

[30]Ibid., p. 169.
[31]Cited in Schieder, *Nationalstaat,* p. 132.

June were heavy with military ceremony: the anniversary of the establishment of the Lehr-Infanterie Battalion, the huge annual Potsdam and Berlin military parades, and the almost daily royal troop reviews for all the regiments stationed in the area. Then came summer, which was a dead time for ritual in Prussia as elsewhere all over Europe. Government virtually stopped, and everyone who could repaired to the beaches, mountains, or spas to wait out the heat. Then, at the beginning of September, the huge fall maneuvers heralded the resumption of public life. Each year a different province was host to the maneuvers, which took place only after several days of celebrations, including parades, dinners, reviews, inspections, speeches, and fireworks. They represented the most concentrated imperial attempts to awe and flatter the locals with royal and military display. After William II's accession to the throne naval maneuvers lengthened the agenda. After such a beginning the rest of the fall was modest, if not disappointing. The opening of the Reichstag was a new ritual. Otherwise, hunts, many of them private or nearly so, filled the weeks until Christmas, which the emperor spent with his family and closest advisers. In addition, at frequent but not regularly scheduled intervals throughout the year the kaiser appeared at swearings-in, regimental dinners, flag nailings, and dedications.

This brief enumeration makes clear how many of the Prussian ceremonies were military. It does not make clear, however, how much time these ceremonies consumed. In the planning stage a simple monument dedication required the services of the assistant to the state secretary of the interior, the court chamberlain, the chief of the civil cabinet, the seconds-in-command of the military and naval cabinets, one representative of the naval office, two assistants to the Prussian minister of the interior, the president of the canal office, and a secretary to record their deliberations.[32] Parades were worse, because they involved more people and because William II insisted upon making sundry decisions himself, for example, the speed at which the cavalry should

---

[32]Protocol of a conference on the unveiling of the Kaiser William Memorial at Holtenau, held in Berlin, 5 June 1900, BA/MA RM 2/85.

ride.[33] Even a costume ball required long rehearsals so that it went off with military precision.[34] The events themselves devoured more time. During May and June, for example, the emperor reviewed troops every day from 7:00 A.M. until late morning. He then frequently lunched with the unit officers at their mess and was thus unavailable for government work until the afternoon. Or again, as one of William's aides estimated, the kaiser spent about an hour a day signing the orders promoting officers from one grade to another. William retained this practice to create "a kind of personal bond [between the recipient and] the Kaiser."[35] A considerably lighter burden of dynastic ritual had already threatened to crush the old emperor, William I. His advisers had tried to curtail ceremonial activity, but the importance of ritual to the Hohenzollerns thwarted these reform efforts.[36] Matters became much worse when William II attempted to transform dynastic into national ritual by expanding the number and scope of the ceremonies. Planning, travel, and execution blotted out hours and days which the kaiser could not spare if he was to rule in the manner he pretended. Public criticism began even in his first year and grew steadily until it was a substantial force opposing ritual altogether as a needless and harmful waste of time.[37]

Nonetheless, ritual was the major way that the Hohenzollerns touched their supporters and subjects. For this reason they could hardly abandon ritual, but they could and did change it. These changes record the monarchy's attempts to adapt ceremony to fit a different world. They are worth considering in some detail because they reflect the contradictory impulses in Prussia's ritual

[33]"Instructions for Parade," 27 August 1910, ibid., RM 2/105; William II's marginal note on a telegram from the chief of the Admiralty, 7 September, 1912, ibid., RM 2/107.

[34]Spitzemberg, *Tagebuch,* p. 352 (16 February 1897).

[35]So remarked Aide-de-Camp Max von Mutius, BA/MA, Nachlass Mutius, 2:171.

[36]Heinrich Otto Meisner, "Zur neueren Geschichte des preussischen Kabinetts," *FzBPG* 36 (1924):201.

[37]For a synopsis of public opinion see Norman Rich and M. H. Fisher, eds., *Die Geheimen Papiere Friedrich von Holsteins,* vol. 3 (Göttingen, Berlin, Frankfurt, 1961), p. 385 n. 2.

life. First, they were the product of the monarchy's sociopolitical preoccupations and its positive efforts to do something about them. However, two different limitations hindered these efforts: an external one imposed by the changed context of dynastic ritual in the late nineteenth century and an internal one, Prussia's own ritual tradition.

The first change in dynastic ritual was consistent with the monarchy's desire to strengthen its social base. Throughout the nineteenth century the Hohenzollerns tried to widen the impact of court ceremonial by involving more persons not just from the nobility but from the bourgeois strata as well. The Austrian ambassador reported that the *Hofgesellschaft* became larger every year.[38] Eight hundred guests constituted a "small" court ball,[39] while a court chronicler called the numbers attending the court reception of 1897 "colossal."[40] William II further inflated the number of participants by establishing new medals and decorations[41] and by awarding them much more often.[42] Furthermore, he increased the number of occasions at which all these people could attend court. In the short carnival week of 1903, for instance, there were no fewer than six court balls.[43]

As was true of all the other ritual changes, not everyone was pleased with these attempts to broaden the court's ceremonial effect, and, as usual, William II received the largest share of the blame for trying to do so. The last kaiser came in for much criticism for diluting Prussian traditions by making it easy to be honored[44]

---

[38]Ladislaus Graf von Szögyényi-Marich to Agenor Graf Goluchowski, 15 January 1898, HHStA, Politisches Archiv des Ministeriums des Äussern (PA) III (Preussen), vol. 151, Varia.

[39]Spitzemberg, *Tagebuch,* pp. 339, 351 (7 February 1895, 10 February 1897).

[40]Fedor von Zobeltitz, *Chronik der Gesellschaft unter dem letzten Kaiserreich 1894–1914,* 2 vols. (Hamburg, 1922), 1:139 (23 January 1897).

[41]Aide-de-Camp Adolf von Deines to his father, 1 February 1893, BA/MA, Nachlass Deines, 12:17; Hugo Graf von Lerchenfeld-Koefering to the Bavarian Prince Regent, 19 January 1901, BGSA, MA III 2679.

[42]Helmuth von Moltke, *Erinnerungen, Briefe, Dokumente 1877–1916* (Stuttgart, 1922), p. 353 (19 September 1909).

[43]Spitzemberg, *Tagebuch,* pp. 436–37 (29 December 1903).

[44]Moltke, *Erinnerungen,* p. 353 (19 September 1909).

or ennobled[45] and for ruining the exclusivity, and therefore presumably the cohesiveness, of the *Hofgesellschaft* by opening it to other circles. One observer felt that the "distinguished families of the land" increasingly avoided Berlin for this reason.[46] William II may have intensified the practice, but the trend was already well established. It was Frederick William IV (1840-61), for example, who began the custom of the Ordensfest. This annual ceremony honored at court all the recipients of medals, citations, or orders, most of whom were bourgeois.[47] And it was probably Frederick William II (1786-97) who founded the annual subscription ball,[48] which served to "bring those Berlin circles which do not really belong to the *Hofgesellschaft* into a certain loose relationship with the court."[49] Those circles consisted of "nobles and bourgeois, officials and scholars, members of the industrial and merchant professions, artists, literati, the greats of the theater, and so forth."[50]William I "loved . . . to mix fairly intimately in these circles, liked to converse with artists and actresses, with gentlemen and ladies whom he spotted, whose names he would ask and then pull into conversation."[51]

To bring court ceremonial into the modern world by widening the audience and participants was not enough; the court had to compete with bourgeois standards of elegance as well. This may seem paradoxical, because, influenced by the French model, one tends to associate luxury with the royal court and functional plainness with the bourgeoisie. The Prussian court, however, inherited a long tradition of extreme austerity. It was more "typically Prussian," and therefore admirable, to spend money on the army than to waste it on mere show. That most exalted Hohenzollern Frederick the Great (1740-86) was famous for his misanthropy,

[45]Spitzemberg, *Tagebuch,* pp. 392-93 (5 January 1900).
[46]Szögyényi to Goluchowski, 15 January 1898 HHStA, PA III, vol. 151, Varia.
[47]Mathilde Gräfin von Keller, *Vierzig Jahre im Dienst der Kaiserin. Ein Kulturbild aus den Jahren 1881-1921* (Leipzig, 1935), pp. 95-96.
[48]Zobeltitz, *Chronik,* 1:147.
[49]Keller, *Vierzig Jahre,* p. 51.
[50]Ibid.
[51]Zobeltitz, *Chronik,* 1:147.

hard work, and worn-out blue uniform jacket, not for a brilliant court society. Prussia's colors were not black and white for nothing. But in the nineteenth century this asceticism became increasingly dated. It was unseemly for dinners and balls whose sumptuousness rested on commerce or finance to eclipse those of the Prussian court.[52] The court fought back in two ways: by imitation and by emphasis on its tradition against new practices. These two remedies, of course, contradicted one another and produced inconsistency and confusion that undercut the monarchy's efforts. Nonetheless, the court gamely competed with bourgeois values by gradually increasing its own luxury and brilliant effect, until, under Kaiser William II, it had "developed . . . a tremendous splendor," as the minister of war was forced to admit.[53] Again, William II received the blame: "What haven't people babbled on about his tendency toward superficiality!"[54] But even modest William I had not been above embellishing the Johanniterorden investiture to underscore the central role of the monarchy.[55] In any case, Prussian severity proved difficult to overcome, and even under William II the Berlin court was less luxurious than most others, including Great Britain's.[56]

The second way in which the court tried to rival bourgeois swank was to underscore tradition: new money could not buy old custom. Unfortunately, the court suffered under both its historic austerity and its relative newness; it was the least established court in Europe. William II tried to rectify this by introducing pageantry and institutions supposed to recall, if not the Middle Ages, at least that distant and happier time when the court was the undisputed center of society. Since older European courts had ladies of the court (*Palastdamen*), William too established

[52]Baron Hugo von Freytag-Loringhoven, *Menschen und Dinge wie ich sie in meinem Leben sah* (Berlin, 1923), pp. 67–68.

[53]Karl von Einem, *Kriegsminister unter Wilhelm II: Erinnerungen eines Soldaten, 1853–1933* (Leipzig, 1933), pp. 124–25.

[54]Freytag-Loringhoven, *Menschen und Dinge,* p. 67.

[55]Georg Hinzpeter to Karl Count Schlitz gen. von Görtz, 21 August 1883, Hessisches Staatsarchiv Darmstadt, Nachlass Görtz.

[56]Einem, *Kriegsminister,* pp. 124–25; BA/MA, Nachlass Friedrich von der Schulenburg-Tressow, 1:35.

this position for the first time in 1904.[57] Nine years later William honored some of his generals by naming them chiefs of certain regiments. This marked a return to a Prussian practice that had faded into disuse.[58] Usually, however, William limited himself to nondisruptive revivals, that is, to uniforms. In 1907 he inaugurated an impressive red uniform for the Johanniterorden to replace the old one, which looked like "the dress coat of a mediatized noble estate owner from Mecklenburg" (hardly a compliment). The same person who made this comment liked the new uniform, except for the "curious opera hat" that went with it.[59] For the twenty-fifth anniversary of William's entrance into the First Guard Regiment he changed that unit's dress helmets back to the style of those of Frederick the Great.[60] He did the same thing to the entire uniform of the queen's twenty-one-man equestrian honor guard.[61] William exercised his love of old uniforms and manners most emphatically in the costume balls held at court each year. The response to the real or artificial vestiges of times past varied from enthusiastic (". . . the ceremony with its medieval pomp was highly interesting")[62] to defensive (". . . one can laugh at [such ceremonies], but without doubt they guarantee a completely painterly impression"; "That is the high point of the ceremony, an incursion of medieval chivalry into a barely romantic present"),[63] to downright embarrassment (". . . it's as if the dead had stood up with pigtail and powder").[64] But despite occasional lapses into medieval romanticizing, the

[57]Szögyényi to Goluchowski, 19 February 1904, HHStA, PA III 160.

[58]Austrian Military Attaché to the Chief of Staff, 21 June 1913, ÖKrA, Militär Attaché Berlin, fasc. 13.

[59]Zobeltitz, *Chronik,* 2:114–15.

[60]Keller, *Vierzig Jahre,* pp. 155–56 (13 February 1894).

[61]Lerchenfeld-Koefering to Krafft Baron von Crailsheim, 4 August 1889, BGSA, Gesandtschaft Berlin, 1054.

[62]On the Schwarzer Adler Orden investiture see Keller, *Vierzig Jahre,* p. 95 (19 January 1889).

[63]On the Johanniterorden investiture see Zobeltitz, *Chronik,* 2:117–18 (19 March 1907).

[64]Moltke, *Erinnerungen,* p. 316 (9 February 1905), about a court ball; see also Bogdan von Hutten-Czapski, *Sechzig Jahre Politik und Gesellschaft,* 2 vols. (Berlin, 1935), 1:409.

Berlin court remained considerably more modern than either the Russian[65] or the Austrian.

The one change that never occurred in dynastic ritual was the abolition of an old ceremony. At most a baroque detail dated by taste or overdifficult to achieve might fall away. So it was with the train that the Prussian queen wore to the Ordensfest. This was a heavy affair with an embroidered Prussian eagle and was evidently too much trouble for the younger princesses to manage easily. They asked that it be eliminated; the queen agreed, and in 1909 she dropped it along with the accompanying diadem and heavy jewelry and replaced them with the less burdensome formal attire used for parades.[66] In the same manner William II altered the *Fackeltanz* (torchlight dance). This was the high point of the ceremony surrounding the marriage of royal personages at court. It was not really a dance but more of a round, initiated by twelve ministers bearing lighted wax torches.[67] Some liberal journals opined that such a ceremony was beneath the ministers' dignity. William II also thought that "old men like the ministers were not suitable" for this activity and substituted pages and shortened the function.[68] While William's action may have accorded for once with liberal opinion, it had an ironic symbolic effect, for the *Fackeltanz* was the only court ceremony where ministers had a central role. Otherwise, they ranked below generals and were eclipsed by the splendid uniforms. In cutting them out of an important ritual, William underscored the increasingly peripheral position of civilians at court and in decision making.[69]

Changes in the military ceremonies indicate at once the unrivaled importance of the military to the monarchy's conception of its own stability and future and the growing nervousness that this utter dependence fostered. Under Kaiser William II army and

---

[65]Gerhard Mutius, *Abgeschlossene Zeiten* (Herrmannstadt, 1925), p. 114.

[66]Keller, *Vierzig Jahre,* pp. 96, 265.

[67]See "Instruktion für den Fackeltanz," Berlin, 21 June 1889, in BA, Nachlass Boetticher, 69.

[68]Ibid., marginal note by Karl von Boetticher; Keller, *Vierzig Jahre,* pp. 25-26, 245, 248, 292.

[69]See Hull, *Entourage,* chaps. 7-9.

navy expansion swept "untrustworthy" elements into these institutions, that is, Social Democrats into the ranks and ratings and bourgeois into the formerly noble officer corps. To counteract potential disloyalty, William I had begun administering the oaths personally to the new recruits.[70] The army considered the oath taking the most important step in a recruit's career,[71] and the kaiser's presence underscored this attitude, as did the unusual solicitude toward particularist sentiment. The future chief of staff, Helmuth von Moltke, described such a ritual in 1889:

> It was a completely ceremonial act. The exercise building [was] decorated with flags and shields; in the middle under a purple canopy the field altar was set up, from which first the Protestant and then the Catholic garrison chaplain held an address. Numerous generals and all the flags were present. . . . One gets an intimation of our divided political circumstances from the reading of the different oath forms. First, the Prussian subjects swear, [among them first] the evangelicals, [then] the Catholics. Then, those from Braunschweig, then Württemberg, then the subjects of the rest of the small federal states, and finally those from Alsace-Lorraine, all their special oaths![72]

William II further impressed upon the recruits the importance of the oath by having both his own and the two chaplains' addresses printed beforehand and distributed to them.[73] The kaiser also made an effort to loosen police security at certain public military events so that some of the salutary effect would rub off on civilian onlookers.[74] This practice met with short-lived success, however, for the Bavarian diplomatic representative to Berlin complained at the time of the crown prince's wedding that "the Berlin police, as always on such occasions, went way beyond the necessary bounds. Order may gain by this, but . . . the impression of gran-

[70]Austrian Military Attaché to Chief of Staff, February 1912, ÖKrA, Militär Attaché Berlin, fasc. 12.

[71]Martin Kitchen, *The German Officer Corps, 1890–1914* (Oxford, 1968), pp. 172–73.

[72]Moltke, *Erinnerungen,* pp. 153–54 (18 November 1889).

[73]*Freisinnige Zeitung,* no. 251, 24 October 1908.

[74]Zobeltitz, *Chronik,* 1:169 (28 October 1897).

deur is lost."[75] One final example of the monarchy's growing mistrust of its own soldiery was the Schrippenfest, the celebration of the founding of the Lehr-Infanterie Battalion. Under William I this ceremony ended with the officers visiting local pubs, where their men danced and enjoyed themselves. In later years the Schrippenfest became truncated, in keeping with the growing isolation of the officer corps from the rest of society.[76]

These were the major changes in dynastic ritual under the empire. It is now time to turn to the second aspect of the problem posed at the beginning: How did the reception of dynastic ritual change? This is naturally a much harder question, one which cannot be answered with the precision that modern opinion polls may allow. One is thrown upon less reliable sources, like memoirs, or on the chance utterance in a letter or a diary. Nonetheless, contemporaries' interest in ceremony and its interpretation permits us to discern some trends. It must be added that the reception which concerns us here is not that of the public at large but that of the *Hofgesellschaftler,* whose attitude toward dynastic ritual faithfully reflected their confidence in the monarchy and in themselves as part of it.

We might begin by considering the least successful dynastic rituals, the usual court balls and receptions, the formal dinners, the kaiser's birthday, and the Christmas and New Year's celebrations. Occasionally a ball, reception, or dinner charmed someone, especially a newcomer, but on the whole these events were a chore. In 1907 a French diplomat's niece described her impression:

> The ball was a great bore. Everything went off according to rigid schedule, and we [nonnobles] were not allowed to dance. Instead, we had to look on while young women of the highest nobility and officers of the Imperial Guards danced the "française" and minuets, which they had rehearsed for months with the instructresses of the Palace. After the ball, we went into the supper room, where, at last, we were permitted to talk.[77]

[75]Lerchenfeld-Koefering to Prince Regent Luitpold, 7 June 1905, no. 339/xx, BGSA, MA III 2683.

[76]Keller, *Vierzig Jahre,* pp. 31–32.

[77]Genevieve Tabouis, *They Called me Cassandra* (New York, 1942), p. 28.

Berlin ceremonies distinguished themselves in their "sharply deline-
ated form, in the dignified, seemingly effortless behavior, which,
however, moved entirely within the bounds of the prescribed."[78]
This was precisely the problem: nothing ever changed; nothing
was spontaneous. Within a single month the admittedly sarcastic
chief of the naval cabinet recorded the following diary entries:
"The usual Christmas celebration at the Neues Palais," "New
Year's celebration as always," "the usual Prince's dinner," "the
usual Kaiser's birthday celebration."[79] Things had become so
perfunctory and the ceremonial use of time so burdensome that
even many private dinners ended precisely at ten,[80] while the
balls ended at midnight.[81] We have seen how some *Hofgesellschaftler* resented the influx of new blood into court ceremonies.
Nonetheless, they were bored by the same old faces. This partly
explains the popularity of the two best-loved events, the Ordensfest
and the subscription ball.

"I always liked the opening of the Ordensfest best of all," wrote
a minister. "This festival tried to make itself popular [*sich
volkstümlich darzustellen*], to reward with equal warmth every
rank, every merit. A bourgeois spirit breathed through it."[82] The
nobility liked it too. Baron Gustav von Senden-Bibran, chief of
the naval cabinet, was overjoyed that men and women "of all
classes" could mingle with the court.[83] For Adolf von Deines,
military attaché and aide-de-camp, the Ordensfest "has the advantage that one sees and speaks to people" instead of to the same
old crowd.[84] We have already seen how much Kaiser William I
enjoyed himself at the subscription balls. These most bourgeois
of the court ceremonies pleased because they were the opposite

[78]Adolf Wermuth, *Ein Beamtenleben* (Berlin, 1922), p. 299.

[79]Naval Cabinet Chief Georg von Müller's diary entries for 24 December 1910,
1, 26, 27 January 1911, BA/MA, Nachlass Müller, vol. 4.

[80]Wermuth, *Beamtenleben,* p. 299.

[81]Heinrich Prinz von Schönburg-Waldenburg, *Erinnerungen aus kaiserlicher
Zeit* (Leipzig, 1929), p. 62.

[82]Wermuth, *Beamtenleben,* p. 298.

[83]BA/MA, Nachlass Senden-Bibran, 2:13–14 (22 January 1888).

[84]Adolf von Deines to his father, 14 January 1893, BA/MA, Nachlass Deines,
12:3–4.

of the older occasions: they were never the same twice, offered real conversation instead of mere formalities, allowed one to widen one's sphere of acquaintances, and showed unmistakably that other classes besides the nobility supported the monarchy. This last was doubtless the greatest relief. Court chronicler Fedor von Zobeltitz recorded with satisfaction how on Ordensfest day "flags fly even from the tower of the 'red house,' in which our democratic city government meets."[85]

This last point brings us to the most important trend in the reaction of the *Hofgesellschaftler* to ritual: their creeping unease about the future of the monarchy. They expressed anxiety by questioning rituals that they had hitherto enjoyed, approved of, or taken for granted. They adopted, in spite of themselves, the quizzical, disparaging stance toward dynastic ritual that the Social Democrats had shown from the beginning.[86] They began to share the widespread revulsion against Wilhelmian "superficiality and vainglory." Thus the optimistic Zobeltitz must look over his shoulder in 1907: "One can laugh at [such ceremonies], but. . . ."[87] Chief of Staff Helmuth von Moltke, whose approving description of an oath-taking ceremony in 1889 appears above, had changed his tune by 1905:

Next Sunday there will be a large [flag] nailing in the *Zeughaus* [arsenal]. We still seem to think that we can win victory in a life-and-death struggle with a patch of embroidered cloth! We are caught in a dreadfully peaceable frame of mind. It makes me sick when I see this nonsense, which makes us completely forget the main thing, which is to prepare ourselves earnestly and with bitter energy for war. And so we deck people with multicolored ribbons as insignia, which only get in the way of handling the weapons. We encourage ambition through every possible external symbol, instead of developing a sense of duty. Uniforms become more and more flashy, instead of camouflaged for war. Maneuvers are now parade-like theatrical productions. Decoration is the order of the day, and behind all this folderol [*firlefanz*] grins the Gorgon head of war.[88]

[85]Zobeltitz, *Chronik*, 1:177 (22 January 1898).
[86]See Blessing, "Cult of Monarchy," pp. 369–71.
[87]See n. 62 above.
[88]Moltke, *Erinnerungen*, pp. 337–38 (25 August 1905).

It was not just single-minded warriors who thought something was wrong. Baronness Hildegard von Spitzemberg, whose unparalleled connections and insight have left us the best diary of the period, attended the unveiling of the memorial to Frederick II on 24 January 1912. It caused her to reflect upon the ritual and political state of the monarchy:

One becomes heavyhearted [*schwül zumute*] at these monarchical celebrations, which are pitted against such a Reichstag election [the Social Democrat party had just won over four million votes, its high point] and such a popular mood! And as in all such times, the central participants do not suspect the seriousness of the situation, partly do not wish to see it. So, when Ambassador Metternich was recently here, the Kaiser, instead of briefing himself about the clearly critical political situation, talked at dinner only about nonsense.[89]

Mathilde, Countess von Keller, the queen's lady-in-waiting, arrived at a similar state of despair from intimate acquaintance with court life. All of the countess's duties revolved around ceremony, and her diary-memoir contains the best inside description of Wilhelmian ritual. In the end even she came to doubt the value of it all. She at first consoled herself that display was a sign of the times. In 1903 she noted:

... life is always filled, often with downright worthless things, which I find increasingly wearisome because the times are so unspeakably serious—secret suffrage, the Jesuit law! ... the Social Democrats. ... it makes one anxious and with this, the limitless superficiality in wide circles, the luxury, which grows in public as well as in small private houses. We have often observed that things are simpler at court than in other circles.[90]

Three years later, however, this excuse no longer solaced her. She wrote on William's birthday:

Now the ceremonies begin again; one has less than ever a taste for them. Things are just too serious in the world, even here. ... One has the feeling that one is standing on a volcano, and there is something terribly antipathetic about having to busy oneself with

[89]Spitzemberg, *Tagebuch,* p. 540 (25 January 1912).
[90]Keller, *Vierzig Jahre,* pp. 234–35 (8 February 1903).

all these superficial things, which for us belong to the duties of life.[91]

There are several criticisms buried in these negative sentiments. Moltke felt that the Wilhelmian obsession with ritual was stupid and suicidal. It substituted decorative for imperative action. Zobeltitz was upset because dynastic ritual was no longer effective in awing and thus controlling the nonnoble strata. The two women shared that observation. Countess von Keller blamed this failure on luxury introduced by the upper bourgeoisie. As always, Baroness von Spitzemberg was more political. She believed that mere ritual could not counter divisive social movements and that the fault lay with William II and his advisers, who (here she echoes Moltke) fiddled with ceremonial brilliance while Berlin burned. Despite differences in emphasis all four commentators perceived that dynastic ritual was locked in a fatal crisis. As the central participants and audience of dynastic ritual they understood that the crisis engulfed them all, for when they lost confidence in ritual, they lost confidence in themselves and in their role in Germany.

This very brief exploration of a most complex problem has taken place entirely from the viewpoint of the monarchy and the nobility. Their blinders have caused us to ignore several important aspects of political ritual. We have not discussed aesthetics, for example, because aesthetic considerations took a back seat to functional ones for the noble contemporaries. We have not looked at the working class because the court establishment tried to hold it at arm's length, to control it through the military and not to involve it in any other way with ritual. The discussion of the bourgeois strata has been similarly skewed. They appear not by virtue of their own independent activity, its causes or effects, but because of the way the court establishment reacted to them, or, more indirectly still, to their specter. In addition, a complete appraisal of late-nineteenth-century German political ritual would have to analyze the military's startling success in saturating especially the bourgeois strata with its symbols and

---

[91]Ibid., p. 247 (17 January 1906).

values and the transformation of William II from mere kaiser to the symbol of Germany's future (in his Caesarist guise) and of Germany's fall. All these topics would reveal much more about Wilhelmian political ritual than we currently know.

Despite its narrowness relative to political ritual as a whole, dynastic ritual, even considered from the limited standpoint of the court establishment, provides an interesting commentary on the Wilhelmian period. The concern of the monarchy and the nobility to suppress social and political change, to save Prussia by freezing and then magnifying its peculiarities—in short, to control rigidly and absolutely the various forces that threatened their historic positions—this concern had its direct counterpart in the ritual sphere. The court establishment's functionalist approach to ritual was in one sense merely the logical outgrowth of its general mania for control. George Mosse argues that precisely its rigidity and distrust of genuine popular sentiment made the dynasty incapable of developing real national ritual.[92] It still seems paradoxical, however, that a regime so successful in neutralizing actual political or social threats to its existence (liberalism, social democracy) should have been such a failure when it came to creating positive ritual to fill the vacuum. But this paradox dissolves upon closer examination.

In fact, the dynasty and its nobility had locked themselves into an impossible situation. Their desire to control everything and to change nothing conflicted with their other perceptions of modern times. I have remarked above that the context for dynastic ritual changed in response to the popular demand for a nation-state. This was possible only because the court establishment had acquiesced to the changed context. It did so when it recognized that dynastic ritual should appeal not just to the nobility but also to the bourgeoisie. This meant adopting a bourgeois framework for judging ritual, and, to that extent, it meant that the court establishment relinquished some of its former control over dynastic ritual. Furthermore, it did so at just the time when ritual became even more important to the dynasty for coopting other

[92]Mosse, *Masses,* pp. 82–83, 91–92.

strata, since the dynasty was so dead-set against making concessions in any other sphere.[93] Unfortunately, the nobility was
highly ambivalent about granting concessions even in dynastic
ritual. William I's complete hostility toward national ritual and
his utter determination to preserve dynastic ritual for Prussia and
its nobility were doubtless comforting to the nobility after the
turmoil surrounding unification. But William II disturbed that
comfort.

Kaiser William II acknowledged, however obliquely, the importance of both the bourgeoisie and its nationalism by trying to
modernize Prussian dynastic ritual, in order both to involve the
bourgeoisie and to compete with it. To this end he expanded the
Hofgesellschaft, though not comprehensively enough, increased
court luxury, and introduced medieval-appearing costumes and
customs. However, the very structure of Prussian tradition defeated
these maneuvers. Prussian dynastic ritual was based historically
on the very opposite principles: noble exclusivity, frugality, and
lack of ostentation. Although the bourgeoisie was never significantly
integrated into Prussia's dynastic ritual, William's efforts had
profound effects upon the nobility. On the one hand, this class
objected to William's tampering with Prussian tradition. It resented
the "bourgeois" luxury, the display, the larger *Hofgesellschaft,*
because these changes affronted noble privilege, its history, and
the basis of noble social domination (birth, not wealth). At the
same time the nobles regretted the failure of William's efforts, for
they too accepted the changed context of dynastic ritual and
agreed that its audience had to be widened.

The significance of the nobility's paradoxical response is simply that structurally there was no way for the nobles to avoid
becoming self-doubting and pessimistic. They were damned if
they did and damned if they didn't. In a sense the ritual sphere
gave the court establishment a clearer view of the future than the
one it received from random political or social observations,

---

[93]Much has been written about the paralysis that afflicted the Kaisserreich in
its later years. See, for example, Volker Berghahn, "Das Kaiserreich in der
Sackgasse," *Neue politische Literatur* 16 (1971): 494–504.

because rituals are times specifically set aside for reflection about the larger questions of social existence. The nobles looked for significance in every ritual detail and found again and again the bleakness of their social isolation. The nobles' self-definition was intimately connected with ritual that demonstrated hierarchy, privilege, and obedience. It was an existential matter. The perceived failure of dynastic ritual to reach further into society symbolically undermined their power position and signaled that Germany had slipped beyond their control, even though they still monopolized the concrete bastions of power.

There were, of course, other causes for the nobility's pessimism, events which substantiated the black picture that ritual projected. And there were also flashes of optimism that flickered in the gathering darkness. In 1913 the celebrations surrounding the twenty-fifth anniversary of William's reign brought a brief respite from the nobility's gloom and showed how strong was the desire to believe in the dynasty.[94] Nonetheless, the nobles' loss of self-confidence, their despair, mirrored in their interpretation of ritual, is of crucial importance if we are to understand their desperate leap into the World War.[95] But, as Herr von Briest told his wife in Theodor Fontane's brilliant depiction of Wilhelmian society, *Effi Briest,* "That is *too* big a subject."

[94]Anton Monts's diary entry 17 January 1913, printed in Theodor Wolff, *Der Marsch durch zwei Jahrzehnte* (Amsterdam, 1936), p. 78.

[95]See Volker R. Berghahn, *Germany and the Approach of War in 1914* (London, 1973), pp. 171-73; Hull, *Entourage,* chap. 9.

2

The German Foreign Ministry and the Question of War Guilt in 1918–1919

ERICH J. C. HAHN

In June 1925, two months after he became president of the German Republic, seventy-seven-year-old Field Marshal Paul von Hindenburg noted with geriatric curtness how he dealt with the question of German war guilt: "On such matters you do not debate, but state your decided opinion, and that's that."[1] In electing an avowed monarchist and hero of the lost war as head of state of their young democracy, many Germans expressed uncritical attachment to the defunct empire. Such remarkable continuity in political attitudes was possible, despite the revolution of 1918-19, partly because the record of the German imperial government, especially its role in the outbreak of the World War, had not yet been fully examined.

The question of German war guilt, like the related question of German war aims, on which Hans W. Gatzke wrote the pioneering work,[2] touches on the fundamental purposes of imperial Germany's domestic and foreign policies. In recent years there has been an important debate about the relationship between domestic and foreign policy in imperial Germany. Following Eckart Kehr, historians such as Fritz Fischer, Hans-Ulrich Wehler, and Volker

---

[1]Paul von Hindenburg, notation on a report of a visit to England by Hermann Lutz, 24 June 1925, DZA, Präsidialkanzelei, no. 688, Schuld am Kriege, vol. 1, fol. 97.

[2]Hans W. Gatzke, *Germany's Drive to the West: A Study of the Western War Aims During the First World War* (Baltimore, Md., 1950, reprint, 1978).

Berghahn have suggested that the imperial government's foreign policy was largely an "integration strategy" dictated by domestic concerns. They argue that an outdated, authoritarian, imperial system, threatened by the rise of social democracy, tried to extend its life expectancy through an aggressive foreign policy. Specifically, in 1914 the imperial government assumed a calculated risk of war in a desperate attempt to unite a nation divided by class conflict. The aims of imperial foreign policy were not clarified after the revolution of 1918–19 by unhindered historical investigation. Every government during the Weimar Republic blocked full disclosure of the empire's role in the outbreak of the war and engaged in a political cover-up through semiofficial propaganda that reaffirmed the explanations of imperial policy from 1914. The foreign ministry took the lead in November 1918. Former imperial diplomats, whose integrity and position were at stake, found that personal interest coincided with patriotic duty. They fended off leftist demands for purges and salvaged their personal credibility at home (though not abroad) by claiming that the victors had fabricated the "lie" of German war guilt in order to exact huge reparations from the losers. Foreign Minister Ulrich von Brockdorff-Rantzau and his officials set the course of German policy on war guilt at Versailles. They were so determined to refute German guilt that they exceeded cabinet guidelines and disregarded directives. As a result, by the summer of 1919 the republic was firmly committed to defend the foreign policy and vindicate the historical reputation of the empire.

Germany's responsibility for the outbreak of war became a crucial issue of domestic and foreign policy in the last days of July 1914, when Chancellor Theobald von Bethmann Hollweg was less concerned to preserve peace at all costs than to avoid the suspicion of German guilt. He calculated that the long-standing social and political divisions which jeopardized Germany's chances of military success could be overcome only if Germany appeared

THE WEIMAR REPUBLIC

Legend

- TERRITORY LOST BY VERSAILLES TREATY
- FORMER GERMAN BORDER
- OCCUPIED TERRITORY
- BORDER OF DEMILITARIZED ZONE
- SAAR DISTRICT

MILES
0 50 100 200

Regions and places labeled: MEMELLAND, BALTIC SEA, EAST PRUSSIA, DANZIG, WEST PRUSSIA, POSEN, POLAND, WARSAW, Vistula River, UPPER SILESIA, DENMARK, SCHLESWIG, KIEL, LÜBECK, HAMBURG, BREMEN, Elbe River, BERLIN, Oder River, LEIPZIG, WEIMAR, COLOGNE, KOBLENZ, MAINZ, Rhine River, SAAR, STUTTGART, MUNICH, CZECHOSLOVAKIA, Danube River, VIENNA, AUSTRIA (ANSCHLUSS PREVENTED), BUDAPEST, HUNGARY, SWITZERLAND, ALSACE, LORRAINE, LUXEMBURG, EUPEN, MALMEDY, BELGIUM, FRANCE, HOLLAND, ENGLAND

to have been "forced into war."[3] By seemingly taking the Socialist party leaders into his confidence, he laid the basis for the unprecedented domestic accord (*Burgfriede*) of the early war years.[4] The complete success of Bethmann's domestic strategy in July 1914, which contrasts sharply with the miscalculated risks of his foreign policy, rested on a fundamental falsehood. Before the Reichstag on 4 August 1914 the emperor and the chancellor covered up Germany's role in the July crisis by placing all responsibility on Russia and France, alleging that the former had mobilized too soon and that the latter had violated German territory. From then on, censorship and propaganda reaffirmed the official view that an encircled Germany was fighting for survival. Even leading Social Democrats declared that the war was defensive. The deputy Eduard David stated this opinion so effectively at the Stockholm Socialist Congress in 1917 that his address was warmly endorsed by the Berlin Foreign Ministry official who monitored accounts of the origins of the war.[5]

In the fall of 1917 serious differences over war aims arose between the government and the Reichstag. Since uncensored revelations about the outbreak of the war could deepen the domestic discord, the government issued a secret censorship decree which assigned the Foreign Ministry to review before distribution any publication dealing with foreign policy, war guilt, and the political and military preparations for war. This effort "to avoid at all costs inconsistencies and contradictions from which foreign propaganda could forge weapons against us"[6] may have

---

[3]Bethmann Hollweg to Tschirschky, postscript, 27 July 1914, in Karl Kautsky, Max Montgelas, and Walter Schücking, eds., *Die Deutschen Dokumente zum Kriegsausbruch,* 4 vols. (Charlottenburg, 1919), 1:268.

[4]Konrad H. Jarausch, *The Enigmatic Chancellor: Bethmann Hollweg and the Hubris of Imperial Germany* (New Haven, Conn., 1973), pp. 168–69; Dieter Groh, *Negative Integration und Revolutionärer Attentismus* (Frankfurt, 1973), pp. 628–728.

[5]Susanne Miller, *Burgfrieden und Klassenkampf: Die Deutsche Sozialdemokratie im Ersten Weltkrieg* (Düsseldorf, 1974), pp. 183–90; Eduard David, *Wer trägt die Schuld am Kriege?* (Berlin, 1917), pp. 38–39; Bülow to Lersner, 18 October 1918, PA, Weltkrieg, adh. 4, Vorgeschichte des Krieges, vol. 12.

[6]Von Braun, secret decree, 20 October 1917, PA, Weltkrieg, adh. 4, Vorgeschichte des Krieges, vol. 8.

been a response to the circulation of a memoir by Prince Karl
Max Lichnowsky, German ambassador to Great Britain in 1914.
He denounced Germany's relentless naval buildup and inept
foreign policy and declared that he was not surprised that "the
whole civilized world outside Germany places the entire responsibility for the World War upon our shoulders."[7]

The role of Foreign Ministry watchdog was given to Legation
Secretary Bernhard Wilhelm von Bülow. An ardent patriot and a
zealous official, Bülow did not restrict himself to surveillance but
prepared a rebuttal to Lichnowsky and new documentation
supporting the official explanation of the outbreak of the war. In
the summer of 1918, Bülow also developed a long-term strategy
of preemptive historiography which became the basis of later
official efforts during the Weimar Republic to clear Germany of
charges of war guilt. He took for granted that the ministry itself
had to stay aloof in public debate. Material which the ministry
compiled would be publicized by a "politically trained" historian
who was free to engage in "aggressive polemics" because he
disavowed all ties to the ministry. Bülow estimated that with
continual clandestine coaching the right candidate would be able
to steer the war-guilt debate into the right channels:

> Such a task can be entrusted only to a man who is determined
> from the start to write nothing that would be detrimental to his
> fatherland; assuming sound intelligence [*gesunden Verstand*], this
> is not a danger in light of the sources. Aside from this condition,
> he would rely on his own judgment, and would not be subject to
> any kind of tutelage. To be sure, a special relationship of trust
> should be established, so that our [the Foreign Ministry's] judgment,
> resting as it does on even more complete knowledge of the sources,
> is taken into account, just in case historical research adheres to
> errors or is trapped in dead ends—a situation which may possibly
> never arise.[8]

Bülow's scheme to "stiffen the nation's will to resist" was not put

---

[7]Harry F. Young, *Prince Lichnowsky and the Great War* (Athens, Ga., 1977),
p. 149.

[8]Bülow to Smend, 20 June 1918, PA, Weltkrieg, adh. 4, Vorgeschichte des
Krieges, vol. 11.

to the test before the November 1918 revolution. But it shows that the imperial government, in particular the Foreign Ministry, feared all along that a free debate would make the official account of the outbreak of war less tenable.

Germany's catastrophic defeat gave the war-guilt question a new, revolutionary potential, best summed up by the Independent Socialist Karl Kautsky in the fall of 1919:

> Since the outbreak of the World War, one question occupies all minds: who brought this terrible misfortune upon us; which persons, which institutions are the causes? This is not only a scholarly question for historians. It is an eminently practical question for politicians. The answer contains the death sentence—not in a physical, but certainly in a political sense—for all those identified as authors [of the war]. The persons and institutions whose authority brought about such terrifying [events] must be cast among the politically dead, they must be stripped of all power.[9]

Yet the political demise of persons and institutions which Kautsky thought inevitable did not occur. The high bureaucracy was not interested in purges.[10] In the Foreign Ministry some junior officials issued a "November Manifesto" supporting the republic. But they never demanded that the senior statesmen and diplomats of the empire be held accountable.[11] All major political parties, including the Majority Socialist Party, were hamstrung by their wartime record. They could not expose the sins of the imperial government without assuming some responsibility for those sins.

Only the Independent Socialists demanded vigorously to tell all and spare no one. In this spirit Kurt Eisner, head of the revolutionary government in Munich, released reports to show that in July 1914 Germany had backed Austria despite prior knowledge of the ultimatum to Serbia. Eisner hoped to discredit both the old regime and the new Berlin government in order to steer Germany's

---

[9]Karl Kautsky, *Wie der Weltkrieg entstand: Dargestellt nach dem Aktenmaterial des Deutschen Auswärtigen Amts* (Berlin, 1919), p. 13.

[10]Wolfgang Elben, *Das Problem der Kontinuität in der deutschen Revolution* (Düsseldorf, 1965).

[11]Friedrich von Prittwitz und Gaffron, *Zwischen Petersburg und Washington: Ein Diplomatenleben* (Munich, 1952), p. 233.

November revolution into a more radical course. He thought that the Foreign Ministry in particular had to be purged so that only representatives of the new revolutionary Germany would negotiate the armistice and the peace.[12] In response to Eisner's revelations, which were of questionable accuracy, the Berlin government took the first steps to bring to light German foreign policy of 1914. It placed the most important imperial archives under its protection to ensure that nothing was destroyed[13] and commissioned Karl Kautsky to prepare an edition of Foreign Ministry documents on the outbreak of war. Like other Independent Socialists, Kautsky believed that all Germans had a right to know the truth about imperial policy during the July crisis. He also hoped that conclusive proof that the republic rejected the aims and methods of the empire might temper the victors' vengeance. To this end speed was essential. Kautsky and a small staff had their selection of documents ready for the press by late March 1919, well before the peace treaty was drafted.[14]

The Independent Socialists' sense of urgency about breaking with the old regime was confirmed by the cool reception which the German delegation met at the Berne Socialists' Conference in early 1919. The Germans were split. The Independents hoped to win international sympathy and support by openly conceding German war guilt. To the same end the Majority Socialists introduced a war-guilt resolution calling for full-scale publication of documents by all governments and the prosecution of guilty statesmen. The new Germany would show the way: "The young German Republic has no reason whatever to spare a single individual whenever it finds responsibility for the unleashing of international slaughter [*Völkermorden*]. German social democracy will use all its influence so that those who are responsible will be

---

[12]Herbert Michaelis and E. Schraepler, eds., *Ursachen und Folgen vom deutschen Zusammenbruch 1918 und 1945 bis zur staatlichen Neuordnung in der Gegenwart* (Berlin, n.d.), 111:26.

[13]Erich Matthias and Susanne Miller, eds., *Die Regierung der Volksbeauftragten, 1918-19: Quellen zur Geschichte des Parlamentarismus und der politischen Parteien* (Düsseldorf, 1969), 1st ser., 6:139 n. 8.

[14]Kautsky, *Wie der Weltkrieg entstand*, pp. 7-12.

prosecuted."[15] The full reckoning demanded by the Independent Socialists seemed assured. Yet the very next day, the Majority Socialist leader Hermann Müller backed off. In a major speech he blamed the war on long-standing economic rivalries among the powers.[16] By reiterating this commonplace of socialism, Müller played down individual responsibility and exonerated imperial Germany from particular blame. While the congress voted to readmit the Germans into the Socialist International, this did not mean full rehabilitation. Eduard Bernstein warned from Berne that the International would not support Germany's call for a truly just peace (*Rechtsfrieden*) without conclusive proof that the imperial past was overcome. Some continuities were tolerable in the administration, the judiciary, and the economic system. Bernstein continued:

> However, when one also persists in treating the question of the responsibility for the outbreak of war as if on this issue there were continuity between imperial and republican Germany,...then there is no hope of convincing the democracies of Europe that the German people, in parting company with the *Imperator,* have also taken leave of the imperialistic spirit.[17]

As Bernstein realized, only government policy could give evidence of deeper change. But the new government had a compelling reason not to expose or disavow the old regime.

In late November 1918 the German government learned from an official of the United States Embassy in The Hague that the victors would probably base their demand for reparations on Germany's guilt for the outbreak of the war. The informant recommended that Germany ward off this danger by calling for an international enquiry into war guilt, atrocities, and the blockade. The Foreign Ministry in Berlin immediately proposed a neutral international commission to examine all archives, question the

[15]*Vorwärts,* no. 86, 16 February 1919, report by H. Müller, copy in PA, Weltkrieg, no. 2c, Sozialistenkonferenzen..., Bern, vol. 13; Wolff Telegraphen Büro (WTB) release no. 280, 5 February 1919, ibid.

[16]WTB release nos. 286, 289, 6 February 1919, ibid.

[17]Bernstein to Foreign Ministry, 16 February 1919, ibid.; the report was forwarded to President Friedrich Ebert.

leading politicians of 1914, and reach a just verdict on war guilt.[18] The victors ignored this self-serving suggestion to put war guilt on ice, thereby eliminating the controversy from the peace negotiations and from German domestic politics as well. In early March 1919, Britain and France finally announced that an enquiry was superfluous because "the responsibility of Germany has been long ago incontestably proved." The Berlin Foreign Ministry rejected this summary verdict, charging that the victors, who rightly belonged among the accused, were acting as prosecutor and judge.[19] While the ministry was quite correct that the Allies' verdict was premature and partisan, the same was true of its own policy on war guilt.

Ever since the November 1918 warning, the Foreign Ministry had believed that the victors would base their reparation demands on the presumption of German guilt and ignored the possibility that enormous reparations might be exacted on other grounds.[20] Germany's economic future seemed at stake. The Foreign Ministry's investigations of war guilt were designed to undermine the victors' case. The prevailing attitude is revealed in minutes of a meeting convened in late February 1919 by the Foreign Ministry's Office for Peace Negotiations (Geschäftsstelle für die Friedensverhandlungen) to draft guidelines for research into the outbreak of war, atrocities, and William II's responsibility. The participants in the meeting first agreed, properly, to use only unimpeachable sources. But then they specified what conclusions were to be drawn: the navy and army would refute charges that Germany had made military and economic preparations for war in 1914, and the very principals responsible for German policy in 1914, former Secretary of State Gottlieb von Jagow or the head of the political division, Wilhelm von Stumm, would explain the outbreak of the war. A general staff representative suggested that they should show how France before the war had been "totally dominated by

---

[18]Peter Krüger, *Deutschland und die Reparationen, 1918–19* (Stuttgart, 1973), pp. 46–47.

[19]Michaelis and Schraepler, eds., *Ursachen und Folgen,* 111:331–32; cf. Krüger, *Deutschland und die Reparationen,* pp. 47, 147 n. 108.

[20]Krüger, *Deutschland und die Reparationen,* p. 47.

the policy of *revanche* for Alsace-Lorraine."[21] Thus two leading German statesmen of 1914 were to conduct their own prosecution and defense, with the acquittal already decided. The Foreign Ministry ignored this naïve proposal and turned to its war-guilt expert Bernhard von Bülow, whose approach was more subtle but no less partisan. He compiled "defense" and "offense" files (revealing the spirit in which he addressed his task), combed the victors' "colored books" (their official publications regarding the outbreak of the war) for inaccuracies,[22] and wrote essays on prewar diplomacy. In fact, Bülow himself assumed the role of the "politically trained" historian he had tried to recruit in 1918.

Bülow's efforts to exonerate imperial Germany were threatened in the latter part of March 1919, when Kautsky completed the documentation of German prewar policy. The collection revealed that Germany had energetically backed Austria, shielding it from foreign intervention even at the conscious risk of general war. Worse still, Kautsky had included the Kaiser's all-too-frequent spontaneous, truculent, puerile marginalia; whatever their influence, they were a highly quotable, devastating self-indictment of the man and the system. Kautsky noted with malicious glee that the imperial marginalia afforded a rare amusement: " . . . for once the people get to see an emperor in underwear."[23]

Kautsky's selection created a dilemma for the government which had promised to publish it. A Foreign Ministry review pointed out that if the documents were suppressed the victors could claim that the sinister record of imperial Germany was being concealed; if they were released, they could cite damaging passages out of context to justify harsh peace terms. The ministry also predicted that the German people would not believe docu-

[21]Minutes, 22 February 1919, PA, Geschäftsstelle für die Friedensverhandlungen, Protokolle und Protokollmaterial, vol. 1.

[22]PA, Weltkrieg, Handakten betr. Vorwürfe unserer Gegner die zu wiederlegen sind, Defensivmappe L.S. von Bülow, 1 vol.; Handakten betr. Anklagen die gegen unsere Gegner zu erheben sind, Offensivmappe L.S. von Bülow, 2 vols. The file PA, Handakten Gaus, no. 63, Anklagen die hinsichtlich der Schuld am Kriege gegen unsere Feinde zu erheben sind, is in fact also part of Bülow's papers.

[23]Kautsky, *Wie der Weltkrieg entstand,* p. 11. Kautsky's collection was published in late 1919; see n. 3 above.

ments that helped the victors' cause, particularly if they suspected that a desire to discredit the old regime had inspired "the quest for historical truth and determination to hide nothing."[24] By insinuating that the documentation bore the stigma of treasonable socialism, officials in the Foreign Ministry rejected Kautsky's aim to dissociate the republic from the empire. They proposed that a new commission, including Kautsky, should round out his selection with material from the War Ministry, the general staff, and even foreign publications. A project of such scope would have suspended informed debate on war guilt until long after the peace treaty. Doubtless that was the ministry's aim. But first the cabinet had to agree.

The cabinet decided on the fate of Kautsky's documentation at the same time that it defined guidelines for the German peace negotiators, in late March and early April 1919. Because the victors were expected to justify harsh peace terms by invoking German war guilt, the strategy the cabinet adopted to rebut this accusation determined the immediate fate of Kautsky's work. At first opinion was divided. Adolf Müller, the envoy in Berne, wanted "all suitable material" published. In the cabinet Matthias Erzberger thought that speedy publication might even benefit the peace negotiations. But Foreign Minister Ulrich von Brockdorff-Rantzau was not the man to expose the imperial government whose aims he had served so loyally. Nor would he risk a doctored publication, for fear of betrayal: " . . . the more radical elements [in the cabinet] could attack us in the rear with unwelcome revelations." In mid-March he informed the cabinet that "a unilateral publication would hardly improve" the German case.[25] Eduard David, an Independent Socialist, agreed but nonetheless opted for immediate publication. After seeing Kautsky's selection,

[24]Freytag, memorandum, n.d., "Aktenveröffentlichung über den Kriegsausbruch," PA, Weltkrieg, adh. 4, no. 2, vol. 2; unsigned memorandum with corrections by Bülow, n.d., ibid.; GFM 8849H/E615656–66.

[25]Dieckhoff to Bülow, 5 March 1919; PA, Schuldreferat, Agentenberichte, 123/1–5; cf. cabinet minutes, 17 March 1919, Hagen Schulze, ed., *Das Kabinett Scheidemann. Akten der Reichskanzlei, Weimarer Republik* (Boppard am Rhine, 1971), pp. 63–64.

he told the cabinet that he had to retract his wartime statements defending imperial policy because "moral guilt lay in large measure on the German side."[26] He had support from Walter Simons, head of the Foreign Ministry's legal section, and also from President Friedrich Ebert, who had commissioned Kautsky's work. Both wanted to convince the public at home and abroad that there was no continuity between empire and republic. But since most ministers had not seen Kautsky's selection, Johannes Bell, of the Center party, and David were delegated to submit a report. After hearing from Bell on 8 April that the selection gave a one-sided, unfavorable picture of German policy, the cabinet voted to postpone publication for the time being. David alone dissented.[27]

Yet the official promise to open up the record of imperial foreign policy in 1914 was seemingly not betrayed, only shelved. The cabinet also approved a two-phase inquiry. First, a parliamentary committee (*Untersuchungsausschuss*) acting as prosecutor would investigate whether any Germans shared responsibility for the outbreak of the war, its prolongation, or the eventual defeat. Cases arising from this preliminary inquiry would go before a special tribunal (*Staatsgerichtshof*) made up of high-court judges and parliamentarians.[28] Once again the effect and doubtless also the intent of this plan, which the foreign minister fully endorsed, was to keep documents on the outbreak of the war from the public for an indefinite period. The advantages for German domestic and foreign policy were obvious. At home no incriminating or controversial documents would fire up political debate. Abroad the victors' war-guilt verdict would appear premature and unjust, if not implausible, as long as Germany's parliamentary and judiciary inquiry was under way. The cabinet was so eager to have these political benefits that it ignored two fundamental objections put forward by the jurist Otto von Gierke: any extraordinary tribunal was contrary to German law, and its decisions

[26]Cabinet minutes, 22 March 1919, Schulze, *Kabinett Scheidemann*, pp. 85–91, citation, p. 88.

[27]Cabinet minutes, 8 April 1919, ibid., pp. 146–48.

[28]Ibid., pp. 147–49; p. 148 n. 10 explains the composition of the court.

would constitute ex post facto justice.[29] Legislation to create the inquiry was delayed in the national assembly. On 3 June, when the ultimatum imposing the peace treaty seemed imminent, Brockdorff-Rantzau telegraphed Prime Minister Philipp Scheidemann to speed up passage of the bill so that he could contrast Germany's "uncompromising" will to clear up the war-guilt question with the victors' ruthlessly dictated peace treaty.[30] While his desperate effort failed (the assembly never voted on the bill), it shows that Brockdorff-Rantzau's foremost interest was to gain diplomatic advantage from the appearance of forthrightness.

Contrary to appearances, however, between April and June 1919 the cabinet and the Foreign Ministry did more to suppress discussion than to further "uncompromising" clarification of the guilt question. Public debate entailed the risk of damaging revelations. One minister was even delegated to have "thorough conversations" with conservative leaders so that they would not ask "harmful questions" about war guilt in the national assembly. According to David, the government lived in constant fear that Kautsky might leak his documents before the peace treaty and that questions in the assembly could leave the government no choice but to publish his material to preclude a leak. It was probably for similar reasons that the cabinet turned down a suggestion by Prussia's state government that before any peace talks Germany should proclaim that it would not be saddled with war guilt and would reject all peace terms resting on this charge.[31] Brockdorff-Rantzau reassured the national assembly that an open and truthful answer to the guilt question was being sought, not to

[29]*Deutsche Zeitung,* no. 145, 31 March 1919, copy in DZA, Reichslandbund, no. 9056, Schuld am Kriege innerhalb Deutschlands, vol. 2.

[30]Brockdorff-Rantzau to Paxkonferenz Berlin, 3 June 1919, Schulze, *Kabinett Scheidemann,* p. 427 n. 15. Cf. Brockdorff-Rantzau interview, 4 June 1919, Ulrich von Brockdorff-Rantzau, *Dokumente und Gedanken um Versailles* (Berlin, 1925), pp. 189–90. Fritz Dickmann, *Die Kriegsschuldfrage auf der Friedenskonferenz von Paris* (Munich, 1964, reprint from *HZ* 197 [1963]:69–70), sees no political motives in the scheme to set up a special tribunal.

[31]Karstedt to Westarp, 22 and 25 March 1919, DZA, Nachlass Westarp, no. 41. Annelise Thimme kindly made these letters available. Scheidemann to Hirsch, 20 April 1919, Schulze, *Kabinett Scheidemann,* pp. 189–90.

avenge mistakes of the past but to learn from them. War guilt should be investigated only "as a means for political education."[32] Yet whatever these lessons, he seemed not to see an urgent need for them.

The policy of stifling public debate on war guilt before the conclusion of the peace treaty had two motives. Clearly the cabinet had patriotic reasons. Because the German case proved to be so weak, most ministers supported what appeared to be a temporary cover-up. They did not want to furnish the victors with any evidence that justified a harsh peace but sought to avert long-term harm to the republic. A more delicate reason for suppressing the record of the imperial government from public scrutiny was that the new republic depended heavily on the cooperation of former imperial officials and institutions. Because of this continuity at all but the highest levels, any revelations that discredited the old regime could do irreparable harm to the credibility of the new one.

Such concerns could not be openly discussed in the cabinet, where each minister had to guard his reputation. One incident illustrating the new government's vulnerability occurred on 27 March in an exchange between the Hamburg banker Max Warburg and the Independent Socialist Eduard Bernstein during a meeting of experts advising the Foreign Ministry on a financial strategy for the peace delegation.[33] After surveying the nation's financial plight, Warburg warned that Germany could not secure the credit necessary for reconstruction unless it denied war guilt from the outset. The Germans, he declared, could quite properly reject any accusation of war guilt because the immediate causes of the war were not yet known and over the long term all nations were equally responsible. Bernstein argued that it was a grave tactical error to stand up for the imperial government because

[32]Brockdorff-Rantzau speech, 4 October 1919, Brockdorff-Rantzau, *Dokumente und Gedanken um Versailles,* p. 69.

[33]Minutes of Finance Committee, 27 March 1919, A.M., PA, Geschäftsstelle für die Friedensverhandlungen, Protokolle und Protokollmaterial, vol. 3. There are two manuscripts, the typed original edited by Warburg and the printed final version.

nothing could persuade the French or the British that the Central Powers had not started the war. There was hope for concessions from the victors only if the new Germany demonstrated that it had definitely broken with the old. Thus challenged, Warburg seemed to agree. But his script for proclaiming the break (a passage Warburg edited from the final minutes) has the flavor of Wilhelmian diplomatic insensitivity. The Germans were to declare proudly:

> ... we were driven into the general warlike situation as a result of circumstances as they formerly existed. You did not allow us to rise economically (Bernstein: Oh, wealthy Germany!); during the whole period we could not expand economically one way or another. I worked quite long enough on the colonial agreement with England to see how difficult things were, and how in the end they gave us nothing. [Typed manuscript, p. 59]

By flaunting bitter memories of frustrated world policy or reviving well-worn accusations of encirclement, as Warburg suggested, the republic could hardly prove that it had put the empire behind. Yet he recognized the dilemma which the continuity in persons and institutions created when he warned that the victors would laugh derisively if the Germans arrived saying; "Until now we were criminals; however, from here on we will be different." The victors would say to themselves: "That can't be true, because they themselves can't believe it. They must know better" (typed manuscript, p. 60). Indeed, the foremost problem was the credibility of the German delegates and their government. As Bernstein replied, everything hinged on the word "we":

> The question is not whether we are guilty. I must ask you to use the word "we" with great care. There is not a single issue on which there are more transgressions or lapses than with the word "we." (Warburg: Our predecessors!) Yes, that is the point. Today Germany is a Republic and has broken with the old system. One thing must be stated: the new Germany is not the same as the old, it is not liable. Joint liability [*Solidarität*] must be rejected and by rejecting it one puts the new Germany in a much better position abroad than it has been up to now. [Printed manuscript, p. 24]

Bernstein asked the German peace negotiators to do the impossible, just as David did in the cabinet. In 1919 there were no prominent officials (except Social Democrats) whose political reputations had not been made in the empire or who had not represented its interests and supported or at least condoned its aspirations. Doubtless everyone had questioned some aspects of imperial policy. But no one who had risen in the service of the empire could suddenly denounce it and claim to be a democratic republican without inviting incredulous smiles. Even as Warburg protested his readiness to cut loose from the past, he gave himself away twice, once when he slipped into the traditional apologia for Wilhelmian world policy and again when he recalled how he had represented that policy in international negotiations. The issue was not only the credibility of the republic and its delegation in concluding financial agreements, as Warburg suggested. Equally at stake were the personal honor and political credibility of every imperial official who, in response to Ebert's appeal, had remained in public life after November 1918. For this reason the republic could not suddenly disavow the empire, as the Independent Socialists demanded.

On 21 April the cabinet agreed to a policy on war guilt submitted by the Foreign Ministry.[34] The German delegation would try to eliminate the issue from the agenda by rejecting the victors' attempt to base their terms on alleged German guilt. The Germans would argue that the role of each nation in the outbreak of the war was not yet known and had to be assessed in the broader context of European politics going back to 1871. Since the victors had turned down the German proposal for a neutral international inquiry, Germany would launch one alone, and until that investigation was completed, it "must decline discussion of the war-guilt question." Finally, the delegation would declare that the issue did not have to be settled before peace negotiations, because in the armistice Germany had already assumed specific obligations to make reparations (this was a reference to the Lansing note of 5 November 1918, by which Germany had agreed to make compen-

[34]"Richtlinien für die deutschen Friedensunterhändler", 21 April 1919, Schulze, *Kabinett Scheidemann,* pp. 203–204. Cf. Scheidemann to Hirsch, 20 April 1919, ibid., pp. 189–90.

sation "for all damage done to the civilian population of the Allies and their property by the aggression of Germany by land, by sea, and from the air"). The manner of carrying out this moderate, inoffensive protest was left to Brockdorff-Rantzau and the peace delegation.

In Versailles the Germans learned that there would be no direct negotiations. The ceremony at which they received the draft peace treaty was their only chance to address the victors face to face. Brockdorff-Rantzau and his colleagues were aware of the perils of this opportunity and debated his response almost to the last minute. From several drafts the foreign minister chose the harshest and delivered it in a most offensive manner. With the treaty still unopened before him, he accused the victors of intense hatred and a passionate wish to punish Germany and make it pay. Twice he denounced the treaty for charging Germany with unilateral war guilt, which it did not do. Then he proposed other reasons for the war—the imperial rivalries of the previous half century, the denial of national self-determination and, of course, Russia's mobilization—and called again for a neutral inquiry into war guilt and war crimes. These issues took up nearly half of the address. In the other half Brockdorff-Rantzau reminded the victors that the prearmistice agreements were the only legally binding basis for a just peace and outlined what he regarded to be Germany's commitments to make reparations to Belgium and France only.[35]

By his manner and his address Brockdorff-Rantzau served notice that the journey to Versailles would not become a "march to Canossa," an analogy made several weeks earlier by Bernhard von Bülow.[36] But the cabinet guidelines of 21 April did not call for instant and aggressive denial of German war guilt. As other drafts show, Brockdorff-Rantzau could have taken up the issue in

[35]Brockdorff-Rantzau address, 7 May 1919, *Das Deutsche Weissbuch über die Schuld am Kriege: Materialien, betreffend die Friedensverhandlungen,* pt. 6, (Charlottenburg, 1919), pp. 1–4.

[36]Bülow manuscript, "Weltdemokratie oder Weltrevolution, pt. 3, Der Gang nach Versailles," n.d., PA, Nachlass St.S. B.W. von Bülow, Pariser Friedenskonferenz, vol. 3.

more temperate tones or ignored it altogether until the treaty had at least been studied.[37] Why he chose to abandon the reserve of a seasoned diplomat is unclear. He gave a studied performance of contempt from the moment he remained seated while reading his speech to his exit, when he affected Bismarckian disdain by lighting a cigarette. Outwardly the delegation supported him, as did the cabinet and most of the German people. Only the Independent Socialists did not join in the rejectionist clamor, which they believed was futile.

Brockdorff-Rantzau had accepted his portfolio on condition that he could reject a humiliating, ruinous peace. This policy could succeed only if the whole nation backed the government. Unlike the military, financial, and territorial provisions of the treaty, which were often highly technical and appealed to sectional interests, war guilt, presented as a question of national honor, touched all Germans—statesmen, soldiers, and civilians—who could not admit that their incalculable sacrifices had been made for an immoral cause. While no known document suggests that Brockdorff-Rantzau decided to play up war guilt in order to re-create something like the domestic accord (*Burgfriede*) of 1914, the foreign minister's fulminations appear to have been part of his strategy to prepare and unite the country to reject the treaty. The cabinet soon objected that such emphasis was given to war guilt. But the German delegation ignored its directives.[38]

The Germans ultimately had only three weeks to examine the draft treaty. In that time they submitted a spate of seventeen notes to prove that the treaty violated the spirit of Woodrow Wilson's principles and the letter of the armistice agreements and was unfulfillable as well. Three notes dealt with war guilt. The German attack concentrated on Article 231, which seemed to link the victors' reparations claims to German war guilt. The article states:

[37] Alma Luckau, *The German Delegation at the Paris Peace Conference* (New York, 1941), pp. 65, 213–20.

[38] Udo Wengst, *Graf Brockdorff-Rantzau und die aussenpolitischen Anfänge der Weimarer Republik* (Frankfurt, 1973), p. 57.

The Allied and Associated Governments affirm and Germany accepts the responsibility of Germany and her allies for causing all the loss and damage to which the Allied and Associated Governments and their nationals have been subjected as a consequence of the war imposed upon them by the aggression of Germany and her allies.

For the Germans this was unacceptable on two counts. First, the victors were breaking the prearmistice agreements to clear the way for higher reparations. There was just cause for this view, though the Germans, interpreting the armistice to their advantage, clung to false hopes about the size of their reparations payments.[39] Second, the article seemed to amount to a confession that imperial Germany had been the "aggressor." Even though all the victors held this opinion, in Article 231 they did not intend to express a moral verdict; "aggression" referred to the declarations of war and the violation of Belgian neutrality, which the imperial government had always admitted.[40]

The Germans proceeded on two mistaken assumptions: that Article 231 was the keystone holding up much of the treaty and that this article was based on a report written by a ten-power commission which the Allies had set up in January 1919 to examine war guilt, war crimes, and the possibility of trials. In the first chapter, "Responsibility of the Authors of the War," the commission had concluded that in 1914 the Central Powers had premeditated war and made it unavoidable by deliberately blocking conciliation efforts.[41] The German delegation in Versailles had come into possession of the report in the beginning of May and had decided, by refuting it, to strike at Article 231 and the treaty itself.

[39]Krüger, *Deutschland und die Reparationen,* pp. 50–51. Cf. Hajo Holborn, "Diplomats and Diplomacy in the Early Weimar Republic," in *Germany and Europe,* (New York, 1970), pp. 187, 190.

[40]Fritz Dickmann, *Die Kriegsschuldfrage auf der Friedenskonferenz in Paris 1919,* pp. 8–11, 15–17. On the origins of Article 231 see ibid., pp. 43–59; Holborn, "Diplomats and Diplomacy in the Early Weimar Republic," pp. 186–88.

[41]"Rapport présenté à la Conférence des Préliminaires de Paix par la Commission des Responsabilités des Auteurs de la Guerre et Sanctions, 29 Mars 1919." The first part of the report dealing with war guilt is reprinted in *Das Deutsche Weissbuch,* pp. 12–27; see n. 35 above.

Bernhard von Bülow, who was in Versailles as the Foreign Ministry's expert on war guilt, outlined the procedure on 13 May.[42] As an overture the Germans would discredit the various "colored books," the main sources of the Allied report. Bülow had already written critiques to show that the official British, French, Belgian, and Rumanian collections were incomplete, inaccurate, and biased. These articles appeared in the *Deutsche Allgemeine Zeitung* under an editorial comment that the Allied War Guilt Commission had based its conclusions on questionable sources.[43] To discredit the report, Brockdorff-Rantzau invited four respectable scholars to Versailles: Hans Delbrück, Count Max Montgelas, Albrecht Mendelssohn Bartholdy, and Max Weber. They belonged to the Heidelberg Association for a Policy of Justice, a select group of political moderates with international connections. Prince Max von Baden had sponsored it in February 1919 to refute the victors' verdict of German war guilt and to lobby for a peace of reconciliation.[44] Ostensibly the four men were to write a critique of the Allied commission's report on responsibility. In fact, they were expected to sign a memorandum prepared for them, probably by Bülow. This is clear from Brockdorff-Rantzau's instructions: "The necessary material is here [in Versailles], the rebuttal nearly completed. It is a question of enhancing the value of our material by the authority of these gentlemen. Therefore,

[42]Bülow to Freytag, 13 May 1919, PA, Schuldreferat 15/30, Korrespondenz Bülow-Freytag.
    [43]Ibid.; Haniel to Naumann & Freytag, 13 May 1919, PA, Handakten Bernstorff, vol. 5. The series ran in the *Deutsche Allgemeine Zeitung*, no. 235, 17 May 1919, to no. 246, 22 May 1919. Manuscripts of the series are in PA Handakten Gaus, no. 63, a file originating with Bülow.
    [44]The papers of the Heidelberg Association seem to be lost. They are not in the archive of Prince Max von Baden (letter from Sekretariat Schloss Salem, 6 April 1978) or in the papers of Kurt Hahn (personal information from Frau Henriette von Arnswald, Warnsdorf) or in the papers of Count Maximilian Montgelas, whose extensive correspondence appears to be no longer extant. The Montgelas Papers consist mainly of well-ordered manuscripts and clippings from the postwar period. I am grateful to Ludwig Count Montgelas (Bubing-Ampfing, Bavaria) for granting me generous access to this material.

please extend the invitation so courteously that there may be no refusals."[45]

Evidently Brockdorff-Rantzau feared the candidates would reject his invitation if they learned of his intentions. Weber did not know the reason for his summons and was even misinformed when he called at the Foreign Ministry before leaving for Versailles. Brockdorff-Rantzau expected Montgelas to resist his call.[46] Probably only Delbrück knew his role. He postponed his departure to make contact with Jagow and to visit Bethmann Hollweg in Hohenfinow. These contacts put Delbrück in a position to prevent discrepancies between the memoirs that both statesmen were about to publish and the rebuttal being prepared in Versailles. Bethmann even gave Delbrück galley proofs of his memoirs and explained various damaging revelations.[47]

By bringing the scholars to Versailles, Brockdorff-Rantzau trapped them neatly. If they left without producing a strong professorial refutation of the Allied report, they would appear less than patriotic and weaken the German position. Yet a scholarly critique was hardly possible, since they had few documents at their disposal and not even a week to reach agreement. Apparently they saw some Foreign Ministry files, including "Weltkrieg, vols. 1–16, July–August 1914," about which there is a curious passage in a letter from Bülow: "I have telegraphed for the files today and you were so kind to see to the necessary small additions."[48] These may have been justified and harmless, but

[45]Brockdorff-Rantzau to Foreign Ministry, 13 May 1919 (draft by Bülow), PA, Deutsche Friedensdelegation in Versailles, pol. 7, Die Vorgeschichte des Krieges und die Schuldfrage, vol. 1, GFM 4662H/E213294-95.

[46]Wolfgang J. Mommsen, *Max Weber und die deutsche Politik, 1890-1920* (Tübingen, 1974), pp. 341 n. 132, 349 n. 162. On Montgelas see Bernstorff to Müller (Berne), 14 May 1919, and reply, 15 May 1919, PA, Handakten Bernstorff, no. 1.

[47]Delbrück to Jagow, 17 May 1919; draft of reply, 20 May 1919, BA, Nachlass Delbrück, no. 78, p. 245; Bethmann Hollweg to Jagow, 20 May 1919, PA, Nachlass Jagow, no. 7.

[48]See n. 42 above. On returning the files to Berlin, Bülow instructed Freytag to lock them away in a special safe so that, "in case the entente should demand them, they can be got out of the way easily"; 28 May 1919, PA, Schuldreferat 15/30, Bülow-Freytag Correspondence.

Brockdorff-Rantzau kept from the scholars in Versailles important evidence that did not fit his strategy. Roderich Goos, a historian in the Austrian Foreign Ministry, found material suggesting that Bethmann Hollweg had warmly endorsed the British mediation offer of 29 July 1914 while Austria-Hungary's foreign secretary, Count Leopold Berchtold, had deliberately scuttled it to ensure that war would break out between Germany and Russia.[49] Goos took this material to Berlin, and the Foreign Ministry officials were so impressed that they sent him on to Versailles.[50] Brockdorff-Rantzau regarded the new evidence as more incriminating than helpful, though his reasoning was a bit confused: "Unfortunately it shows that while the impotence of our foreign policy makers of that time does completely vindicate our policy in a moral sense, we nevertheless failed miserably, intellectually and politically."[51] He ignored the Austrian offer to publish the material immediately. To shift responsibility onto Austria-Hungary was no advantage. Bülow had already noted in November 1918 that Germany would still be blamed for supporting its reckless ally.[52] The Goos material also did not fit into the Foreign Ministry's plan to fix blame on imperial Russia. For these tactical reasons the scholars in Versailles were allowed mere glimpses of the Austrian documents.[53] Brockdorff-Rantzau did not want a critical review of all the evidence, only prestigious autographs to

[49]Wedel to Brockdorff-Rantzau, 26 and 30 April 1919, PA, Weltkrieg, adh. 4, Sammlung von Schriftstücken zur Vorgeschichte des Krieges, vol. 15, GFM 8860/E617828–29 and 841–42. Cf. Roderick Goos, *Das Wiener Kabinett und die Entstehung des Weltkrieges* (Berlin, 1919), pp. 232–42.

[50]Wedel to Bauer, 4 April [sic, should be May] 1919, and reply, 7 May 1919, HHStA, Deutsch-Öesterreich 13/1, Veröffentlichung der Dokumente betr. den Kriegsausbruch, 1919; Langwerth to Brockdorff-Rantzau, 9 May 1919, PA, Weltkrieg, adh. 4, vol. 15, GFM 8860/E617852.

[51]Brockdorff-Rantzau to Langwerth, 3 May 1919, GFM 8860/E617844; for the citation see cabinet minutes, 19 May 1919, Schulze, *Kabinett Scheidemann*, p. 351.

[52]Bülow to Schwertfeger, 6 November 1918, BA, Nachlass Schwertfeger, no. 77; cf. undated memorandum, PA, Nachlass Brockdorff-Rantzau, Versailles 1, vol. 1, GFM 9015/H235320–21.

[53]Brockdorff-Rantzau to Foreign Ministry, 14 May 1919, PA, Weltkrieg, adh. 4, vol. 15, GFM 8860/E617858; for Ebert, Brockdorff-Rantzau to Langwerth, 26 May 1919, GFM 8860/E617887.

give a political document the hallmark of independent scholarship. He succeeded admirably. Even today the document is still known as the "professors' memorandum." How much or how little of it the professors wrote is impossible to reconstruct. Coached by Bülow and others who had intimate knowledge of the sources and a clear idea of the political needs of the day, the academics eventually submitted a text on 27 May that was acceptable to the German delegation.[54] Actually, with the exception of Brockdorff-Rantzau the delegates were very skeptical of the entire scheme and at first suggested that the professors should simply publish their work on their own.[55]

Predictably, the professors' memorandum blamed the Russians' mobilization for war. Lesser villains were revanchist France and mistrustful Britain, though the mood in the latter was deemed understandable in light of Germany's naval program. Supporting the memorandum were "heavy-caliber" appendices from Bülow's file "Accusations Regarding War Guilt That Should Be Leveled Against Our Enemies."[56] Bülow used evidence from captured Serbian archives to show that Russia had for years conspired with Balkan states, Serbia in particular, to diminish Austria's position in that area. The collection ended with articles reprinted from *Pravda* which blamed imperial Russia, France, and Britain more than the Central Powers but also argued that imperialism in general had caused the war. On several occasions Brockdorff-Rantzau himself had taken up this Leninist interpretation, which spread responsibility very broadly and blamed no one in particular.[57]

Before Brockdorff-Rantzau could deliver the professors' memo-

---

[54]Schulze, *Kabinett Scheidemann,* p. 384 n. 19. Individual contributions to the professors' memorandum might be sorted out if the Bonn Foreign Ministry Archive discovers the file Handakten Simons, no. 14, Bemerkungen zum Bericht der Kommission . . . über die Verantwortlichkeiten der Urheber des Krieges.

[55]Delegation Versailles, minutes, 25 May 1919, 6:00 P.M., GFM 4662H/E212249.

[56]*Das Deutsche Weissbuch,* n. 35 above, esp. pp. 58–67. For the Bülow appendices see PA, Handakten Gaus, no. 63, n. 22 above.

[57]Brockdorff-Rantzau, speeches, 15 January 1919, 14 February 1919, Graf Brockdorff-Rantzau, *Dokumente und Gedanken um Versailles,* 7 May 1919 (Berlin, 1925), pp. 41, 46–47, 70.

randum and appendices to the victors and distribute it simultaneously at home and abroad, the cabinet in Weimar had to consent. It did not approve how the foreign minister had played up the war-guilt question in Versailles. In a note of 13 May he had challenged the victors to hand over their evidence. Allied compliance would have given the report by the Commission on Responsibility status as a peace-conference document that Germany could challenge officially.[58] The cabinet found the note too provocative. After David saw the Goos material and warned that any mention of war guilt only invited "a political setback and a hefty diplomatic slap in the face," the cabinet ordered the delegation in Versailles to suspend further declarations on the subject and study the evidence.[59] It did not want to provoke the victors and jeopardize the overriding objective of the German notes and counterproposals: to achieve negotiations. Since there were additional disagreements between Weimar and Versailles, members from each side conferred in Spa, Belgium, on 18 May. Brockdorff-Rantzau maintained that he had been authorized to make policy in Versailles, in consultation with his delegation and without interference from Weimar. He denied exceeding the cabinet's guidelines in his note on war guilt of 13 May and gave no hint of the preparations under way to deliver more notes on the topic.[60] On 24 May another note warned the victors that if they reverted to secret diplomacy to decide the war-guilt question Germany might make it the public issue it ought to be.[61] The material for this offensive, which was strictly against cabinet directives, was the professors' memorandum with its appendices. In a rare telephone call to Berlin on 27 May, Bülow asked for immediate cabinet approval to submit this package to the victors. But the cabinet, which had not seen the material, again ordered the delegation not to issue any note on war

[58]Brockdorff-Rantzau to Clemenceau, 13 May 1919, *Deutsche Weissbuch,* p. 5.

[59]Cabinet minutes, 14 May 1919, Schulze, *Kabinett Scheidemann,* pp. 322 n. 5, 323; citation from Brockdorff-Rantzau, memorandum, 19 May 1919, ibid., p. 351.

[60]Brockdorff-Rantzau, memorandum, 19 May 1919, ibid., pp. 349–51.

[61]Brockdorff-Rantzau to Clemenceau, 24 May 1919, *Deutsche Weissbuch,* pp. 8–11.

guilt.[62] This injunction did not stop Brockdorff-Rantzau. On 28 May,"after heavy battles and against the will of the cabinet," he submitted the complete material to the victors and released it simultaneously as a new *German White Book*.[63] When several ministers protested this highhanded disregard of a cabinet order, Brockdorff-Rantzau tried to dismiss the professors' memorandum as the work of four pacifists that was supposed to flush out the victors' evidence.[64] This was certainly not true. Bülow's hurried efforts to have the *White Book* translated, distributed in hundreds of copies at home and abroad, and reviewed in the press show that its purpose was to mobilize domestic and foreign opinion against the treaty.[65] After the great strain of preparing the German case, Bülow made a rare, candid estimate of his efforts in a personal letter:

> As long as we live the guilt question will be disputed. For us, Russia—the imperial one, of course—must remain the scapegoat. However, any nation can be charged successfully only on the basis of its own documents. I would undertake "to prove" conclusively from the archives of any nation that it, and it alone, is responsible for the war—or for whatever else you like.[66]

The passage expresses the spirit in which the Foreign Ministry conducted its campaign against the charge of German war guilt. Behind the public pretense of seeking historical truth, behind the academic façade, political expediency ruled. Imperial Russia was the logical scapegoat. Bethmann Hollweg had already cast it in this role in 1914, and it no longer had official defenders. Moreover, if the victors conceded a measure of Russian responsibility, they

[62]Bülow-Dieckhoff, telephone transcript, [27 May 1919], PA, Handakten Bernstorff, vols. 1-2. Cabinet minutes, 27 May 1919, Schulze, *Kabinett Scheidemann*, p. 384.

[63]Bülow to Freytag, 28 May 1919, PA, Schuldreferat 15/30, Bülow-Freytag Correspondence. Delegation Versailles, minutes, 28 May 1919, GFM 4662H/E212591.

[64]Schulze, *Kabinett Scheidemann*, pp. 384–85 n. 10; cabinet minutes, ibid., 30 May 1919, pp. 402–403; cabinet minutes, 2 June 1919, ibid., p. 416.

[65]On the distribution and translation of the *White Book* in early June see PA, Handakten Bernstorff, no. 4; Schuldreferat, Bülow-Freytag Correspondence; Handakten Simons, no. 113; Nachlass Bülow, Pariser Friedenskonferenz, vol. 3.

[66]Bülow to Freytag, 31 May 1919, PA, Schuldreferat 15/30, Bülow-Freytag Correspondence.

admitted inadvertently their own complicity as Russia's former allies. But this "total plan" (*Gesamtplan*), as Bülow called it,[67] was too clever and failed completely. On 16 June the victors issued an ultimatum that included only minor revisions of the treaty but reasserted German war guilt in the strongest terms. Thus Brockdorff-Rantzau's insistent refutations provoked the diplomatic slap in the face that David had predicted. Abroad, sympathy for Germany's situation was always restricted to marginal groups. At home, the war-guilt question did not galvanize public opinion. On his return Brockdorff-Rantzau indirectly conceded the failure of his tactic. He omitted war guilt entirely from two speeches which he hoped would persuade the cabinet and the Reichstag not to sign the treaty.[68]

By making a refutation of Germany's alleged unilateral war guilt official policy at Versailles, Brockdorff-Rantzau left a fateful legacy. The Foreign Ministry continued the campaign in his spirit over the next fifteen years through a small War Guilt Section (Schuldreferat), which monitored and directed research and discussion at home and abroad. One of its purposes was to shift debate from the July crisis to the long-range policies of all the European states. In March 1919, Count Bernstorff ventured in the cabinet that 1870 was the year to start. The monumental publication of Foreign Ministry documents *Die Grosse Politik der Europäischen Kabinette, 1871–1914* (1922–27) realized this suggestion. The unprecedented speed of publication and wealth of material forced any student of prewar diplomacy to rely heavily on German sources selected under Foreign Ministry auspices.[69]

[67]Bülow to Haniel, 4 June 1919, GFM 8860/E617924–25.

[68]Brockdorff-Rantzau, draft speeches for the cabinet and the national assembly, 17 June 1919, PA, Nachlass Brockdorff-Rantzau, Versailles 1, vol. 1, GFM 9015/235432–47, 466–74.

[69]Herman J. Wittgens, "War Guilt Propaganda Conducted by the German Foreign Ministry During the 1920s" (unpublished paper presented at the Annual Meeting of the Canadian Historical Association, Montreal, 1980), p. 5. See also Annelise Thimme, "Friedrich Thimme als politischer Publizist im Ersten Weltkrieg und in der Kriegsschuldkontroverse," in Alexander Fischer, Gunter Moltmann,

In the German antiwar-guilt campaign of 1918–19 men and institutions rooted in the old regime revealed their inability to break with the past. Only the Socialists could readily turn against the empire which had stigmatized them as outsiders. However, as novices in government and diplomacy they had to call on imperial elites to help ensure domestic stability and negotiate peace. The Socialist leaders proved no match for resolute institutional infighters like Brockdorff-Rantzau and Bülow, who were determined to defend their "good cause."[70] There was more to this cause than winning international support for milder terms at Versailles, or rallying German opinion, in the manner of prewar integration strategy, to reject a humiliating dictated peace. In any case the November revolution had made that strategy obsolete by establishing parliamentary government. Thereafter the traditional elite in the Foreign Ministry had to ensure its political survival by defending its credibility at home and abroad. The war-guilt question served a function similar to the stab-in-the-back legend which allowed the army to escape the political consequences of defeat. By claiming to defend Germany against the charge of unilateral war guilt (which was a blatant distortion), the diplomats were in effect trying to elude the consequences of the miscalculated risks of 1914. For this reason the antiwar-guilt campaign had to be kept alive even after the peace was signed. Through the 1920s the Foreign Ministry's antiwar-guilt propaganda stifled a critical reassessment of Germany's role in Europe and possibly post-

and Klaus Schwabe, eds., *Russland Deutschland Amerika: Festschrift für Fritz T. Epstein zum 80. Geburtstag* (Wiesbaden, 1978), pp. 212–38, esp. pp. 223–38. After World War II the scholarly standards of *Die Grosse Politik* were superseded in the *Akten zur deutschen auswärtigen Politik, 1918–1945*. Since 1969, Hans W. Gatzke has had a great share in maintaining these standards as United States editor-in-chief of this unique international project. See Hans W. Gatzke, "The Quadripartite Project: *Akten zur deutschen auswärtigen Politik, 1918–1945:* Experiment in International Historiography," in *Russland Deutschland Amerika,* pp. 333–41.

[70]Bülow used this phrase in July 1918 when recruiting a historian to publicize the Foreign Ministry's view on the outbreak of the war; see n. 8 above.

poned a break with the traditions and aspirations of imperial foreign policy. The resulting continuity in political culture helps explain why the German electorate could choose a backward-looking, defeated Prussian general as president and cheer the revanchist beer-hall braggadocio of an Austrian lance corporal.[71]

[71]Grants from the Canada Council and the Deutscher Akademischer Austauschdienst made possible the archival research for this article. I presented an earlier version at the Annual Meeting of the Canadian Historical Association in Montreal in 1980. The careful criticism of several colleagues helped me improve substance and style.

3

German Army Doctrine, 1918–1939, and the Post-1945 Theory of "Blitzkrieg Strategy"

WILLIAMSON MURRAY

For obvious reasons the period between 1933 and 1945 has been one of the most widely studied in German history. Yet historians have shown little or no interest in some aspects of the period. The scholarly literature exhaustively explores the political history of the German army and the gradual process of "coordination" (*Gleichschaltung*) through which the National Socialist system absorbed it but has left the evolution of German military doctrine, tactics, and strategic thought in the interwar period relatively untouched.[1] Military historians have for the most part begun their studies with the outbreak of the World War II,[2] while other historians have looked at this period in German history as if a mere mention of rearmament were sufficient to dispose of the entire thorny topic.

Yet the doctrines which the German army developed between the wars not only made possible the complete destruction of the

[1] For works on the political relations between the army and the party see Klaus-Jürgen Müller, *Das Heer und Hitler* (Stuttgart, 1966); Robert J. O'Neill, *The German Army and the Nazi Party* (London, 1966); Manfred Messerschmidt, *Die Wehrmacht im NS-Staat* (Hamburg, 1969); Telford Taylor, *Sword and Swastika* (New York, 1952); John Wheeler-Bennett, *The Nemesis of Power* (New York, 1952). A work that attempts to examine doctrine is T. N. Dupuy, *A Genius for War* (Englewood Cliffs, N.J., 1977), but Dupuy makes hardly any use of primary sources.

[2] See particularly B. H. Liddell Hart, *The History of the Second World War* (London, 1970).

European balance of power between 1939 and 1941 but also enabled a beleaguered and outnumbered Germany to hold out well beyond the theoretical limits of its economic and military potential in the face of the overwhelming superiority of the United States, the Soviet Union, and Great Britain. Germany's remarkable performance suggests several questions: How did German doctrine develop between the wars? What factors influenced German thinking? Most important, what was the relationship between German foreign policy and grand strategy, on the one hand, and German doctrine, particularly the doctrine of the so-called blitzkrieg, on the other?

Any discussion of German military thought between the wars must begin with the lessons of the Great War. Throughout that war the Germans had proved themselves more imaginative and realistic than their opponents in their adaptation to new tactical and operational conditions.[3] Nevertheless, by 1916 the armies of Germany, Britain, and France had reached a stalemate on the Western Front. This deadlock had produced a combination of spiraling casualties and diminishing results. The Germans therefore exchanged their strategy of attrition (Verdun) and unwillingness to abandon any territory (the Somme) for a more flexible response on both strategic and tactical levels. General Erich Ludendorff, the prime molder of German strategy in the last two years of the war, abandoned attrition in the West in favor of a concentrated attempt to destroy Russia. In France and Flanders the Germans stood on the defensive. In 1917 a major operational withdrawal from the bulge of the German lines in France to more defensible positions freed a number of divisions. In addition, this retreat from an exposed salient took the sting out of General Robert Nivelle's disastrous spring 1917 offensive.

Tactically, Ludendorff discarded the doctrine that front-line troops abandon no territory. Instead of packing infantry into front-line trenches, the Germans now held forward positions with a thin screen of machine gunners, who delayed the attackers and

---

[3]In particular see the fine study of G. C. Wynne, *If Germany Attacks* (London, 1940). It was largely ignored when it appeared.

gained time for the artillery and infantry reserves to counter enemy moves. The bulk of German forces formed counterattack units at local, operational, or strategic levels.[4] The German success against the Nivelle offensive and the British attacks at Passchendaele indicate how close the Germans had come to solving the problem of defensive warfare—that of inflicting maximum casualties while suffering minimum losses in territory and manpower. The successful German counterattack at Cambrai in 1917 after the initial shattering impact of the British tank assault exemplifies the effectiveness of German "offensive-defensive" tactics.

In the east the wide-ranging military operations freed the German high command from the "trench mentality" that characterized Allied military leadership both during and after the war. Nevertheless, while Ludendorff's armies had achieved operational freedom, they had failed to turn operational successes into a decisive strategic success. German armies never managed to trap a significant body of Russian troops except at Tannenberg, where the Russians marched into the encirclement.

With the collapse of Russia in 1917, German attention returned to the West. Ludendorff's first blow, against the Italians at Caporetto, demonstrated that the Germans had solved the problem of achieving operational freedom in the West as well but did not yet possess the means to turn a breakthrough into a decisive strategic success. The German pursuit came to rest on the banks of the Piave after almost but not quite knocking Italy out of the war.[5] The great German attacks of 1918 followed a similar pattern. They hit an enemy who had learned little from the

[4]In this chapter I use the German system of "tactics," "operations," and "strategy," since this system is better adapted to delineating military events than the Anglo-Saxon convention of "tactics" and "strategy." In the German conception the term "tactics" refers to actions up to divisional and corps level and involves the fundamentals of training, doctrine, and weapons. The term "operations" involves corps and army-size formations and their employment in the immediate theater of operations. "Strategy" means the use of these units to achieve a wider purpose.

[5]For a graphic account of what German tactics did to the Italians, see Erwin Rommel, *Infantrie greift an* (Berlin, 1939).

successful German defensive tactics of the previous year. The Allies were still packing their troops in the forward trenches. Reserves were too far in the rear or were unavailable. Defense was static rather than based on a flexible response. Cooperation among the Allied armies was minimal. These factors produced defeats that almost led to strategic disaster.

The Germans achieved their great victories in 1918 by emphasizing surprise and concentrating superior forces and artillery on one particular segment of the front. The initial thrust against the British Fifth Army south of Arras caught one-third of the defending troops in the front line, where the intense bombardment massacred them.[6] Nevertheless, the German breakthrough that destroyed much of the Fifth Army (70,000 prisoners, 1,100 guns) did not produce a strategic victory.[7] The Germans did not succeed in driving the British back to the Channel ports but instead merely acquired a longer, weaker front to defend. They were thus the strategic losers, and their victories in April in Flanders and in May at the Chemin des Dames had similar results.

Historians have argued that one of the Germans' major errors in World War I was their failure to recognize the value of the tank. In fact, however, the German error lay more in failure to appreciate the danger that the tank posed to their own defensive positions than in any offensive value the slow and mechanically unreliable tanks of 1916–18 might have had for the German armies.

There were several reasons for German lack of interest. As the British victories in 1918 showed, tanks did not yet have the capability for strategic exploitation. Open warfare in the East did not require a slow-moving, costly machine to cross the space between the trenches, while in the West the Germans had stood on the defensive for most of the war. By 1918 they had evolved a tactical doctrine that enabled them to break into and through Allied positions in the West and thus had little need for a weapon

---

[6]Oberkommando des Heeres, *Der Weltkrieg,* vol. 14 (Berlin, 1944), chap. 3.

[7]Llewellyn Woodward, *Great Britain and the War of 1914–1918* (London, 1967), pp. 384–89.

that could only break into an enemy's trench system. Nevertheless, the weight of the British tank attacks in 1918 did make an indelible impression, and this impression helps explain why the German army was so willing to experiment with the new weapon in the postwar period. It also helps explain why the German army was one of the few in Europe before 1939 to make significant preparation for antitank warfare.

The Treaty of Versailles forced the Germans to limit their army to 100,000 men with a proportionately small officer corps, to eliminate the general staff, and to demilitarize a zone fifty kilometers east of the Rhine. The treaty also prohibited tanks and aircraft. All too often historians have cited these limitations and the loss of the war as the major reasons for the German receptiveness to new ideas.[8] Indeed, these provisions did help provide the Germans with a small, coherent officer corps. Defeat did make the Germans more receptive to new ideas. But most important was that the German army had been the *most* flexible and innovative of the armies that had engaged in the 1914–18 war— except with respect to the tank. German army performance in the Great War makes unsurprising its preeminence among the European armies in the 1920s and 1930s in facing the tactical and operational problems of modern warfare. Versailles provided the incentive to adapt, but flexibility and willingness to innovate were already characteristics of the German army. Moreover, unlike the British, who seemed bent on forgetting the war as quickly as possible, the Germans continued to regard the military as a serious and important occupation.[9] It is also worth noting that much of the German public reacted to the war in a very different fashion from that of the French and the British. Erich Maria Remarque and Arnold Zweig had many counterparts in Britain and France, but it is hard to think of a British equivalent of Ernst Jünger's gleeful celebration of the warrior elite of the trenches.

[8]For those who believe that the small size of the German army was instrumental in its learning the lessons of World War I and in preparing for the next, R. Paxton, *Parades and Politics at Vichy* (Princeton, N.J., 1966) should prove instructive.

[9]Michael Howard, "The Liddell Hart Memoirs," *Journal of the Royal United Services Institute,* February 1966, p. 61.

This new, restricted German army faced considerable difficulties. With a new long-service (twelve years) military force the Germans could no longer depend on a conscript army to defend their frontiers. French and Polish numerical superiority and Germany's extensive frontiers in the East compounded the problem. The only solution apparent to General Hans von Seeckt and his Reichswehr planners was some form of mobile defense. Since the German army was not allowed tanks, initial German experiments aimed at increasing defensive mobility through use of trucks and other vehicles.[10] In 1922 a small exercise in the Harz Mountains began the development of German motorized and mechanized forces. Seeckt was so interested in the maneuver that he wrote a covering letter to the War Ministry report on this experiment. He commented:

> I fully approve of the conception and leadership of the Harz exercise, but there is still much that is not clear about the specific tactical use of motor vehicles. I therefore order that the following report be made available by all staffs and independent commands as a topic for lectures and study. Troop commanders must see to it that experience in this area is widened by practical exercises. We must recognize that mobility is an important aid for our weak military power.[11]

Shortages of money for new weapons and severe treaty restrictions constrained German progress. On the other hand, unlike its Continental neighbors the German army did not have to train large batches of recruits and could focus upon the theoretical and, as far as possible, practical development of new tactics. Concentration on study, combined with the dictum that operations meant movement ("Operation ist Bewegung") was Seeckt's legacy to the Reichswehr. In effect Seeckt's emphasis on mobility completed the German army's break with trench warfare and represented a major advantage that the German army was to possess against numerically superior armies in the first years of

---

[10]Motor vehicles had served in World War I only to move troops behind a static front line, as in the French reinforcement of Verdun.

[11]Reichswehrministerium, Chef der Heeresleitung, "Harzübung, 8.1.22.," NARS T-79/65/000622.

World War II.[12] Moreover, the Treaty of Versailles helped the Germans by restricting their weapons. Thus mountains of obsolete equipment did not limit the vision of German commanders, who could concentrate upon a weapon's future possibilities rather than its immediate capabilities.[13] Theory had its limitations, however. Cooperation with the Russians in the mid-1920s had less to do with studying the application of armored tactics than with finding out how to build and repair a tank.[14] In 1928 the army sent Heinz Guderian, the future tank commander, to Sweden to see the last prototype German tank from World War I and to ride in a tank for the first time.[15] Seeckt, for all his brilliance as a leader, was not a revolutionary thinker. He failed to grasp the tank's potential and appears to have believed that cavalry would again play the role that it had lost in World War I. While Seeckt did much to further the concept of mobile military operations, he neither helped nor hindered the development of the tank. In 1928 he wrote that motorization was one of the most important developments for modern armies but added: "Many prophets already see the whole army equipped with armored vehicles and the complete replacement of the horsemen by the motorized soldier. We have not yet progressed that far."[16]

While using canvas dummies and cars covered with sheet metal to represent tanks, the Germans paid close attention to developments in other lands. In the early 1930s, General Werner

[12]See particularly Jehuda Wallach, *Das Dogma der Vernichtungsschlacht* (Frankfurt, 1967), p. 342.

[13]Erich Wagner, "Gedanken über den Wert von Kriegserinnerung und Kriegserfahrung," *Militärwissenschaftliche Rundschau* 2 (1937):232. Rommel also makes the same claim in his papers: Erwin Rommel, *The Rommel Papers,* ed. B. H. Liddell Hart (New York, 1953), p. 516.

[14]Heinz Guderian, "Spitzenvertretung der Panzertruppe in der Obersten Führung des Heeres, 1938–1945" (manuscript, Foreign Military Studies, U.S. Army Europe, P041, 1948), p. 4.

[15]Heinz Guderian, *Panzer Leader* (New York, 1957), p. 23.

[16]Oberstleutnant Matzky, "Kritische Untersuchung der Lehren von Douhet, Hart, Fuller, und Seeckt," Wehrmachtakadmie, no. 90/35 g.K., Berlin, November 1935, p. 44, BA/MA W 10-1/9.

von Blomberg, military district commander in East Prussia, and his chief of staff, Colonel Walter von Reichenau, read and translated works of such British theorists as B. H. Liddell Hart and J. F. C. Fuller.[17] Both Liddell Hart and Fuller also influenced Guderian, although it would seem that Fuller was the more important thinker for Guderian's development.[18] While one should not minimize the influence of the British writers, the Germans also paid close attention to British experiments and maneuvers with armored forces in the 1920s and early 1930s. The impact of intelligence reports on these maneuvers may well have had more influence on the development of German doctrine than did the writings of British theorists. The German intelligence service also managed to acquire the current British field manual on the employment of armored fighting vehicles, and this manual formed the framework for theoretical studies on armored warfare before German rearmament actually began.[19]

German reports on British maneuvers are an indicator of the interest within the Reichswehr. A War Ministry report of November 1926 discussed that summer's British maneuvers with armored forces in considerable detail and noted that improvements in speed and maneuverability had broadened the role of the tank: the pace of the infantry no longer had to tie down armored vehicles. With their increased speed they could strike out either on their own or in the company of motorized infantry and artillery as well as cavalry. The report underlined that a combination of swifter tanks and mobile troops would make possible fuller exploitation of breaches in the enemy front line. The study suggested the lessons that the German army should draw from these changes:

> In addition, with existing models, one can now clarify what will happen with tanks behind the enemy's main line of resistance after

[17]B. H. Liddell Hart, *The German Generals Talk* (New York, 1958), p. 22.

[18]Kenneth Macksey, *Guderian* (London, 1975), p. 41.

[19]Guderian, *Panzer Leader,* pp. 20-22. The British field manual to which Guderian refers is probably Broad's pamphlet *Mechanized and Armoured Formations,* which a certain Captain Stuart sold to the Germans (Kenneth Macksey, *Tank Warfare* [London, 1971], pp. 85-86).

a successful breakthrough. Tanks can be used for attacks on the enemy's rear positions, against advancing reserves, as well as against command posts and artillery emplacements. For such tasks, present-day tanks are far more capable than older models. We, therefore, recommend that in exercises armored fighting vehicles be allowed to break through repeatedly in order to portray this method of fighting and thus to collect added experience.[20]

A War Ministry report on the British experimental maneuvers with motorized and mechanized forces held in 1929 emphasized the size of the exercise area and the speed of movement. The study also pointed out that parceling out tanks in the slow-moving infantry had hindered the armor without speeding up the infantry.[21]

Speculation and practice maneuvers with dummy tanks changed to the real thing after January 1933. Blomberg and Reichenau became the key figures in the War Ministry, but while their political role was of great importance, they did not determine the development of doctrine within the army. Their leader, Adolf Hitler, also exhibited an interest in new military developments but for the most part remained in the background until after the Fritsch-Blomberg crisis of January, 1938.[22] This is not to say that Hitler was not willing to overrule the military. On the question of the pace of rearmament Hitler forced the army to accept more divisions than the general staff had originally suggested, and he remilitarized the Rhineland against the warnings of his military and diplomatic advisers. But on questions of weapons, tactics, and organization Hitler played little or no role in the initial rearmament effort. When Hitler appeared at a demonstration of mobile forces at Kummersdorf in 1934, he does not seem to have grasped the potential of the new doctrine, although he did make several approving comments.[23]

The men who determined the shape of the new German army

---

[20]Reichswehrministerium, Berlin, 10 November 1926, "Darstellung neuzeitlicher Kampfwagen," NARS T-79/62/000789.

[21]Reichswehrministerium, "England: Die Manöver mit motorisierten Truppen, September 1929," NARS T-79/30/000983.

[22]See particularly Friedrich Hossbach, *Zwischen Wehrmacht und Hitler, 1934–1938* (Hannover, 1949), p. 39; see also Taylor, *Sword and Swastika,* p. 116.

[23]Macksey, *Guderian,* p. 58.

were General Werner Freiherr von Fritsch, its commander-in-chief; General Ludwig Beck, chief of staff; and General Erich von Manstein, Beck's assistant. In a one-sided judgment Guderian singled out Beck in his memoirs as the primary opponent of panzer divisions and armored tactics within the German army.[24] Beck and Fritsch, however, faced enormous difficulties in planning rearmament, and the question of armor was just one among a host of problems. Beck, in fact, did allow experimentation and allotted considerable resources for this relatively unproved weapon, without excluding the development of other weapons. From the German army's point of view in 1934, tanks were a risky investment. They were expensive and consumed large quantities of gasoline, a scarce resource for Germany in wartime. Steel was also in short supply. Finally, only the light-skinned Mark I, armed with machine guns, was ready for production, and it was clear that it would take German industry considerable time to produce heavier models. As it turned out, nearly five years passed before the first medium tanks (the Mark IIIs and Mark IVs) appeared in operational units in 1939.[25]

Beck, at least in his writings, does not seem to have foreseen armor's strategic possibilities. Nevertheless, he played an important role in persuading Fritsch and Blomberg that the army should establish panzer divisions. Beck watched the results of the British summer maneuvers of 1934 with particular interest. In spite of claims since the war that by 1929 German armor development had surpassed the British,[26] Beck's comments on this maneuver show that the Germans still regarded the British as pioneers:

The maneuver caused a great sensation in England and resulted in many challenges. Once again results showed that the leadership of large mechanized formations, even in an army as motorized as the English, which has the most extensive experience in the world,

[24]Guderian, *Panzer Leader*, pp. 21-22. Macksey echoes Guderian's unfair charges (Macksey, *Guderian*, p. 61).

[25]Erich von Manstein, *Aus einem Soldaten-Leben, 1887-1939* (Bonn, 1958), pp. 241-42.

[26]F. W. von Mellenthin, *Panzer Battles* (London, 1955), p. xv (U.S. ed., Norman, Okla., 1956).

nevertheless ran into considerable difficulties and that reality can be disappointing. On the other hand, one gains the impression that English tank troops were brilliantly led and performed in outstanding fashion. British military leadership seems completely aware of present difficulties. Therefore, it will be especially instructive to watch the direction which the next development of the English army will take in the area of motorization.[27]

General Oswald Lutz, the first commander of the new German armored force, told Sir John Dill in 1935 "with some pride that the German tank corps had been modelled on the British."[28] Ironically, however, by 1937 the German view of the British army had undergone a fundamental change, largely owing to the failure of the British to expand on the experiences that they had gained with their early armor experiments. An Army High Command (OKH) intelligence summary of 1937 reported that leadership in the British army was rigid and slow. German intelligence doubted (accurately, as it turned out) whether the British high command could handle large-scale movement of motorized forces.[29]

Thus British and German tank development followed opposite courses: the former toward the subordination of armor to infantry, the latter toward the expansion of the new arm into independent divisions, corps, and finally armies. In the spring of 1935, Beck conducted a general staff tour on the use of a panzer corps, though the first panzer division had not yet been formed. In the following year the annual tour studied the uses of a hypothetical panzer army.[30] In the maneuvers of 1935 tanks did well enough to convince Blomberg and Fritsch that their day had come.[31] This led to the formation of three armored divisions in the fall of

[27]Der Chef des Truppenamts, Dez. 1934: "England; Manöver des Panzerverbandes, 18. bis 21.9.34.," NARS T-79/16/000790.

[28]DRC 31, 9 October 1935, p. 271. Cab 16/112.

[29]Oberkommando des Heeres, 15 December 1937, "Zusammenstellung der wichtigsten Veränderungen in den fremdländischen Heeren im Jahre 1937," NARS T-79/134/000958.

[30]Manstein, *Aus einem Soldaten-Leben,* p. 241.

[31]R. O'Neill, "Doctrine and Training in the German Army," in Michael Howard, ed., *The Theory and Practice of War* (New York, 1966), p. 157.

1935.[32] In addition, the army formed independent tank brigades for cooperation with the infantry and, as a sop to the cavalry, three so-called light divisions. The latter possessed a battalion of tanks and were designed to perform long-range reconnaissance, the old role of the cavalry.[33] The impressive performance of panzer divisions on maneuvers led to the amalgamation of the independent tank brigades into new armored divisions by the end of the 1930s.[34] The light divisions survived until after the Polish campaign, in which Guderian's prewar criticism that they did not possess the staying power of panzer divisions and that the Luftwaffe could perform long-range reconnaissance more accurately proved correct.[35] During the winter of 1939–40 the army converted the light divisions into panzer divisions. Finally, four regular infantry divisions received motorized support and the title "motorized infantry divisions." They did not make a substantial contribution to the striking capability of the mechanized force but combined with the panzer divisions in corps proved themselves an admirable supporting formation in mobile operations throughout the war.

Beck in particular has come in for much ex post facto criticism because of the number of different types of motorized and mechanized formations the army established in 1935. But Beck's motive was justifiable in view of the lack of precedent for such formations: he desired to experiment to find the proper mix of weapons. Significantly, by the end of the Polish campaign the Germans had narrowed their experimentation to two basic formations: armored and motorized infantry divisions.

Once provided with the necessary support, German tank advocates set to work. The basic principle of the new panzer divisions

[32]Guderian, *Panzer Leader,* pp. 36–37.

[33]Taylor, *Sword and Swastika,* p. 109.

[34]The Twenty-fifth Panzer Regiment appeared in an independent role as late as September 1938.

[35]Heinz Guderian, "Schnelle Truppen einst und jetzt," *Militärwissenschaftliche Rundschau* 2 (1939): 241; 7.Pz. Division (2. Leichte Division), Gera, 19 October 1939, la Nr. 393/39, geh., "Erfahrungen bei den Operationen im Osten," NARS T-315/436/000480.

was that the new force would depend on a combination of arms. The initial table of organization called for a motorized rifle brigade, an antitank battalion, an armored reconnaissance battalion, an artillery regiment, a signal battalion, a light-engineer company, and a panzer brigade of two regiments.[36]

Along with an understanding that effective armored warfare required the combination of arms, German tank pioneers understood how to use the new formations. From the beginning German tank doctrine stressed the use of armored division units in close and explosive cooperation.[37] In 1936, Lutz pointed out to his subordinate commanders that armored warfare relied on the close cooperation of the panzer division's components and on the concentration of their attacking strength:

> I have the impression that the two most important principles of panzer tactics, "surprise and mass," with which theoretically each panzer officer should be familiar, in reality are not given enough attention. I urge that during the officers' theoretical training in the winter, and during unit training, commanders direct special attention to this point.

Lutz argued further that the key to armored operations was flexibility. Sometimes exploitation would involve all arms and at other times one particular arm. All units had to be prepared to push on immediately after they had achieved their initial goals.[38]

In 1937, Lutz expanded this directive. He urged that tank units exploit breakthroughs immediately. After reaching their first objectives, tank units should proceed at once against second and third objectives. They were to smash unprepared enemy reserves, while at the same time panzer division reserves would move forward to exploit opportunities on the exposed enemy flanks and rear areas. Lutz warned that every minute lost favored the creation of a new enemy front. He demanded a thorough briefing of all the participants in an offensive on leadership, objectives,

[36]Guderian, *Panzer Leader,* app. 24.

[37]Guderian, "Schnelle Truppen einst und jetzt," p. 241.

[38]Kommando der Panzertruppen, Ia op. Nr. 4300, Berlin, 10 November 1936, "Bemerkungen des kommandierenden Generals der Panzertruppen im Jahre 1936 und Hinweise für die Ausbildung 1936/37," NARS T-79/30/000913.

the planned cooperation between the different arms, and radio discipline. Finally, tank leaders belonged at the front, where they could immediately exploit the developing and fluid situation.[39] As even nonarmored officers recognized, unless a tank break-through was broad, powerful, and rapid, it would not be effective.[40] By 1939, Lutz and Guderian had created a system and doctrine which met these requirements. The new panzer divisions could concentrate rapidly, launch a sudden blow, and exploit any breach in the enemy front. Germany possessed an arm which could gain not only operational but also strategic freedom, something which the other European armies were not able to counter until 1942.

As in other armies, many German officers doubted that the tank advocates were on the right track. However, for the most part the conservative opposition was quite different in nature from the opposition to armor in the British army. German doubts mainly concerned deep-penetration tactics rather than the question of whether the tank was a useful weapon. Like Fuller in Britain, Guderian exacerbated the conflict by his outspokenness. Nevertheless, German military journals continued to print his articles throughout the 1930s even if they remained unsympathetic to his cause. In 1939 he sarcastically commented in the principal German military periodical: "The motor is a German discovery. Unfortunately, militarily this piece of genius found greater understanding abroad than here. . . . Our military press provides the proof of this as it with astonishing persistence favors the slow against motorized and mechanized forces."[41]

General Otto von Stülpnagel remarked to Guderian that his ideas were utopian and that large armored units were militarily impossible. General Gerd von Rundstedt pithily commented, "Alles Unsinn, mein lieber Guderian, alles Unsinn" ("All nonsense,

---

[39]Kommando der Panzertruppen, Ia Nr. 3770/37, Berlin, 15 November 1937, "Besichtigungsbemerkungen des kommandierenden Generals des Kommandos der Panzertruppen im Jahre 1937," NARS T-79/30/000937.

[40]H. Gr. Nord, Gru. Kdo. 2., "Der Stellungskrieg, 24.2.38.," NARS T-311/124/7167953.

[41]Guderian, "Schnelle Truppen einst und jetzt," p. 235.

my dear Guderian, all nonsense").[42] Soon after Munich the German military attaché in Prague agreed with his British opposite number that tanks had some reconnaissance value and a restricted offensive role. But both felt that the tank "had little or no future."[43] As late as 1940 a German infantry manual claimed that the infantry was the chief branch and that other weapons merely supported it.[44] Another writer commented that the tank was a weapon of the present. Antitank weapons would soon compel it to share the fate of the horse.[45] One commentator in the *Militärwissenschaftliche Rundschau* even followed the same line that many British reactionaires were taking:

> It remains to be pointed out that the tank attacks of the Entente in 1918 occurred under the most favorable circumstances, namely without having to push through fortified positions and without finding antitank guns. It is the fate of each new weapon to be able to reach greatest effectiveness only so long as it is new, until finally the required defense is developed. The war came to an end in 1918 before antitank weapons were developed.[46]

In reply Guderian sarcastically challenged his critics to offer "some new and better method of making a successful land attack other than self-massacre" and insisted that tanks, properly employed, were the "best means available" for the offensive.[47]

What separated the German army from the other European armies was the fact that most German army leaders, while remaining skeptical about the armor school's seemingly extravagant claims, acquiesced in the development of the new arm. Moreover, many of the opponents of an independent role for

[42]M. Plettenberg, *Guderian: Hintergründe des deutschen Schicksals, 1918–1945* (Düsseldorf, 1950), p. 14.

[43]Newton [Prague] to Halifax, 1 November 1938, FO 371/21746, C 13400/1941/18.

[44]H. Senff, "Die Entwicklung der Panzerwaffe im deutschen Heer zwischen den beiden Weltkriegen," *Wehrwissenschaftliche Rundschau* (August, 1969), p. 442.

[45]M. Ludwig, "Gedanken über den Angriff im Bewegungskrieg," *Militärwissenschaftliche Rundschau* (1936):154.

[46]Oberst Lindemann, "Feuer und Bewegung im Landkrieg der Gegenwart," *Militärwissenschaftliche Rundschau* (1937):369.

[47]Guderian, *Panzer Leader,* pp. 39–40.

armor showed themselves surprisingly adaptable to tank warfare once it had proved itself. Erwin Rommel was a leading opponent of armor in the prewar period, yet three weeks in Poland were sufficient to persuade him that the tank was the weapon of World War II. Despite his inexperience he asked for and received command of the Seventh Panzer Division. Rundstedt found what he saw of armored operations in Poland so convincing that he became one of the leading proponents of the great armored push through the Ardennes in 1940.

Nevertheless, serious differences on armored tactics continued well into the war. Guderian reports that, at the war game dealing with the proposed thrust through the Ardennes in 1940, General Franz Halder, Beck's replacement as chief of staff, proposed that the panzer divisions only push bridgeheads across the Meuse and then wait for the infantry to come up—precisely what the French expected. Only a conference of army commanders, army group commanders, Guderian, Halder, and Hitler resolved the fundamental conflict between the chief of staff and the panzer leaders in favor of the latter. But some remained unconvinced. General Ernst Busch, commander of the Sixteenth Army, announced at the end of the meeting that he did not believe the armored forces would even get across the river.[48] Halder's insistence a year later that the infantry divisions lead the breakthrough at the start of the Russian campaign indicated an uncertain grasp of mobile warfare at best.

The development of armored doctrine was only one facet of the German rearmament effort. German infantry doctrine, based on the tactics proved at Caporetto and in the West in 1918, emphasized speed, firepower, and surprise; not by chance had a study of German infantry tactics in the World War inspired Liddell Hart's early, revolutionary work on armored-warfare theory.[49] Above all, German infantry doctrine emphasized aggressiveness, and it was the very aggressiveness demanded by the

---

[48]Ibid., pp. 90–92.

[49]See Jay Luvaas, *The Education of an Army* (Chicago, 1964); B. H. Liddell Hart, *Memoirs,* vol. 1 (London, 1965).

doctrine that made infantry officers like Rommel such superb tank commanders. The magnitude of armor's success in 1940 has tended to obscure the achievement of German infantry in the first war years. In France in 1940, General Fedor von Bock's Army Group B, consisting largely of infantry divisions, not only managed to fix Allied attention in northern Belgium but also played a major role in herding the British and French armies into the Dunkirk perimeter. Erich von Manstein's handling of an infantry corps in the second and final phase of the French campaign reflected not only the capabilities of that commander but those of the German infantry as well.[50] While the German armored forces won the great victories of 1939–41, the performance of the German infantry in the subsequent period of defeat demonstrated the effectiveness of interwar German doctrine—especially interwar defensive doctrine.

German defensive doctrine in the late 1930s was a further elaboration of World War I doctrine. General Wilhelm von Leeb's work *Die Abwehr,* which appeared in serialized and book form in 1937, represented a crystallization of German thinking on defensive warfare. Leeb's work advocated an active, aggressive defense. Light, well-armed units were to hold the front line, while reserves, concentrating on the threatened sectors, would seal up enemy penetrations. The defense would not remain passive but would launch counterattacks as soon as possible.[51] Another German commentator noted in 1938:

> At all times [in the Great War] we achieved excellent results when, on the defensive, rather than remaining passive, we staggered the enemy with surprise attacks. The massive counteroffensive is without doubt the best means the defender has to spoil the plans of the attacker.[52]

At approximately the same time a major army group command put German defensive doctrine in the following terms:

---

[50]Erich von Manstein, *Lost Victories* (Chicago, 1958), pp. 134–47.

[51]General Ritter von Leeb, "Die Abwehr," *Militärwissenschaftliche Rundschau* 6 (1936):1, 2; 3 (1937).

[52]General Erfurth, "Die Überraschung im Kriege," *Militärwissenschaftliche Rundschau* (1938), p. 335.

The defense has to calculate that the enemy will break through with surprise, swiftness and great impact. It must therefore be ready for immediate countermeasures and dispose of sufficient mobile reserves. The composition of an operational reserve results from its tasks. One needs mobile units with stopping power, such as aircraft, machine-gun formations, antitank units, motorized artillery, motorized engineer units, and mobile units with strong firepower and impetus such as tank units.[53]

Thus German doctrine, unlike that of the French, recognized the importance not only of reserves but also of mobile, quick-reaction reserves that could respond to an enemy breakthrough with speed and power.[54] Nevertheless, the Germans seem to have neglected the use of tanks in a strategically defensive role, a role Liddell Hart was already urging for armor in 1938–39.[55] The Germans saw the tank primarily as an offensive weapon, and Leeb commented typically that it had no other role in defensive warfare except to counterattack.[56]

Combined with German defensive doctrine went a recognition that the tank would pose a serious threat on the battlefield of the future. Recollection of the battering the German troops had received from Allied tanks in 1918 played a major role in the German emphasis on antitank defense.[57] While the British and French armies underlined the supposed inferiority of tanks against antitank weapons but made little effort to meet an armored threat, the Germans made considerable preparation to ensure the

[53]H. Gr. Nord, Gru. Kdo. 2., "Der Stellungskrieg, 24.2.38.," T-311/124/7167953.

[54]For the most thorough examination of French doctrine see Philip Bankwitz, *Maxime Weygand and Civil-Military Relations in Modern France* (Cambridge, Mass., 1967).

[55]See particularly B. H. Liddell Hart, *The Defence of Britain* (London, 1939).

[56]Leeb, "Die Abwehr," *Militärwissenschaftliche Rundschau* 3 (1937):282.

[57]The East German historian Gerhard Förster, in his *Totaler Krieg und Blitzkrieg* (Berlin, 1967), p. 143, is highly critical of German antitank development between the wars and claims with some justification that German antitank weaponry proved ineffective in Russia. However, his criticism benefits from hindsight. The Germans devoted more attention to antitank defense than did the other European armies.

protection of infantry units against tank attacks.[58] In the rearmament period German infantry divisions received more antitank weapons than did the equivalent formations of other armies. As a result they were better equipped to meet tank attacks.[59] By 1939 the Germans were emphasizing mobile antitank units as the answer to large-scale armored attacks. Because the enemy would probably not commit its task force until the front had broken, German doctrine emphasized that mobile antitank guns should be held back from the front line. Only when the enemy had committed its armor would they be used.[60] The panzer divisions stressed antitank measures. Lutz's instructions for 1938 demanded that tank units work closely with their Panzer Abwehr Abteilung (antitank detachments) in both defensive and offensive operations.[61]

All these developments in doctrine could not have achieved the results the German army accomplished in World War II had not the German officer corps been willing to work long and hard at its profession.[62] The Wehrmacht set standards which it *expected* its units to meet and did not consider overall success a reliable indicator of excellence. *Erfahrungsberichte* (after-action reports) from the Anschluss and the Czech crisis were heavily critical of the performance of many units. Significantly, the higher the

---

[58]Abteilung des Generalstabes des Heeres, "Die Entwicklung der deutschen Infanterie im Weltkriege, 1914–1918," *Militärwissenschaftliche Rundschau* (1938), pp. 399–400.

[59]Gkdo. VII A.K., München, 5 January 1938, "Verwendung von Panzereinheiten im Kampf der verbundenen Waffen," NARS T-79/64/000317. See also H. Rosinski, "Reichswehr Today," *Foreign Affairs,* April, 1939, p. 548.

[60]Oberkommando des Heeres, Gen St d H, 11. Abt. (11b), 3 March, 1939, "Panzer Abwehr in Festungskampffeldern," NARS T-314/403/000154.

[61]Kommando der Panzertruppen, Ia Nr. 3770/37, Berlin, 15 November, 1937, "Besichtigungsbemerkungen des kommandierenden Generals des Kommandos der Panzertruppen im Jahre 1937," p. 11, NARS T-79/30/000937. These remarks clearly foreshadow the brilliant use Rommel made of antitank guns and armor in combination in North Africa.

[62]On the subject of conducting useful military exercises as opposed to polishing buttons and holding parades, consult Hermann Teske's description of how the German army prepared for the 1940 campaign: *Bewegungskrieg* (Heidelberg, 1955), p. 15.

reporting headquarters the more critical these reports became.[63]
Even as late as the Polish campaign after-action reports expressed
severe displeasure at the combat efficiency of most units, in spite
of the overwhelming victory.[64]

After tracing the development of German doctrine between
the wars, the time has come to answer the question posed at the
beginning of this article. What was the relationship between
German doctrine on the one hand and German foreign policy
and grand strategy on the other? Economic historians from Burton
Klein to Berenice Carroll and Alan S. Milward have discerned at
the root of German rearmament something they call "blitzkrieg
strategy."[65] They argue that Hitler and the army high command
recognized that Germany could not fight a long war and as a
result developed a special strategy and a tactical organization
designed to gain quick, decisive victories. Supposedly the Germans deliberately planned for short campaigns followed by periods
of recuperation and thus structured German doctrine and strategy around panzer divisions and close air support as a means of
escaping the inability of their economic base to support a long

[63]See particularly Williamson Murray, "The Change in the European Balance
of Power, 1938-1939" (Ph.D. diss., Yale University, 1975), Chaps. 10, 14.

[64]Among others, see 8. Division, "Erfahrungsbericht," 15 October 1939, NARS
T-314/372; OKH, GenStdH O Qu I, "Taktische Erfahrungen im polnischen
Feldzug," 15 October 1939, NARS T-315/671; Generalkommando VIII A.K. Abt.
Ia, "Erfahrungsbericht über den Feldzug in Polen, September 1939," NARS
T-315/372; 7. Panzer Division (2. Leichte Division), "Erfahrungen bei den
Operationen im Osten," NARS T-315/436.

[65]See particularly Burton Klein, *Germany's Economic Preparations for War*
(Cambridge, Mass., 1959); Alan S. Milward, *The German Economy at War*
(London, 1965); Berenice Carroll, *Design for Total War: Arms and Economics in
the Third Reich* (The Hague, 1966); and Milward, "Der Einfluss ökonomischer
und nicht-ökonomischer Faktoren auf die Strategie des Blitzkrieges," in Friedrich
Forstmeier and Hans-Erich Volkmann, eds., *Wirtschaft und Rüstung am Vorabend
des Zweiten Weltkrieges* (Düsseldorf, 1975). All devote great attention to economic matters but little to the development of "blitzkrieg strategy." They offer no
evidence to support their claim of a connection between "blitzkrieg strategy" and
economic requirements. For a recent criticism of their assumptions see Matthew
Cooper, *The German Army, 1933-1945* (London, 1978). Unfortunately Cooper's
work contains serious misunderstandings of armored tactics and suffers overmuch
from the influence of Liddell Hart's "strategy of indirect approach."

war. This blitzkrieg strategy theory seemed to provide a rational explanation for Hitler's refusal to let Germany's disadvantageous economic position daunt him, and has therefore exerted wide influence on the massive literature on German foreign policy.[66]

In reality, however, almost no connection existed between Germany's economic problems and the development of blitzkrieg warfare. The German economy certainly constrained rearmament, and the Nazi regime did not fully utilize the resources at its disposal. The general staff and its economic section had good reason to fear the strain of a long war. But the German rearmament effort up to the opening of World War II created a military instrument which consisted mostly of World War I–type infantry divisions that marched to battle while horses pulled their supplies, artillery, and ammunition. In the French campaign the panzer divisions made up less than 10 percent of the German divisions deployed in the West.[67] Thus a small percentage of the total forces mobilized won the great German victories of the first years of World War II. That this force existed was the consequence of the professional expertise of the German army, not of the designs of German political or economic strategists. The coincidence between the development of the doctrine that won the great victories of 1939–41 and the strategic needs of the German economy was no more than that: sheer coincidence. That the Germans deliberately aimed for periods of calm following major military efforts was the result of immediate military requirements, not deep-laid plans, as Hitler's initial insistence on attacking the West prematurely in the fall of 1939 demonstrates.[68] Nor did Hitler play much of a role in the development of German army doctrine before 1938; he seems to have failed

[66]See, among many others, Gerhard L. Weinberg, *The Foreign Policy of Hitler's Germany: Starting World War II, 1937–1939* (Chicago, 1980), pp. 19–22.

[67]Only 10 of the 155 divisions in the German army in April 1940 were panzer divisions. For the invasion of France the German army deployed only 136 divisions in the West. See Telford Taylor, *The March of Conquest* (New York, 1958), pp. 17, 154.

[68]See particularly Murray, "The Change in the European Balance of Power, 1938–1939," Chap. 5.

to grasp the strategic potential that armored forces offered.[69]

Hitler's rearmament program did make one indirect contribution to the development of an armored force. The tremendous increase in resources and funds available after 1933 probably made the OKH more willing to invest in the creation of an experimental armored force of three divisions. This force was large enough to examine the question of how mechanized corps and armies would operate. Had the Nazi regime not provided funding on such a scale or had Hitler allowed the army to follow its own smaller program (twenty-one versus thirty-six divisions),[70] the OKH might have devoted the same percentage of resources to the new, untested armored force. The result would have been a smaller armored and motorized core. Such an outcome might have led the Germans down the same path as the British, for the failure of the British army to carry its experimentation beyond the stage of the 1934 maneuvers reflected the paucity of funds and the small size of the British army as well as the much-described incompetence of its officer corps.[71]

The word *blitzkrieg* itself conceals a semantic problem. In the traditional sense *blitzschnell* (lightning) warfare had always been present in German strategy from the time of the elder Helmuth von Moltke: Germany had to win quickly before the weight of a two-front war could crush it. In this sense "blitzkrieg strategy" was not new.[72] But its more specialized definition as a particular

---

[69]See Hossbach, *Zwischen Wehrmacht und Hitler,* p. 39; Gerhard L. Weinberg, *The Foreign Policy of Hitler's Germany: Diplomatic Revolution in Europe, 1933–1936* (Chicago, 1970), p. 178. It is worth noting that the German memoir sources on the development of armored tactics make no mention of interest by Hitler or OKH strategists in the strategic possibilities of armor. Interest centered rather on the operational and tactical use of tank forces.

[70]IMT, *TMWC,* 20:603.

[71]It is only fair to point out that the British army's rearmament program never really got off the ground. The British government could not make up its mind about the army's strategic role: defense of the empire or support for Britain's friends on the Continent. Until Chamberlain decided in favor of a Continental commitment in February 1939, the army did not receive funds to prepare even its infantry for service there.

[72]See Larry Addington, *The Blitzkrieg Era and the German General Staff, 1865–1941* (New Brunswick, N.J., 1971), for this broader meaning of "blitzkrieg strategy." The most thoughtful and comprehensive general work on German strategy is Wallach, *Dogma der Vernichtungsschlacht.*

kind of war—involving cooperation among tanks, aircraft, dive bombers, and motorized infantry and artillery to carry out wide-ranging mobile operations—was a new tactical method with strategic implications. That a broader definition had always been present in German strategy is not proof that Hitler and the OKH pushed the development of new tactical doctrine as the answer to Germany's traditional need to conduct a *blitzschnell* war. The skepticism of the OKH and most generals in the prewar period indicates that the German army did not develop armored tactics to meet strategic needs. Much of the military establishment opposed war in 1938 and 1939 precisely *because* they did not regard armor as the solution to Germany's strategic problems.

The German victories of 1939–41 resulted not from numerical or qualitative superiority in manpower and weapons, but rather from the application of a new system of tactics and operations. It was precisely this new system that roused serious skepticism in the German officer corps. However, German skeptics were more willing to concede that the tank might be a useful weapon and that armored formations might have a role in warfare than were their counterparts in other armies. For all the doubts about the use of armored divisions in an independent role, the German tank prophets remained an integral part of the German army establishment.[73] Arguments about the tank, if at times heated, rarely degenerated into the diatribes characteristic of debates in

---

[73]The treatment that leading tank pioneers received in Germany, Britain, and France may well serve as an indicator of receptiveness to new ideas. In Germany, Guderian became head of the armored forces in 1938, a position from which he directly influenced the training and organization of the new formations. In Britain, on the other hand, Fuller received promotion to major general in the early 1930s but never occupied an active command. Percy Hobart, one of the most perceptive British armored officers in the late 1930s, lost his position as commander of the British armored division in Egypt; summer 1940 found him serving in the Home Guard. Charles de Gaulle, despite his theoretical work on the subject, did not secure a command in the French armored and motorized forces until shortly before the débâcle of May 1940. In 1935, General Maurice Gamelin had gone so far as to decree that his high command, as the sole arbiter of doctrine, must pass on all articles, lectures, and books by serving French officers. As André Beaufre comments, "Everyone got the message, and a profound silence reigned until the awakening of 1940" (André Beaufre, *1940: The Fall of France* [New York, 1968], p. 47).

Great Britain. Moreover, the intellectual effort, the study and hard work that the German military customarily devoted to its craft, helps explain the flexibility of many German officers in adapting to armored warfare after the campaign in Poland had proved the capabilities of the new formations.

German success in evolving the new tactical doctrines shook the foundation of European civilization. While panzer forces made up only a small percentage of the German army throughout World War II, German armor destroyed nearly all of the armies it faced and yielded in the end only to crushing numerical superiority. The German army high command not only provided sufficient funds for the development of the armored force but also allowed its armor pioneers to develop their doctrine and train their forces largely free from outside interference. The results for Europe were tragic. They were doubly tragic because the efficiency of German infantry and defensive doctrine enabled the Germans, after conquering most of the European continent in two years, to fend off an overwhelming coalition for four more years.

4

William II and His Russian "Colleagues"

LAMAR CECIL

There was nothing in which William II, the last German kaiser and king of Prussia, took greater delight than diplomacy. He had no patience with the routine obligations of kingship but an enormous relish for royal pomp and fanfaronade. Diplomacy, with its peripatetic visitations to foreign courts, fed the kaiser's boundless appetite for ceremony. Since these royal pageants enthroned him at center stage but placed his attendant statesmen in secondary roles, diplomacy gratified the overweening self-importance that was such a fundamental ingredient of William's personality. In intellect William II was certainly the equal of any of his "colleagues," as he was pleased to refer to his fellow rulers. He had a kingly talent for tongues, an astounding memory, and an eclectic interest in the arts and sciences. But these attributes came close to being nullified by a number of delinquencies of personality and mind. William's vainglory persuaded him that he was Germany's premier diplomat, both by right of station and because of his imagined virtuosity in the labyrinthine intricacies of European *Grosse Politik*. Although the kaiser could on occasion exercise a sort of loquacious charm, tactlessness and indiscretion were more dependable features of his personality. William II's extensive demonology, which embraced American Indians, modern Greeks, Jews, Slavs, Latins, and sundry others, might have caused no harm had he been able to keep his dislikes to himself; but the kaiser had an irresistible urge to communicate his feelings to the most inappropriate audiences. He could with complete sangfroid proclaim in the presence of a French military attaché that Napoleon had been a parvenu or observe to an Italian envoy that "next to the French, the people I hate the most are diplomats and deputies."[1]

Unfortunately, there were few monarchs more poorly suited for diplomacy and more maladroit in its exercise than the kaiser. William II, far from realizing that he suffered from weaknesses of personality and intellect that would have been fatal in any uncrowned diplomat, believed that his personal superiority entitled him to give the commanding word on all matters. Anyone who attempted to assert a professional or constitutional right to fashion diplomacy was denounced in imperial tirades as an incompetent trespassing on what was an exclusively royal prerogative. Nothing could safely be entrusted to German parliamentarians or envoys, and William himself would therefore have to assume the diplomatic burden of the empire. "The Foreign Office [?]—I am the Foreign Office," he was accustomed to assure other rulers as well as the diplomats accredited to his court.[2] This was, for once, no rhetorical effusion, for the kaiser meant what he said. William II did not insist on doing everything, but he was determined that nothing was to occur without his approval. While German officials could conceive and elaborate policies, it was pointless for them to try to launch diplomatic offensives that did not coincide with the kaiser's views or that he could not be persuaded to adopt as his own.

William's insistence on being accorded a respectful consideration in affairs of state did not imply a similar obligation on his part to those who served him. He often did not bother either to consult or to inform the Wilhelmstrasse, doing and saying as he

---

[1]Holstein diary, 11 November 1888, *HP,* 2:283. On another occasion the kaiser described diplomats as "freaks." See W. H.-H. Waters, *Potsdam and Doorn* (London, 1935), pp. 129–30.

[2]Stamfordham to Reischach, 21 July 1929, RA GV M2530/2; William II to Edward VII, 30 December 1901, RA X 37/51; Prince Bernhard von Bülow, *Denkwürdigkeiten,* 4 vols. (Berlin, 1930–31), 2:512; Hatzfeldt to Holstein, 17 September 1893 and 14 August 1895, *HP,* 3:438–40, 544; Ludwig Raschdau, *Unter Bismarck und Caprivi: Erinnerungen eines deutschen Diplomaten aus den Jahren 1886–1894* (Berlin, 1939), pp. 174–75.

pleased. The kaiser did not hesitate to name favorites as envoys, give them private instructions, and encourage them to report directly to the crown rather than to the Foreign Office. German diplomats quickly learned that successful careers could best be furthered by agreeing with the kaiser, and the result was that everything that emerged from the Wilhelmstrasse was tailored to William II's tastes. In his long reign German diplomacy, next only to naval policy, was the most conspicuous emblem of the imperial *persönliches Regiment* (personal regime).[3] All European statesmen recognized the preeminent role of the kaiser as the arbiter of German diplomacy, and in the formulation of responses to Berlin they kept William II squarely at the center of their calculations.

Although William II chose to isolate himself on an exalted plane above his statesmen as well as his subjects, he believed that he was by no means alone. The kaiser was certain that he could enlist his fellow sovereigns in the struggle to defend European civilization against the many perils which threatened it. William's conception of diplomatic method consisted largely of his own association with other rulers, and the royal barometer of relations with foreign powers often reflected little more than his current attitude toward a particular "colleague."[4] William's inconstancy was notorious, and his feelings often moved swiftly between exaggerated extremes. The cause of these sudden changes was usually the kaiser's perception of the degree to which he was or was not treated with the respect and deference he believed to be his due. In the case of the Russian czars, Alexander III and Nicholas II, presently to be examined, William's behavior often proceeded from such considerations and was a farrago of adulation and bossiness, flattery and bluster. The kaiser was always eager to meet as frequently as possible with the crowned heads of Europe, and he was firmly convinced that these encounters led to

[3]On this point see most recently Paul M. Kennedy, *The Rise of the Anglo-German Antagonism, 1860–1914* (London, 1980), pp. 403–409; Lamar Cecil, *The German Diplomatic Service, 1871–1914* (Princeton, N.J., 1976), pp. 220–25.

[4]Eulenburg to Holstein, 4 February 1889, *HP,* 3:307; Karl Rosner, ed., *Erinnerungen des Kronprinzen Wilhelm* (Stuttgart and Berlin, 1922), p. 84; Bülow, *Denkwürdigkeiten,* 1:80, 2:62, 397.

improved relations. The Three weeks after ascending the throne in 1888, he wrote to his grandmother Queen Victoria that he believed that "monarchs should meet often and confer together to look out for dangers which threaten the monarchical principle from democratical and republican parties in all parts of the world." Bismarck had prescribed an annual royal conclave and believed, so William assured the Prince of Wales, that such conversations were worth ten times any ten diplomatic dispatches.[5]

Sustained by the Iron Chancellor's injunction, the kaiser journeyed incessantly from court to court. He had little appreciation of what either diplomacy or good manners required of a guest, and consequently he usually left a wake of exhaustion and irritation.[6] The kaiser's first trip to Italy after his ascension is an instructive and typical case. Rome required all of the diplomatic finesse a visiting ruler could bring to bear, because it was the residence of both the pope and his archrival, the king of Italy. William II managed to exasperate papists, monarchists, and republicans alike. He was offensively noisy to everyone, ridiculed the ancient Leo XIII behind his back, made salacious allusions to the naïve and sheltered heir to the Italian throne, and treated the legislators who were presented to him with autocratic disdain. The Prussian envoy at the Vatican wrote in dismay after the kaiser's welcome departure that "I have observed him for the first time as a statesman, which is what he aspires to be. Unfortunately, I can detect few diplomatic qualities. One saw only affected conceit and exaggerated behavior."[7]

In dealing with the kaiser, his "colleagues" seldom managed to remain unscathed by his bizarre behavior. William was pitiless in making fun of physical shortcomings, and few rulers escaped his

[5]6 July 1888, RA 156/84; 1 December 1899, RA L4/81.

[6]Prince Nicholas of Greece, *My Fifty Years* (London, n.d.), p. 94; Viscount Chilston, *W. H. Smith* (London, 1965), p. 350; Kenneth Young, *Arthur James Balfour* (London, 1963), pp. 121–22; Sir Henry Lucy, *The Diary of a Journalist,* 3 vols. (London, 1923), 2:20 (21 June 1891).

[7]Kurd von Schlozer, *Letzte Römische Briefe, 1882–1894* (Stuttgart, 1924), pp. 130–31; Ernst Feder, ed., *Bismarcks Grosses Spiel: Die geheimen Tagebücher Ludwig Bambergers* (Frankfurt am Main, 1933), p. 430 (17 November 1888); Bülow, *Denkwürdigkeiten,* 4:337–38.

effulgent malice. The self-styled Czar Ferdinand of Bulgaria, to take but one example, was a very ugly man, disfigured by an enormous nose. William was not content merely to slap Ferdinand on his rear whenever they met and unfeelingly refer to him as "Fernando Naso" but declared in public and in a deliberately loud voice that his Balkan colleague was a hermaphrodite.[8] Even when not spewing insults, the kaiser knew how to bait other rulers. He once insinuated, quite unnecessarily, to King Edward VII that it had been the Prussian field marshal Blücher, not Wellington, who had saved the day at Waterloo, to which his uncle had huffily replied—with accuracy on at least the first two counts—that the kaiser's observation was "foolish, injudicious and historically untrue."[9] Many of William II's insults were diplomatically smothered but undoubtedly not forgotten. Sir Frank Lascelles, for many years the British ambassador in Berlin, once declared to a German official that "if I were to report to London all that Your Most Sublime Ruler has said to me we would twenty times over have had war between England and Germany."[10]

William II's personal diplomacy proved to have an almost entirely negative impact. Among Europe's rulers only Queen Wilhelmina of the Netherlands, the Habsburg emperor Franz Joseph, King Oscar of Sweden, and a few of the more insignificant German princelings seem to have had any affection for the kaiser; his own relatives certainly did not. While William contributed greatly to his own unpopularity, the monarchical partners

[8]W. H.-H. Waters, *"Secret and Confidential": The Experiences of a Military Attaché* (New York, 1926), p. 331; Rudolf Vierhaus, ed., *Das Tagebuch der Baronin Spitzemberg: Aufzeichnungen aus der Hofgesellschaft des Hohenzollernreiches* (Göttingen, 1960), p. 517 (12 January 1901); Joseph M. Baernreither, *Fragments of a Political Diary* (London, 1930), p. 277 (12 March 1914); William II to Archduke Franz Ferdinand, 31 December 1908, HHStA, Franz Ferdinand Nachlass, X/11; Szögyényi to Goluchowski, 20 August 1897, HHStA, Preussen III, vol. 148, Varia; Szögyényi to Aehrenthal, 18 August 1910, vol. 169, Varia. All subsequent references to HHStA files are from Preussen III except where otherwise noted. For another royal victim, the "dwarf" Victor Emmanuel III, see Michael Balfour, *The Kaiser and His Times* (London, 1964), p. 146.

[9]Knollys to Lascelles, 23 December 1905, Lascelles Papers, FO 800 12.

[10]Count Robert Zedlitz-Trützschler, *Zwölf Jahre am deutschen Kaiserhof: Aufzeichnungen* (Berlin and Leipzig, 1924), pp. 132-33 (10 October 1905).

through whom he hoped to manage Europe's affairs were a royal lot in the face of whose peculiarities even the most ingratiating of princes might have been ineffective. William II was not Europe's only royal eccentric. There were other sovereigns, and indeed entire regal houses, who were also infected with the regrettable qualities so apparent in the kaiser. Wittelsbach vanity surpassed the kaiser at his most pretentious; Ferdinand of Bulgaria's theatricality left William's own considerable gift for histrionics in the shade; for fatuity, of which the kaiser was certainly not bereft, the Habsburgs vied with the Spanish Bourbons for pride of place. The Hanoverians excelled all others in obstinacy, while the morose Romanovs were the unchallenged monuments not only of tyranny but of churlishness as well. Not all of the problems that emerged between the kaiser and other royalties were his fault, and there were times when William could rise to genuine, if often clumsy, attempts to rectify past wrongs and improve relations.

Unfortunately, the kaiser most frequently directed his efforts to quarters where they were least likely to succeed. William II did not distribute the attention he paid to other rulers in equal measure, for in his estimation monarchs were to be valued in proportion to their autocratic power or forcefulness of personality. He confided in King Leopold II of the Belgians, whose credentials for tyranny were irreproachable, if not at home, then certainly in the Congo, that he "could not respect a monarch who felt himself responsible to parliamentarians and ministers rather than to Our Father in Heaven."[11] The kaiser deplored pusillanimous rulers such as his brother-in-law King Constantine II of the Hellenes or Victor Emmanuel III of Italy. Weak sovereigns whose kingdoms were of limited significance William dismissed forthwith, for they could contribute little to his notion of diplomacy among "colleagues." France was powerful, but the kaiser recognized that there were no alliances to be made with the revanchists in Paris. Austria-Hungary, on the other hand, was a trustworthy if fragile ally. As a result William II's highly personal diplomatic offensives

[11]Bülow, *Denkwürdigkeiten,* 2:75.

tended to concentrate on Russia and England, the two great monarchies whose sovereigns were his relatives but whose loyalty he did not feel was secure.

It was unfortunate that London and Saint Petersburg should have assumed the burden of William II's diplomacy, for in both capitals the kaiser encountered colleagues whose amour propre was quite as inflated as his own. There was no sovereign in Europe as easily ruffled and as determined to have her way as Queen Victoria. Her son Edward VII was similarly vigilant in guarding against assaults on his dignity. William never succeeded in establishing a satisfactory relationship with either of these formidable personalities, a misfortune which was certainly not entirely his fault. The Russian majesties Alexander III and Nicholas II were equally touchy and even more difficult. Both Alexander III and his heir were introspective and reclusive, suspicious of outsiders who might invade their privacy or disturb the leaden complacency that prevailed at the Russian court. The Russian monarchs, in their difficult personalities and matchless power, were the most forbidding of all European sovereigns. Moreover, Alexander III's consort, Czarina Maria Feodorovna, was a princess of the Danish royal house, which for decades had been obsessively anti-Prussian. The enmity of the Danes was an inheritance for which the kaiser was blameless but which did much to spoil his association with the Russian monarchs. To establish fruitful relations with the Romanovs or with their vengeful relatives in Copenhagen would have taxed the talents of any ruler. For William II, with his blustering and officious manner, it proved impossible.

The establishment of sound Russo-German relations had been a fundamental, if ultimately elusive, element of Bismarck's diplomacy, and it was a goal which, for somewhat different purposes, Berhard von Bülow revived in the late 1890s. In league with Admiral Alfred von Tirpitz and with William II's approval Bülow embarked on an aggressive weltpolitik which had an anti-English and pro-Russian configuration. A German alliance with Saint Petersburg was his primary aim, for this would provide the basis for Germany's Continental security and make possible an eventual challenge to Britain's maritime domination of the world.[12] In the accomplishment of this goal the leading consideration in Berlin's Russian policy would be the autocratic czar, without whose cooperation a Russo-German alliance would be impossible.[13] Bismarck had frequently argued that the czar's opinion was decisive, a fact which made a diplomatic post in Russia far more arduous than one in France. In Paris an envoy could blame the constantly changing ministry for his inability to secure results, whereas in Saint Petersburg, "where all hangs on the czar, one always knows what ground he has to conquer."[14] Berlin's exaggerated estimation of the power of the Russian sovereign, a view which tended gradually to be corrected after the Iron Chancellor's fall from office, in turn promoted William II's importance, for Alexander III had no confidence in Bismarck's successors and refused to deal with them. The indolent Nicholas II did not like to mix with diplomats and largely confined such attention as he gave to diplomacy to heads of state. Therefore, the kaiser had by default to serve as Berlin's agent in winning over the two czars to a pro-German policy. The behavior of Russian diplomats, who were convinced that anything that was to be accomplished in Germany had to be pursued through William II, further enhanced the kaiser's central role in Russo-German relations.[15]

The relationship between the Romanov and Hohenzollern rulers, however, was never the paramount factor in Germany's relations with Russia, and German diplomats belatedly learned that Nicholas II exercised less authority over the Russian government than they

---

[12]See especially Peter Winzen, *Bülows Weltmachtkonzept: Untersuchungen zur Frühphase seiner Aussenpolitik, 1897–1901* (Boppard, 1977); Barbara Vogel, *Deutsche Russlandpolitik: Das Scheitern der deutschen Weltpolitik unter Bülow, 1900–1906* (Düsseldorf, 1973).

[13]Vogel, *Deutsche Russlandpolitik*, pp. 46–47.

[14]Herbette to Goblet, 17 June 1888, *DDF*, 1st ser., 7: 159; Bülow to Eulenburg, 8 February 1892, John C. G. Röhl, ed., *Philipp Eulenburgs politische Korrespondenz*, 3 vols. (Berlin, 1976–83), 2: 760–61; Raschdau, *Unter Bismarck und Caprivi*, p. 146. Herbert von Bismarck agreed. "Herbert von Bismarcks Not[izen], Herbst 1891" [hereafter cited as "Not[izen]"] Prince Otto von Bismarck-Schönhausen Nachlass, BA, FC 3018/234–36.

[15]Barrère to Hanotaux, 30 September 1896, *DDF*, 1st ser., 12:763–64.

had believed. Even the despotic Alexander III was incapable of resisting the flood of pan-Slav forces in his empire which were directed primarily against Germany and its ally Austria-Hungary. In Berlin diplomatic, economic, and military considerations, which had certainly to be measured in terms of William's predilections, were always more significant than the kaiser's interaction with his Russian colleagues. But the personal ties between the kaiser and his Russian counterparts were important considerations in Russo-German affairs, for two reasons. First, statesmen, in assessing the behavior of a rival power, attributed the greatest import to the most seemingly trivial episodes of royal conduct. A toast by the czar to the kaiser, if too short or too perfunctory or delivered in French rather than in German or even English, might be registered as a sign of deteriorating relations. A trip too often postponed, or made to some place other than the capital, might be regarded as an equally negative portent. The apparent failure of the kaiser and the czar to get on well with one another therefore tended to become one more weapon in the arsenal of diplomats in both Saint Petersburg and Berlin who regarded attempts at Russo-German rapprochement with either pessimism or disapproval.

Second, a cordial footing between the rulers could assuage irritations or disappointments occasioned by policies adopted by their governments and even promote cooperation between the two empires. If the czar and the kaiser were on good terms, a valuable avenue of communication and even conciliation could be maintained, and the problems that arose, though seldom capable of elimination, could at least be partly defused. The constructive role of the sovereigns had been exhibited during the 1860s and early 1870s in the friendship between William I and his Russian nephew Alexander II. Alexander III did not share his father's positive view of Germany but nevertheless made no move to sever the tie with Berlin after coming to the Russian throne in 1881. Although Berlin and Saint Petersburg often disagreed and finally after 1878 began to turn against one another, the sovereigns maintained a mutually affectionate and respectful attitude that helped attenuate the growing antagonism reflected both in diplomacy and in public opinion. But when relations between the rulers soured, as they did after William's ascension in 1888, not only did royal rivalries begin to constitute yet another cause of Russo-German friction, but they also eliminated a last restraining influence on the mounting hostility between the two powers.

William II regarded Russia as a special preserve for his alleged diplomatic expertise. Even before coming to the throne, he had crowed to a German diplomat apropos of a problem that had arisen between Germany and Russia: "Just send me to Saint Petersburg. I know the czar, and within twenty-four hours I'll have things in order."[16] William was referring to the gruff and morose Alexander III, whom he met in 1884 on the occasion of his first journey to Russia.[17] William was both awed and captivated by the czar, who always represented to him the beau ideal of a sovereign. "He was truly an autocrat and an emperor," William II told Count Sergei Witte years after Alexander's death, and he liked to say that he wanted the Hohenzollern monarchs to play a more authoritative role, "as in Russia."[18] On his first

[16]Rashdau, *Unter Bismarck und Caprivi,* p. 17.

[17]For William's early favorable impression of the czar see Herbert von Bismarck, "Tagebuch," Bismarck Nachlass, BA, FC 3018/163–64, and his "Not[izen]," ibid., 234–37; Eulenburg to Bülow, 28 February 1887, Röhl, ed., *Eulenburgs Korrespondenz,* 1:220; Eulenburg's notes, 11 June 1887, "Eine Preussische Familiengeschichte," Eulenburg Nachlass, BA, 2:31–32 (all subsequent references to the Eulenburg Nachlass, unless otherwise noted, are to the "Familiengeschichte" by volume number). See also Charles Swaine, memorandum, 20 November 1887, Salisbury Papers, Hatfield House, Herts., ser. A., vol. 61 (all subsequent references to the Salisbury Papers are to series A). For William's trip to Russia in 1884 and a second trip two years later see Herbert to Wilhelm von Bismarck, 13 May 1884, Walter Bussmann, ed., *Staatssekretär Graf Herbert von Bismarck: Aus seiner politischen Privatkorrespondenz* (Göttingen, 1964), p. 236; Heinrich O. Meisner, ed., *Denkwürdigkeiten des General-Feldmarschalls Alfred Grafen von Waldersee,* 3 vols. (Stuttgart and Berlin, 1923–25), 1:238–39, diary, 20 May 1884; William's notes, 11 September 1886, Bismarck Nachlass, BA, FC 2986/342–45; Count Richard von Pfeil, *Neun Jahre in Russischen Diensten unter Kaiser Alexander III* (Leipzig, 1911), pp. 148–50; William II, *Ereignisse und Gestalten aus den Jahren 1878–1918* (Leipzig and Berlin, 1922), pp. 11–13.

[18]Abraham Yarmolinsky, ed., *The Memoirs of Count Witte* (Garden City, N.Y., 1921), p. 403; notes marked "Hollmann," 25 April 1897, Prince Bernhard von Bülow Nachlass, BA, no. 30.

trip and on a second in 1886, William was careful to behave modestly and leave the initiative in conversation to the czar, which pleased Alexander.[19] Indeed, William treated Alexander with a deference so marked that it struck some observers as obsequious.[20]

After leaving Russia, William wrote several letters to the czar in which he was very critical of his mother and father, Queen Victoria, and his uncle the Prince of Wales.[21] He now considered himself to be a specialist in Russian affairs, in which he took a conspicuous interest.[22] It therefore seemed imperative to William that, on becoming kaiser in 1888, his first state visit abroad would be to Alexander III, a palpable indication of his fervent admiration. The kaiser was gratified by the reception accorded him by the czar, but he now began to discover that Alexander's character had a darker side. The czar was alternately arrogant and torpid, besides being excessively insistent on seclusion. This reclusiveness only deepened what William perceived to be Alexander's inclination to fantasy, and he worried that a ruler who suffered from such inertia might someday be fated to share the sanguinary end that had befallen Louis XVI.[23]

---

[19]William's behavior conformed to directions for handling Alexander III given him by Count Herbert von Bismarck, legation secretary in the embassy in Saint Petersburg. See Bismarck, "Tagebuch," Bismarck Nachlass, BA, FC 3018/163–67, 234–41.

[20]Waldersee, *Denkwürdigkeiten*, 2:152, 10 April 1890; Yarmolinsky, ed., *Witte Memoirs*, p. 403; Eugene de Schelking, *Recollections of a Russian Diplomat: The Suicide of Monarchies (William II and Nicholas II)* (New York, 1918), p. 12; Vinck to Chimay, 2 September 1890, Bernhard Schwertfeger, ed., *Amtliche Aktenstücke zur Geschichte der Europäischen Politik, 1885–1914 (die Belgische Dokumente zur Vorgeschichte des Weltkrieges)*, 9 vols. (Berlin, 1925), 1:310; Pourtalès to Holstein, 9 February 1890, *HP*, 3:326.

[21]Four letters between May 1884 and May 1885, copies in the Hohenzollernsche Hausarchiv (hereafter Hausarchiv), rep. 53d, no. 5, Geheimes Staatsarchiv, Berlin-Dahlem, printed in Otto Becker, *Das Französisch-Russische Bündnis* (Berlin, 1925), pp. 286–90.

[22]Herbert von Bismarck's "Not[izen]," Bismarck Nachlass, BA, FC 3018/240.

[23]William II's notes on a report of the German military plenipotentiary in Saint Petersburg, 15 January 1889, GFM NARS T-139/90; Friedrich Curtius, ed.,

After William II had left Saint Petersburg, Alexander III informed the German ambassador that the kaiser's frank and open manner had pleased him greatly.[24] This was little more than diplomatic froth, for the czar had not found much that was appealing in his guest. As kaiser, William had no longer exhibited the modest bearing that Alexander had found attractive during the prince's earlier visits to Saint Petersburg. The czar did not like anyone who was too effervescent, and William II's effusive deference and fussy airs did not conform to Alexander's sense of imperial dignity. The kaiser's bravura was disconcerting, and according to one of the czar's daughters he found William "an exhibitionist and a nuisance."[25] Alexander III was an exemplary family man, and he thoroughly disapproved of the vicious remarks William had made about his parents in his letters and the disrespectful way he had treated them. The kaiser, he declared, was "un petit gamin mal élevé, rempli de mauvaise foi" ("an ill-mannered, dishonest rogue").[26]

Alexander's dislike of the kaiser was not entirely rooted in his objection to William's personality, for he also did not at all approve of the kaiser's domestic or diplomatic policies. William's pronounced interest in social-welfare programs for the benefit of the working class, a prominent concern of the young sovereign in

---

Denkwürdigkeiten des Fürsten Chlodwig zu Hohenlohe-Schillingsfürst, 2 vols. (Stuttgart, 1907), 2:432, 436 (diary, 25 March and 25 May 1888); Szögyényi to Kálnoky, 18 February 1893, HHStA, vol. 143 (Berichte), 6C; William II to Caprivi, 18 November 1892, GP, 7:143–44; William's marginalia on Prince Bismarck's Gedanken und Erinnerungen, 3 vols. (Stuttgart and Berlin, 1921), 3:134, Hausarchiv, rep. 42a, no. 42/1.

[24]Villaume to Bülow, Bülow Nachlass, no. 22; Herbert von Bismarck, memorandum, 25 July 1888, and Schweinitz to Otto von Bismarck, 25 July 1888, GP, 6:326–37; Laboylaye to Goblet, 25 July 1888, DDF, 1st ser., 7:193.

[25]Ian Vorres, The Last Grand Duchess: Her Imperial Highness Grand Duchess Olga Alexandrovich, 1882–1960 (New York, 1964), p. 40; Yarmolinsky, ed., Witte Memoirs, pp. 404–405; Gleb Botkin, The Real Romanovs: As Revealed by the Late Czar's Physician and His Son (New York, 1931), pp. 102–103; Alexander, Grand Duke of Russia, Once a Grand Duke (New York, 1932), p. 174.

[26]Herbert von Bismarck, "IV Not[izen]," Bismarck Nachlass, BA, FC 3018/425; Otto von Bismarck, Gedanken und Erinnerungen, 3:83–84.

the late 1880s, did nothing to endear him to the czar, since in Alexander's opinion such charitable schemes only raised expections that could never be met.[27] Considerably more alarming was the increasingly anti-Russian tone that prevailed in Berlin in the late 1880s. Alexander believed that the kaiser and his confidant, the chief of the general staff, General Count Alfred von Waldersee, rather than Chancellor Bismarck, were responsible for this development. The czar's suspicions were well founded, for Waldersee was in fact working steadily and effectively to persuade William II that Alexander was plotting a sudden attack on Germany and that the only recourse was to arm and plan for a preventive war against Russia. Waldersee's influence on the kaiser was enormous, and under his tutelage William had come by 1887 to share the general's fear of Russia.[28] Pan-Slavism, Prince William declared the next year, had put an end to the traditional policy of Russo-German friendship.[29] Count Philipp zu Eulenburg-Hertefeld, who was even more intimate with William than was Waldersee, was also active in undermining William's regard for the czar.[30]

Alexander III was notorious for baldly expressing his displeasure, and the fact that William II, however personally distasteful or politically unreliable, was the ruler of Russia's most powerful neighbor did not in the least deter the czar from giving vent to his strong and highly undiplomatic feelings. When annoyed, Alexander could be spiteful and nasty, and William II brought out the worst features in the czar's malicious disposition. Alexander III responded to William's pressing overtures by repeatedly making

[27]Wilhelm von Schweinitz, ed., *Denkwürdigkeiten des Botschafters General v. Schweinitz,* 2 vols. (Berlin, 1927) 2:408 (3 April 1890); Pourtalès to Holstein, 19 March 1890, *HP,* 3:330-31.

[28]*HP,* 2:316; Kaiser William II, *Aus meinem Leben, 1859-1888* (Berlin, 1923), p. 326; Waldersee, *Denkwürdigkeiten,* 1:333, 345 (16 November and 17 December 1887).

[29]Herbert von Bismarck to Franz von Rottenburg, 12 April 1888, Rottenburg Nachlass, BA, no. 3.

[30]Eulenburg to Bülow, 28 February 1887, Röhl, ed., *Eulenburgs Korrespondenz,* 1:220; Eulenburg, notes, 11 June 1887, Eulenburg Nachlass, BA, 2:31-32.

fun of him and pointedly neglecting to accord the kaiser the ritualistic courtesies by which all monarchs, and especially William II, laid store. The czar openly denounced the kaiser, and this ill-tempered criticism made its way back to Berlin, to the kaiser's great consternation. His reaction might have been still more tempestuous had not the Foreign Office succeeded in keeping some of Alexander's disparagements from coming to William's attention.[31]

The kaiser soon realized that his state visit to Saint Petersburg, intended as a gracious sign of good will, had instead been interpreted there as a manifestation of weakness. William became incensed when, after a suitable interval had elapsed, Alexander III showed no inclination to make a reciprocal visit to Berlin.[32] Nothing came from the Romanov capital except dismaying reports of the czar's animosity. Acutely wounded by Alexander's effrontery and rudeness, William responded in kind. Like the czar, the kaiser never let considerations of diplomacy bridle his tongue or restrain his gestures. Alexander's hostility, which undoubtedly seemed to William a most ungenerous response to his admiration of the czar, quickly revealed that the kaiser had a gift for insult no less well honed and no less undiplomatic than that of his Russian colleague. William refused to wear his numerous Russian decorations, dismissed the Russians as lunatics, and declared that their behavior made any sort of friendship or understanding quite impossible.[33] If Alexander

---

[31]On the czar's treatment of William II see Peter Jakobs, *Das Werden des Französisch-Russischen Zweibundes, 1890–1914* (Wiesbaden, 1968), p. 45; Pourtalès to Holstein, 9 February 1890, *HP,* 3:326; Schelking, *Recollections,* p. 12. For the kaiser's outraged reaction, see Herbert von Bismarck, "Not[izen]," Bismarck Nachlass, BA, FC 3018/279; Arthur von Brauer, *Im Dienste Bismarcks: Persönliche Erinnerungen* (Berlin, 1936), pp. 116–17.

[32]Villaume to Bülow, November 1889, Bülow Nachlass, BA, no. 22; Hajo Holborn, ed., *Aufzeichnungen und Erinnerungen aus dem Leben des Botschafters Joseph Maria von Radowitz,* 2 vols. (Berlin and Leipzig, 1925), 2:297, 29 May 1888; Malet to Salisbury, 22 June 1889, Salisbury Papers, vol. 62; Waldersee, *Denkwürdigkeiten,* 2:47, 25 March 1889.

[33]Malet to Salisbury, 22 June 1889, Salisbury Papers, vol. 62; Herbert to Otto von Bismarck, 25 September 1888, Bussmann, ed., *Herbert Bismarck,* p. 547.

wanted to see him again, he would have to present himself in Berlin.[34]

The czar dallied until October 1889 before going to Germany, where he behaved correctly but without a trace of enthusiasm.[35] By that time Bismarck's position had seriously eroded, and not long after Alexander returned to Russia, the crisis erupted that culminated in the chancellor's dismissal in March 1890. A subsidiary cause of the friction between William II and the chancellor was Bismarck's assertion that his sovereign's suspicions of Russia were largely unfounded, while the kaiser feared that Bismarck was inclined to sacrifice the alliance Germany had made in 1879 with Austria-Hungary in favor of the defensive Reinsurance Treaty with Russia that the chancellor had engineered in 1887. On March 17, William reproached Bismarck for not having shown him a number of dispatches from the German consul general in Kiev that reported increasing troop movements near the Russo-German frontier, which William, unlike Bismarck, interpreted as preparations for war against Germany.[36] Long annoyed by the chancellor's imperious behavior and his opposition to various internal policies, William II allowed Bismarck to resign on the following day.

The new chancellor, General Leo von Caprivi, shared William II's fear of a Russian attack, and the two decided that when the Reinsurance Treaty expired in June 1890 it would not be renewed. They believed that the Russian pact was incompatible with the alliance with Austria-Hungary, and neither William nor Caprivi, who had no experience in diplomacy, felt equal to the Bismarckian

[34]Malet to Salisbury, 22 June 1889, Salisbury Papers, vol. 62.

[35]On the visit see William II to Kaiser Franz Joseph, 10 October 1889, HHStA, Kabinetts Archiv, Geheim Akten, vol. 2; Waldersee, *Denkwürdigkeiten,* 2:71 (15 October 1889); Giers to Staal, 24 October 1889 N.S., A. Meyendorff, ed., *Correspondence Diplomatique de M. de Staal,* 2 vols (Paris, 1929), 2:51-52. On Alexander III's lack of cordiality see Herbette to Spuller, 13 October 1889, and Barrère to Spuller, 15 October 1889, *DDF,* 1st ser., 7:518, 521.

[36]Bismarck's account is in *Gedanken und Erinnerungen,* 3:88-90; for William's see Waldersee, *Denkwürdigkeiten,* 2:117-18 (17 March 1890); Eulenburg's notes entitled "Als Bismarck ging," Eulenburg Nachlass, BA, No. 76, pp. 26-27.

feat of managing to be a party to both treaties.[37] The kaiser realized that Germany's withdrawal would require considerable delicacy, since he had earlier assured the czar that he intended to continue the alliance.[38] He therefore explained to Alexander that he had not favored renewing the Reinsurance Treaty because it could not be squared with Germany's prior commitment to Vienna.[39] He also disingenuously assured the Russian envoy that Bismarck's dismissal had been occasioned by the aged chancellor's failing health and not because of any objection to Bismarck's long-standing, if sometimes stormy, attachment to Russia.[40] William was confident that the czar accepted these mollifying explanations and that Russia, though deprived of the German treaty, would not form an alliance with France as long as Paris was a republican capital and would not attack Germany unless it had allies. Besides, Russia's acute financial distress and the pitiable economic condition of the peasantry would prevent the czar from entertaining any idea of attacking Russia's neighbors.[41] Nevertheless, while Alexander might want peace, he could one day find himself unable to stop those forces in Russia and France that clamored for a war of annihilation against Germany.[42]

On all counts the kaiser's confidence in the efficacy of his personal diplomacy with the czar proved ill-founded. Alexander had no trust in William's explanations about the collapse of the Reinsurance Treaty, in the continuation of which he in fact had little faith, nor did he believe the kaiser's assurances that Bismarck's

[37]Caprivi memoranda, 22–23 May 1890, Caprivi to Schweinitz, 29 May 1890, *GP,* 7:29–36.

[38]Serge Goriainov, "The End of the Alliance of the Emperors," *AHR* 23, no. 2 (1918):343.

[39]Szögyényi to Goluchowski, 14 November 1896, HHStA, vol. 147 (Berichte), 37A–D.

[40]Goriainov, "End of the Alliance," p. 343.

[41]William II to Queen Victoria, 8 December 1891, RA 159/53; Malet to Salisbury, 22 November 1890, Salisbury Papers, vol. 63; William to Bismarck, 1 May 1888, Bismarck, *Gedanken und Erinnerungen,* 3:138; Münster to Caprivi, 4 January 1891, *GP,* 7:195–96.

[42]Alfred von Bülow to Caprivi, 30 July 1891, Schweinitz to Caprivi, 5 August 1891, Bernhard von Bülow to Caprivi, 4 August 1891, Deines report, 4 November 1891, all with William II's marginalia, *GP,* 7:207–16, 225 n.

dismissal did not portend danger for Russia. "William is as good a liar as his manners are bad," the czar more than once told his brother, Grand Duke Paul.[43] Alexander declared that in Bismarck's fall he had lost his only friend in Germany. Caprivi he could not trust.[44] It appeared to the czar that William II had spurned Russia for Great Britain, with whom Germany on 1 July 1890 signed a treaty exchanging Zanzibar for Heligoland.[45] Alexander was very hostile to Great Britain because London's imperial hegemony had frustrated Russian expansion from Constantinople to China.

Although the czar professed indifference that the Reinsurance Treaty had not been renewed, he indicated his annoyance at Germany's betrayal of Russia's diplomatic friendship by deliberately avoiding Berlin when he passed through Germany en route to visit the czarina's family in Copenhagen.[46] In August 1890, William II paid a second state visit to Alexander, in the course of which he behaved with his accustomed deference toward his Romanov colleague. The czar considered that his guest had invited himself and was not pleased to see him. According to the kaiser, Alexander treated him rudely and refused to consider reducing the number of troops ominously posed along Russia's German and Austrian frontiers.[47] Alexander, who soon heard of the kaiser's complaints about the way he had been treated while he was in Russia, had no patience with William's wounded feelings.

[43]Maurice Paléologue, diary, 16 February 1904, in his *Three Critical Years (1904-05-06)* (New York, 1957), p. 19. For Alexander III's dim view of the treaty see George F. Kennan, *The Decline of Bismarck's European Order: Franco-Russian Relations, 1875-1890* (Princeton, N.J., 1979), p. 409; Goriainov, "End of the Alliance," p. 344.

[44]Brauer, *Im Dienste Bismarcks,* p. 318.

[45]Goriainov, "End of the Alliance," p. 346; ibid, p. 344.

[46]Wladimir von Korostowetz, *Graf Witte: Der Steuermann in der Not* (Berlin, 1929), p. 119; Alexandre Ribot, "L'Alliance Franco-Russe," *Revue d'histoire de la Guerre Mondiale,* 15 (1935): 201-202; Schweinitz to Caprivi, 3 April 1890, *GP,* 7:11-15.

[47] Herbert von Bismarck, "IV Not[izen]," Bismarck Nachlass, BA, FC 3018/425; Russell to chargé, Berlin, 25 September 1890, Berlin embassy file, FO 64/1236. See also William II's marginalia on Pourtalès to Caprivi, 9 July 1890, *GP* 7: 354-55.

When a diplomatic report from Berlin brought the kaiser's dissatisfaction to his attention, the czar tartly noted that William's strictures, like his fervent attentions on other occasions, were in fact revelations of Hohenzollern weakness.[48] Once again the czar's hostile behavior produced countermeasures in Berlin. The kaiser denounced Alexander to some as a madman, to others as a barbarian; complained about the czar's incivility; and pointedly neglected to offer the expected compliments to the Russian majesties on their silver wedding anniversary in 1891.[49] The czar meanwhile made no attempt to conceal his delight that in spite of William II's overtures to the working class the German socialist movement continued to provoke the Hohenzollerns. "The more problems Germany has," Alexander wrote in 1891, "so much the better for us."[50] From 1891 to 1894, Alexander and William avoided one another, but when they did meet, the czar responded to the kaiser's excessive adulation with evident *froideur*.[51] In May 1891, with considerable diplomatic fanfare, the Triple Alliance of Germany, Austria-Hungary, and Italy was renewed, even through it did not expire until the following year, and the kaiser's state visit to London in July raised suspicions in Saint Petersburg that Germany hoped for England's inclusion in the pact. Alexander III was thoroughly alarmed

[48]Viktor A. Wroblewski, "Lamsdorff über Deutschland und seine Zukunft," *Berliner Monatshefte* 14, no. 5 (1936). This was also the view of the German chargé in Saint Petersburg. See Bülow to Eulenburg, 6 April 1892, Röhl, *Eulenburgs Korrespondenz,* 2:844–45.

[49]Marshall von Bieberstein, diary, 17 March 1890, Walther P. Fuchs, ed., *Grossherzog Friedrich I. von Baden und die Reichspolitik, 1871–1907,* 4 vols. (Stuttgart, 1968–80), 2:750; Radziwill to Robilant, 5–6 January 1891, Princess Marie Radziwill, *Lettres de la Princesse Radziwill au Général de Robilant, 1889–1914: Une grand dame d'avant guerre,* 4 vols (Bologna, 1933–34), 1:57–58; William II to Queen Victoria, 8 December 1891, RA 159/53. For another slight of the czar by the kaiser see W. H.-H. Waters, *"Private and Personal": Further Experiences of a Military Attaché* (London, 1928), p. 50.

[50]Wroblewski, "Lamsdorff über Deutschland," p. 352.

[51]*DDF,* 1st ser., 10:584 n. 3; ibid, 11:431 n. 1. At the end of 1891 the Russian ambassador in Berlin declared that as long as Alexander III and William II occupied their thrones the cleft between Russia and Germany would be as profound as that between France and Germany because of Alsace-Lorraine. Herbette to Ribot, 10 December 1891, ibid, 9:158–59.

at the prospect of Russia's isolation, and his response was to initiate overtures to republican France, the very step William II had declared the czar would never take. In July 1891, Alexander invited a French naval squadron to call at Kronstadt, where he treated its officers with conspicuous courtesy.[52]

It was now the kaiser's turn to be frightened, and he quickly abandoned his optimistic view that Russia, emboldened by her new friendship with France, would not attack Germany.[53] William attempted to placate Alexander by supporting a trade treaty with Russia, which was signed in February 1894, but his efforts were to no avail, for the czar believed that Germany might have made more economic concessions to Russia.[54] Alexander, moreover, was apprehensive at the increasing size of the Prussian army and profoundly suspicious of the kaiser, whose youth and ambition made him eager for the laurels of victory that a war against Russia might provide.[55] At the czar's insistence Russia entered into military talks with France, which led to the conclusion of a secret defensive alliance in January 1894.[56] Even though the kaiser did not know the particulars of the alliance, the telltale signs of Franco-Russian accord were an unmistakable repudiation of his personal diplomacy with his Russian colleague. William

[52]For the consternation this caused William see Eulenburg, note, n.d. [ca. 30 July 1893], Eulenburg Nachlass, BA, vol. 25, pp. 326–28.

[53]Capt. von Funcke, report, 13 April 1891, Bülow to Caprivi, 4 August 1891, Schoen to Caprivi, 20 August 1891, all with William II's marginalia, *GP,* 7:201–202, 215–23.

[54]For the kaiser's support of negotiations then in progress for a trade treaty with Russia, see protocol of Kronrat meeting, 18 February 1894, *GP,* 7:451–52; Gen. Friedrich von Bernhardi, *Denkwürdigkeiten aus meinem Leben* (Berlin, 1927), p. 165; Herbette to Casimir Périer, 3 February 1894, *DDF,* 1st ser., 11:54; Eugen von Jagemann, *Fündundsiebzig Jahre des Erlebens und Erfahrens (1849–1924),* (Heidelberg, 1925), pp. 118–19; Waldersee, *Denkwürdigkeiten,* pp. 306, 310 (9 February, 12 March 1894).

[55]Prince Heinrich VII Reuss to Caprivi, 10 March and 1 May 1893, *GP,* 7:428, 434. For Alexander's alarm at the kaiser's bellicose anti-Russian remarks see Waldersee, *Denkwürdigkeiten,* 2:239 (16 April 1892); and Holstein's retrospective note, (31 October 1901), *GP,* 17:104. See also Villaume, memorandum, 24 April 1889, Bismarck Nachlass, BA, FC 2983/791.

[56]On the czar's initiative in the alliance, see Herbette to Ribot, 8 December, 1891, *DDF,* 1st ser., 9:152.

could not believe that Alexander III, the exemplar of monarchical autocracy, could have committed himself to the radical horde in Paris. But he believed that the czar's unintelligible infatuation would cease if France started any trouble, in which case, William predicted, Germany, Austria-Hungary, and Russia would crush the revolutionary fever in Paris. Meanwhile, France could "cook in her own juice."[57]

In the summer of 1894, Alexander III fell victim to an incurable kidney disorder, a turn of events which the kaiser coolly described as a favorable indication for the future of Russo-German relations.[58] The czar died on November 1, and William's lack of regret was conspicuous enough to alarm Queen Victoria. Saint Petersburg immediately suggested that the kaiser's presence at the funeral would not be welcome, though a number of other European royalties were invited. William's retribution was to absent himself from the memorial service held in the Russian church in Berlin.[59]

The kaiser did not, however, propose to allow the difficulties he had had with Alexander to spoil his relationship with the new czar, the twenty-six-year-old Nicholas II. William had a good opinion of "Nicky," whose quiet and modest bearing contrasted so strikingly with the stern manner of his father. Alexander had instilled adulation but also fear in William; for Nicholas II the kaiser felt instead a fraternal interest, a protective and at times patronizing concern. William was almost a decade older than the "loyal" (*ergeben*) Nicholas, who presumably would be inclined to accept the help and counsel the kaiser was quite prepared to

[57]Lobanov to Hanotaux, 24 October 1895, Ibid., 12:261–63.

[58]Eulenburg, note, 28 September 1894, Eulenburg Nachlass, BA, vol. 31, p. 711; Karl A. von Müller, ed., *Fürst Chlodwig zu Hohenlohe-Schillungsfürst: Denkwürdigkeiten der Reichskanzlerzeit* (Stuttgart and Berlin, 1931), p. 24 (diary, 14 December 1894).

[59]On Queen Victoria's reaction see John Wilson, *CB: A Life of Sir Henry Campbell-Bannerman* (London, 1973), p. 136; on the funeral see Holstein to Hatzfeldt, 30 November 1894, Gerhard Ebel, ed., *Botschafter Paul Graf von Hatzfeldt: Nachgelassene Papiere, 1838–1901,* 2 vols. (Boppard, 1976), 2:1006.

offer.[60] William II could now at last dominate the Hohenzollern-Romanov connection and with careful application of his highly personal diplomacy significantly improve the deteriorating relationship between Germany and Russia. The new czar did not share the military interests of his father, and the danger of a Russian attack on Germany, which had appeared very real as long as Alexander was on the throne, now seemed to William be somewhat less likely. Prince Chlodwig zu Hohenlohe-Schillingsfürst, who had replaced Caprivi as chancellor just before Alexander's death, was a Russophile and would assist in fortifying the new Russo-German bond. So would Bernhard von Bülow, the rising light among German diplomats, who became state secretary of the Foreign Office in 1897 and replaced Hohenlohe as chancellor in 1900.

With Nicholas II on the Romanov throne a wider appeal to family ties could be asserted. With Alexander III the genealogical connection had rested on the marriage of the czar's grandfather Nicholas I to a sister of King William I of Prussia, the kaiser's grandfather. With Nicholas II the family connection was on still firmer ground through the czar's marriage to William's first cousin Princess Victoria Alice ("Alix") of Hesse. The kaiser was eager to make the most of this improved situation, for he was convinced that the rapprochement Alexander had made with France could be dissolved. From the beginning of the new czar's reign William II tendered him all the obtrusive attentions that had so disaffected Alexander III.[61] Unfortunately the kaiser's behavior produced the same negative results in Nicholas II.

The only fault that the kaiser had been able to detect in

---

[60]Marshall, diary, 9 June 1896, Fuchs, *Grossherzog Baden,* 3:526 n. 2. A good example of William's gratuitous advice is his letter to the czar, 26 September 1895, in Walter Goetz, ed., *Briefe Wilhelms II. an den Zaren, 1894-1914* (Berlin, n.d. [1920]), pp. 379-83.

[61]On the dissolution of the alliance see Swaine to Malet, 30 August 1895, FO 64/1351; Lascelles to Salisbury, 28 February 1896, Salisbury Papers, vol. 120; Swaine to Lansdowne, 28 February 1901, FO 64/1520. On William's attentions see Waldersee, *Denkwürdigkeiten,* 2:284, 374 (29 January 1893, 25 October 1896); Holstein to Eulenburg, 28 December 1895, Eulenburg Nachlass, BA, vol. 76, pp. 84-85.

Nicholas before his ascension was that he was too much under the influence of his parents and the Russian court. Nicholas himself admitted that he was utterly malleable.[62] William found that the czar, if liberated from these noxious Germanophobes, was in many respects a "charming, agreeable and dear boy." He declared that Nicholas was in fact the best-mannered man in Europe.[63] The kaiser hoped that his new Russian colleague would prove to be an assertive ruler who would curb anti-German influences in Russia, abandon the alliance with France, and bring Russia and Germany back into their traditionally close association. But like many observers, William was apprehensive that the phlegmatic and indecisive Nicholas was unlikely to prove equal to the titanic responsibilities that awaited him. The new czar, even more than his morose father, was unnaturally reclusive, and the kaiser complained that Nicholas II shunned the official conduct of affairs to devote himself to his wife and children.[64] Even in moments of extreme crisis, such as the Revolution of 1905, the czar, to William II's exasperation, would not personally take command of the situation.[65] Nicholas allowed his ministers to do what they pleased (a state of affairs which Alexander III had never permitted and one which William certainly did not countenance in Germany), and many of them pursued anti-German policies. The kaiser especially detested Count Michael Muraviev, the minister of foreign affairs from 1897 to 1900, whom he openly

[62]Nicholas II to Grand Duke Vladimir, 26 November 1896 N.S., in Theodore von Laue, *Sergei Witte and the Industrialization of Russia* (New York and London, 1963), pp. 122–24.

[63]William to Queen Victoria, 28 January 1893, RA 159/98; Viktoria Luise, Princess of Prussia, *Im Strom der Zeit* (Göttingen, 1974), p. 13; Malet to Rosebery, 2 February 1893, Malet Papers, FO 64/1293.

[64]On the czar's domestic priorities see Szögyényi to Goluchowski, 14 November 1900, HHStA, vol. 154 (Berichte), 54, A–J. For William on Nicholas II's weakness see Lascelles to Salisbury, 24 November 1896, 22 December 1898, FO 64/1379, 1439, Lascelles to Salisbury, 9 March 1900, Salisbury Papers, vol. 121; Call to Goluchowski, 26 October 1895, HHStA, vol. 146 (Berichte), 49B; Call to Goluchowski, 11 April 1900, vol. 154 (Varia).

[65]de Laguiche to Étienne, 23 December 1905, *DDF,* 2d ser., 8:373.

denounced.[66] Moreover, the czar, in William's opinion, was incapable of exercising sufficient control over the Russian army, which the kaiser still believed was ready to attack Germany. Urged on by their French allies, the bellicose Russians were not to be trusted.[67]

As far as William II was concerned, the greatest danger which Germany faced as a result of Nicholas II's weakness was the enhanced power of the Romanov court, where the kaiser was assailed as the "enfant terrible."[68] The Russian royal family was solidly arrayed not only against Germany but against William personally, and the kaiser's two most formidable enemies in Saint Petersburg were the czar's wife and his mother.[69] William had taken an active part in promoting the match between Nicholas II and his Hessian cousin Alix.[70] While the marriage proved to be extraordinarily happy, Czarina Alexandra Feodorovna, as she was formally known, felt no gratitude to the kaiser and did not like to be reminded of his contribution to her happiness. A moody, neurotic woman of very constricted intelligence, the czarina was even more anchoritic than her consort and was acutely protective of the privacy of their happy domestic life. She was always English at heart (like William, she was a grandchild of Queen

[66]On the ministers see Lascelles to Salisbury, 24 November 1896, FO 64/1379. On Muraviev see, inter alia, Holstein to Hatzfeldt, 20 March 1895, 14 January 1897, Ebel, ed., *Hatzfeldt Papiere,* 2:1024, 1122 n. 5, and a printed résumé of conversations between the kaiser and Goluchowski in Berlin, 16 January and 19 January 1897, HHStA, vol. 148, Varia; Szögyényi to Vienna, 11 January 1897, ibid., vol. 149.

[67]Lascelles to Salisbury, 22 December 1898, FO 64/1439; Goetz, ed., *Briefe Wilhelms II,* p. 298 (25 October 1895).

[68]Soulange-Bodin to Hanotaux, 8 August 1897, *DDF,* 1st ser., 13:488.

[69]On Romanov hostility to William see Villaume to Herbert von Bismarck, 24 April 1888, Bismarck Nachlass, BA, FC 2983/791; Rex, note, December 1894, *GP,* 9:339–40; Radolin to Hohenlohe, 14 July 1895, ibid., pp. 357–58; Countess Marie Kleinmichel, *Memories of a Shipwrecked World* (New York, 1923), pp. 160–62; Viktoria Luise, *Strom der Zeit,* p. 21.

[70]Two of the czarina's sisters married men who heartily disliked the kaiser: Prince Louis Battenberg and Nicholas II's uncle, Grand Duke Serge. See Gen. Count Gustav von Lambsdorff, *Die Militärbevollmächtigte Kaiser Wilhelms II. am Zarenhofe, 1904–1914* (Berlin, 1937), pp. 330–31; Bülow, *Denkwürdigkeiten,* 2:454–55.

Victoria), and Nicholas II reproached anyone who referred to his wife's German lineage by noting that "She is *English,* remember."[71] The kaiser, unfortunately, was inclined to treat Alexandra Feodorovna as a German princess rather than as a Russian sovereign.[72] The czarina could not bear William's showy manner, which in her opinion was tasteless and masked an essential shallowness. "He thinks he is a superman, and he's really nothing but a clown," she once declared. "He has no real worth."[73] Both she and Nicholas resented the kaiser's snubs to her brother, the grand duke of Hesse, whom William found distasteful because of his childish personality, his marital irregularities, and his liberal politics. The grand duke, of whom both Nicholas and Alix were exceptionally fond, disliked the kaiser and was an effective voice in influencing Nicholas against him.[74] In addition to her hostility to the kaiser, the czarina found his consort, Kaiserin Augusta Victoria, tiresomely prim and moralistic. It was a case of bigot confronting bigot, and the distaste was mutual. The German empress, an exalted Protestant, was never able to forgive the Hessian princess for having embraced Orthodoxy in order to mount the throne of the czars. Alix avoided William and Augusta Victoria whenever possible and restricted her part in their infre-

[71]Giles St. Aubyn, *Edward VII: Prince and King* (New York, 1979), p. 299. On the czarina's lack of gratitude see Bülow, *Denkwürdigkeiten,* 1:101-102, 130; Sigurd von Ilsemann, *Der Kaiser in Holland: Aufzeichnungen,* 2 vols. (Munich, 1967-68), 2:51 (10 March 1927).

[72]Korostowetz, *Graf Witte,* p. 124.

[73]Prince Felix Youssoupoff, *Avant l'Exil, 1887-1919* (Paris, 1952), p. 164; A. A. Mossolov, *At the Court of the Last Tsar* (London, 1935); Waters, *Potsdam and Doorn,* pp. 193-94.

[74]On the grand duke's private life and his politics see Corbett to Grey, Viscount Grey of Fallodon papers, FO 800/1650; Witte, *Memoirs,* p. 405; Ilsemann, *Kaiser in Holland,* 2:51 (10 March 1927); Hohenlohe, *Denkwürdigkeiten der Reichskanzlerzeit,* p. 7 (diary, 2 November 1894); E. J. Dillon, *The Eclipse of Russia* (New York, 1918), pp. 328-29. For the grand duke's hostility to William II see Rodd to Hardinge, 12 May 1908, Lord Hardinge of Penshurst Papers (University Library, Cambridge), vol. 12; Bülow, *Denkwürdigkeiten,* 1:407; Ludwig Raschdau, *In Weimar als Preussischer Gesandter: Ein Buch der Erinnerungen an deutsche Fürstenhöfe* (Berlin, 1939), pp. 100-101; Schelking, *Recollections,* pp. 148-49; Waldersee, *Denkwürdigkeiten,* 2: 374 (25 October 1896).

quent encounters to the barest of civilities.[75] Alexandra Feodorovna's influence on her husband was enormous, and he indulgently tolerated his wife's animosity to the Hohenzollerns, as he did all her other whims.[76]

Of even greater concern to the kaiser was his belief that Nicholas II was a puppet in the hands of his redoubtable mother, Czarina Dowager Maria Feodorovna. Of all William's Russian enemies Maria Feodorovna was the most tenacious, and she was for decades at the heart of a coterie in Saint Petersburg that was implacably set against him. Her father, King Christian IX of Denmark, had lost the duchies of Schleswig and Holstein to Prussia in the war of 1864, fought when William II was only five years old. King Christian bore the kaiser no grudge for this reverse and even tried to serve as mediator between William and the czars.[77] The king's consort, Queen Louise, on the other hand, proved to be the kaiser's nemesis in Copenhagen. By birth a princess of Hesse-Cassel, which had been sequestered by Prussia in 1866, the queen had sworn vengeance on the Hohenzollerns and refused ever to set foot in Berlin. Alone she would not have been a foe of particularly great significance, but she had conceived and realized vast ambitions for her numerous children. One son succeeded to the throne of Denmark and the second became George I of the

---

[75]On the mutual hostility of the two empresses see Eulenburg, note, 12-13 October 1895, Eulenburg Nachlass, BA, vol. 38, pp. 727-32; Raschdau, *In Weimar,* p. 101; Schelking, *Recollections,* pp. 128, 133-34; Maurice Paléologue, *Guillaume II et Nicholas II* (Paris, 1935), p. 77. The czar throughly disliked the kaiserin. See Edward J. Bing, ed., *The Secret Letters of the Last Tsar: Being the Confidential Correspondence Between Nicholas II and his Mother, Dowager Empress Maria Feodorovna* (New York and Toronto, 1938), pp. 121, 135 (13 August 1897, 22 November 1899 N.S.); Princess Anatole Bariatinsky, *My Russian Life* (London, 1923), pp. 82-83. On the czarina's avoidance of German royalty see Mossolov, *Court of the Last Tsar,* p. 203.

[76]Sazonov, *Fateful Years,* p. 116; Witte, *Memoirs,* p. 198.

[77]On King Christian's relations with the kaiser see William II, memorandum, 28 March 1927, Hausarchiv, rep. 53a, no. 33; Brincken to Caprivi, 8 June 1892, *GP,* 8: 407-408; William to Queen Victoria, 8 December 1891, RA 159/53; Lady Walburga Paget, *Embassies of Other Days and Further Recollections,* 2 vols. (London, 1923) 2:488; Lillie de Hegermann-Lindencrone, *The Sunny Side of Diplomatic Life* (London and New York, 1914), p. 295.

Hellenes. Her first and second daughters married the heirs to the British and Russian thrones, who eventually ascended as Edward VII and Alexander III. A third daughter wed the duke of Cumberland, the claimant to the defunct Anglo-German throne of Hanover, which had been seized by the Prussians in the same war that had added neighboring Hesse-Cassel to the Hohenzollern domains.

Although William II had in no way been responsible for any of these Prussian conquests, Queen Louise's wrath was thoroughly fixed on him and on the kaiserin, whom she despised as a member of a family which in the 1860s had contested her husband's claim to the Danish throne.[78] The queen bequeathed her surpassing hatred of Prussia to all her children, and she thrived on intriguing through them against the kaiser. Her offspring visited Copenhagen regularly, and when they were not at home, they were tied to the queen through a vast correspondence. "Cette mère incomparable," as one observer called her, was a resolute and dictatorial woman who overshadowed her benign husband. William knew of the queen's machinations against him, and he disliked her, declaring that the waves of letters emanating from Copenhagen were the cause of many of his troubles.[79] He held the "old spider" responsible for persuading Alexander III not to visit Berlin.[80] When Queen Louise died in 1898, the kaiser took no pains to disguise his lack of regret. He presented himself at the

---

[78]Radziwill, *Lettres,* vol. 1 (22 and 26 November 1891).

[79]Ibid, pp. 65–66 (2–3 March and 24–25 April 1897).; William II to Nicholas II, 2 August 1905, Herman Bernstein, ed., *The Willy-Nicky Correspondence: Being the Secret and Intimate Telegrams Exchanged Between the Kaiser and the Tsar* (New York, 1918), pp. 117–18; Hohenlohe, *Denkwürdigkeiten,* 2:483–84 (13 December 1891); Waldersee, *Denkwürdigkeiten,* 2:160 (16 November 1890); Maurice F. Egan, *Ten Years near the German Frontier: A Retrospect and a Warning* (New York, 1919), pp. 112-13. On the queen's correspondence see Radziwill, *Lettres,* 2: 79 (24–25 April 1897); Bing, ed., *Secret Letters,* p. 117 (7 April 1897 N.S.); Alexander, Grand Duke of Russia, *Always a Grand Duke* (New York, 1933), pp. 198–99.

[80]Prince Albert zu Schleswig-Holstein-Sonderburg-Glücksburg, "Erinnerungen aus meinem Leben" (typescript), Schlossarchiv, Glücksburg-Ostsee, p. 38; Hohenlohe, diary, 13 December 1891, Hohenlohe Nachlass, BA, no. 1455.

Russian embassy to make the necessary representations of sympathy on the demise of the czar's grandmother. "Monsieur l'ambassadeur," William told the envoy, "I extend my most profound condolences. . . . Now that I have fulfilled my official duty, you surely do not expect me to cry about it, do you [?]."[81]

Although relations between Germany and Denmark improved conspicuously after the queen's death, the anti-Prussian legacy she had sown in her children persisted. For decades the duke and duchess of Cumberland scorned the kaiser even though he tried to make conciliatory gestures to them.[82] The Princess of Wales, who was always very sympathetic with the plight of her dispossessed sister, detested the kaiser and gleefully passed along Alexander's criticisms of him. He thought he was Charlemagne, the princess declared, but in fact he was a fool.[83] Her brother, King George of the Hellenes, also had little use for William II, largely because of the exile from Berlin which the kaiser and kaiserin inflicted for several years on the Greek crown princess Sophie, William's sister. She, like Nicholas's bride, had converted to Orthodoxy, a change of faith which neither the kaiser nor his wife could accept.[84] William found the frumpy king and his

[81]Schelking, *Recollections,* p. 149.

[82]On the Cumberland-Hohenzollern relationship see Baron Wilhelm von Schoen, *Erlebtes: Beiträge zur politischen Geschichte der neuesten Zeit* (Stuttgart and Berlin, 1921), pp. 12–13; Radziwill, *Lettres,* 3:56 (6–7 April 1903); Alexander Izvolski, *Recollections of a Foreign Minister* (Garden City, N.Y., 1921), p. 61. The feud ended in 1913 with the marriage of the kaiser's only daughter to the Cumberlands' oldest son.

[83]Cambon to Delcassé, 29 January 1903, *DDF,* 2d ser., 3:67–68; Herbert von Bismarck, "Not[izen]," Bismarck Nachlass, BA, FC 3019/276. In a similar vein see Princess of Wales to Duke of York, 30 August 1890 and 29 April 1900, RA, GV AA31/14 and AA32/21; Augusta, Grand Duchess of Mecklenburg-Strelitz to Princess of Wales, 12 February 1906, RA, GV CC32/19; Holstein to Eulenburg, 30 November 1896, *HP,* 3:659; Georgina Battiscombe, *Queen Alexandra* (London, 1969), pp. 174–75. Queen Alexandra and the kaiserin disliked one another. See Bülow, *Denkwürdigkeiten,* 1:342; and Bülow, "Numerierte Zettel betr. 1859-1910," p. 140, Bülow Nachlass, BA, no. 153.

[84]Count Erhard von Wedel, ed., *Zwischen Kaiser und Kanzler: Aufzeichnungen des General-adjutanten Grafen Carl von Wedel aus den Jahren 1890–1894* (Leipzig, 1943), p. 168 (19 April 1891); Radziwill, *Lettres,* 1:53 (30–31

modest court in Athens insufferably bourgeois and made him the frequent butt of his sarcasm. It is certainly true that King George was not a particularly elegant figure, but he was a decent and kindly man, much beloved by his brothers and sisters, and his consort, Queen Olga, was the favorite first cousin of Alexander III. The kaiser's diatribes against his Greek colleague eventually came to the attention of the king's relatives and contributed to the disaffection of these eminent persons.[85]

It was Czarina Maria Feodorovna, the wife of Alexander III, who of all Queen Louise's progeny was the most thoroughly anti-German. She never developed any liking either for the kaiser or for his consort.[86] As far as William was concerned, the czarina was ruled by a single obsession: revenge on Prussia for the seizure of Schleswig and Holstein. Maria Feodorovna's "most pernicious" influence on her son was, in his opinion, out of all proportion to her meager intelligence.[87] The kaiser believed that the czarina's spell embraced not only her son but also several of

---

December 1890); Empress Frederick to Queen Victoria, 20 January 1891, RA Z50/6; Bülow, *Denkwürdigkeiten,* 2:89; Hohenlohe, diary, 18 January 1891, Helmuth Rogge, ed., *Holstein und Hohenlohe* (Stuttgart, 1957), pp. 345–46; Anne Topham, *Chronicles of the Prussian Court* (London, 1926), pp. 173–74; Bamberger, diary, 21 December 1890, and William II to King George, 17 December 1890, Feder, ed., *Bismarcks grosses Spiel,* pp. 450–51; Waldersee, *Denkwürdigkeiten,* 2:239 (16 April 1892). See also Arthur G. Lee, ed., *The Empress Writes to Sophie, Her Daughter, Crown Princess and Later Queen of the Hellenes: Letters, 1889-1901* (London, n.d.)

[85]Eulenburg, note, 13 October 1894 and diary entry, 14 October 1894, Eulenburg Nachlass, BA, vol. 32, pp. 773–74; Empress Frederick to Queen Victoria, 1 August 1890, 5 September 1891, RA Z48/44, Z51/20; Malet to Salisbury, 20 December 1890, Salisbury Papers, vol. 63; William II, memorandum 28 March 1927, Hausarchiv, rep. 53a no. 33; Radziwill, *Lettres,* 2:68 (6–7 June 1897).

[86]Bing, ed., *Secret Letters,* pp. 129, 150, 260 (3 December 1897, 10 October 1901, 18 November 1910 N.S.); Izvolski, *Recollections,* p. 60; Lambsdorff, *Militärbevollmächtigte,* pp. 366–67; Schweinitz, *Denkwürdigkeiten,* 2:447 (12 December 1892); Bülow, *Denkwürdigkeiten,* 2:130–31; Vorres, *Last Grand Duchess,* pp. 60–61; Viktoria Luise, *Strom der Zeit,* pp. 20, 30.

[87]Szögyényi to Goluchowski, 12 January 1899, HHStA, vol. 152 (Varia); Rogge, ed., *Holstein and Hohenlohe,* p. 334; Hohenlohe, diary, 12 June 1889, William to Nicholas II, 22 August 1905, Goetz, ed., *Briefe Wilhelms II,* p. 377. For

his ministers, notably the hated Muraviev, who had once been posted to Copenhagen and had ingratiated himself with the Danish royal house. The kaiser's association of the czarina with Muraviev was quite correct, for they were allies. On being reminded in 1897 that the newly appointed foreign minister was anti-German, Maria Feodorovna curtly replied, "So much the better."[88] Count Vladimir Lambsdorff, a prominent Russian diplomat, reflecting on the Germanophobe influence the czarina consistently exercised on both her husband and her son, declared that since her arrival in Russia in 1866 the course of Russo-German relations had "indisputably not gone for the best."[89]

Nicholas II's passivity before his mother and wife severely tried the kaiser's patience, for he did not believe that women should be involved in politics. He was gratified whenever he believed that he could detect signs that the czar seemed to be resisting Maria Feodorovna.[90] But such occasions were rare, and with time Dowager Czarina's anti-German influence showed little evidence of decline, while that of Nicholas's anti-Prussian wife was clearly increasing. Nicholas, alas, was a "czar under the rule of his mother," a "ninny," a "whimperer" (*"Schlappier," "Jammerhund"*). In a moment of exasperation the kaiser incautiously told Lord Lansdowne, the British foreign secretary, that the easily influenced czar was "only fit to live in a country house and grow turnips."[91] If Nicholas II did not assert himself, he might end his

---

William's hostile opinion of the czarina see Lascelles to Salisbury, 24 November 1896, FO 64/1379; Radziwill, *Lettres,* 2:64–65 (2-3 March 1897); Schweinitz, note, 29 August 1895, Schweinitz, *Briefwechsel, p.* 327; Herbert to Otto von Bismarck, 5 October 1889, Bussmann, ed., *Herbert Bismarck,* pp. 547–48; Szögyényi to Kálnoky, 21 April 1895, HHStA, vol. 145 (Berichte), 13A–C. On the influence of the empress on her son see Richard Wortman, "The Russian Empress as Mother," in David L. Ransel, ed., *The Family in Russia* (Urbana, Ill., 1978), pp. 60–74.

[88]Radziwill, *Lettres,* 2:60 (14 February 1897).

[89]Wroblewski, "Lamsdorff über Deutschland," p. 362; Greindl to Chimay, 2 September 1890, Schwertfeder, ed., *Amtliche Aktenstücke,* 1:312.

[90]Szögyényi to Goluchowski, 20 August 1897, HHStA, vol. 148 (Varia).

[91]Eulenburg note, 8 November 1896, Eulenburg Nachlass, BA, vol. 44, pp. 753–55; Bülow, *Denkwürdigkeiten,* 1:454–55; Lansdowne, notes, 1901, FO

life as had Louis XVI, martyred by his subjects, or share the fate of Czar Paul, assassinated in 1801 in the course of a palace revolution.[92]

The kaiser believed that, since Nicholas II was so weak-willed, a countercampaign against the czarinas and the anti-German clique in Saint Petersburg was imperative. Much to the dismay of German diplomats, it was to be waged by the kaiser personally. Statecraft was a matter for sovereigns, and William informed the czar that he preferred hearing from him directly rather than through others.[93] Nicholas II, always the premier target of the kaiser's penchant for giving advice, became the victim of the celebrated "Willy-Nicky" letters and also the recipient of many telegrams. The kaiser's purpose in this florid correspondence was to isolate Russia from both France and England and to urge Nicholas to return to the intimate relations that had prevailed between Germany and Russia during most of the nineteenth century. In William's view, as in Bülow's, Russia and Germany were natural allies, bound by tradition, ideological similarity, and a common apprehension about the inordinate power of Great Britain. The kaiser saw in Nicholas II the sovereign with whom he would determine the future of Europe. "We both make history and guide the fates," he proclaimed to the czar in 1902.[94] To ensure that Nicholas did not capitulate to English blandishments, William stressed that perfidy was all that could be expected from London, where many anarchist "beasts" from the Continent were allowed refuge.[95] As for the French, it was preposterous that they should ever have become Russia's allies, and the kaiser did what he could to plant suspicion in the czar's mind. He was

---

800/130; William II's marginalia on dispatch of Prince Reuss to Caprivi, 15 November 1892, *GP,* 7:411-12.

[92]Lascelles to Salisbury, 9 March 1900, Salisbury Papers, vol. 121; Lascelles to Salisbury, 24 November 1896, FO 63/1379.

[93]Goetz, ed., *Briefe Wilhelms II.,* p. 355 (2 January 1905).

[94]Alvensleben to Bülow, 18 February 1902, Vogel, *Deutsche Russlandpolitik,* p. 109.

[95]Goetz, ed., *Briefe Wilhelms II.,* pp. 389–90 (14 June 1906).

always at pains to remind his Russian colleague, whose grandfather had been assassinated and on whose own life many attempts had been made, that France was not only republican but regicide as well. In 1895 the kaiser wrote in his imperfect English to the czar on this subject; the letter is typical of the fervently hortatory character of William's correspondence with Nicholas II:

> The R[épublique] F[rançaise] is from the source of the great Revolution and propagates and is bound to do so, the ideas of it. Don't forget that [President] Fauré ... sits on the throne of the King and Queen of France "by the Grace of God" whose heads Frenchmen Republicans cut off! Has it not staggered from bloodshed to bloodshed? ... Nicky take my word on it the curse of God has stricken that People forever! We Christian Kings and Emperors have one holy duty imposed on us by Heaven, that is to uphold the Principle "von Gottes Gnaden," we can have good relations with the R.F. but never be intime with her![96]

The kaiser's advice provoked little response other than irritation in Saint Petersburg, for Nicholas had no intention of abandoning his French allies. The czar revered his father, and immediately after his succession he declared to the French that he considered it his "sacred duty" to continue Alexander's policy of friendship. It was a conviction that Nicholas frequently expressed and from which he never wavered.[97] He tried to distance himself from the kaiser by declining to continue the traditional practice of exchanging military plenipotentiaries with Berlin.[98] To William II's regret the czar never exhibited the development of will power which he had hoped his advice would engender. Instead, Nicholas remained reclusive, indecisive, and dependent on women. Thus

[96]Ibid., p. 298 (25 October 1895); for similar language see ibid., pp. 379–83 (26 September 1895).

[97]See, for example, Nicholas to Casimir-Périer, 11 November 1894, and Boisdeffre to Hanotaux, 17 November 1894, *DDF,* 1st ser., 11:417, 427; Bompard to Pichon, 15 December 1906, ibid., 2d ser., 10:559; Louis to Pichon, 5 January 1911, and Louis to Crupp, 4 March 1911, ibid., 2d ser., 10:200, 13:313-14.

[98]Nicholas II to William II, November 1895, Hohenlohe Nachlass, BA, no. 1601. The exchange of military plenipotentiaries was resumed in 1904. See Lambsdorff, *Militärbevollmächtigte.*

the czar, who in William's opinion was "weak, idealistic, too peace-loving and unmilitary," remained incapable of standing up to the French or the "Yellow Peril," William's allegorical expression for the expanding Japanese empire.[99] Even as a correspondent Nicholas II did not measure up to the kaiser's expectations, for he did not always mean what he said or quickly forgot what he had written, if indeed he bothered to answer at all. To William's annoyance, the czar passed his letters on to Muraviev and other ministers rather than treating them as the personal and confidential intimacies of a colleague.[100]

Nicholas II's reaction to the kaiser, like that of his father, was a combination of suspicion and distaste. But the last czar, in contrast to Alexander III, concealed it by his laconic manner and scrupulous politeness. As czar, Nicholas could find nothing that was sympathetic in the kaiser, whose talkative, bombastic, and theatrical manner he found alarming.[101] There is no doubt that the czar felt involved in a sort of personal rivalry with William II—certainly the kaiser believed this to be the case.[102] The diminutive Nicholas was annoyed by William II's insistence on being photographed while clasping him on the shoulder, a pose which inevitably made the kaiser appear to be the czar's towering protector.[103] At meetings with William the retiring czar, who had very little conversational prowess, felt ill at ease and inadequate. Nicholas confided to the British prime minister, Lord Salisbury, that he was by nature a quiet person. The kaiser, on the other hand, according to the czar's indictment, was nervous and ill-mannered. Nicholas complained to Salisbury that not only could he never know what tangent the kaiser's feverish conversation

[99]William II's marginalia on a dispatch of Arco, 13 January 1904, *GP,* 19:27 n. 1; Aehrenthal, memorandum, 22-25 February 1910, Ludwig Bittner and Hans Uebersberger, eds., *Österreich-Ungarns Aussenpolitik von der Bosnischen Krise bis zum Kriegsausbruch 1914,* 9 vols. (Vienna, 1931), 2: 724-26.

[100]Lascelles to Salisbury, 10 March 1900, Salisbury Papers, vol. 121; Zedlitz-Trützschler, *Zwölf Jahre,* pp. 102-103 (7 December 1904); Szögyényi to Goluchowski, 2 February 1899, HHStA, vol. 152 (Varia).

[101]Hanotaux, notes, 12 October 1896, *DDF,* 1st ser., 12:781-82.

[102]Derenthall to Hohenlohe, 21 June 1899, *GP,* 13:214; Witte, *Memoirs,* p. 405.

[103]Paléologue, *Three Critical Years,* p. 19 (16 February 1904).

would take but he (like Ferdinand of Bulgaria) had to endure being slapped on the back and poked in the ribs like a schoolboy.[104] The czar also objected to William's tendency, so in keeping with his notion of royal diplomacy, to use their meetings to make impromptu proposals about questions of great importance. Taken by surprise, Nicholas II felt embarrassed and edgy, and he protected himself by avoiding whenever possible any intimate conversations with the kaiser. When an exchange could not be avoided, the czar was careful to restrict himself to vague generalities.[105] Nicholas found that if he expressed himself more concretely William was sure to take improper advantage of what he said. "Thank heaven!" the czar declared at the conclusion of a meeting with the kaiser in 1912. "Now one does not have to watch one's every word lest it be construed in a way one had not even dreamed."[106] Nicholas's long acquaintance with the kaiser persuaded him that he could not be relied upon. The kaiser's glib assurances of solidarity failed to be reflected in his actions, which in the czar's opinion were devious and disloyal.[107]

Confronted by such a garrulous, relentless, and graphomaniacal colleague, the czar retreated still further into the pampered calm of his domestic sanctuary. William's incessant attentions were irritating interruptions of Nicholas II's comfortable family life,

[104]Margaret M. Jefferson, "Lord Salisbury's Conversations with the Tsar at Balmoral, 27 and 29 September 1896," *Slavonic and East European Review* 39, no. 22 (1960):220; Schelking, *Recollections,* pp. 129-30; Mossolov, *Court of the Last Tsar,* pp. 202-03; Admiral Alfred von Tirpitz, *Erinnerungen* (Leipzig, 1919), p. 147.

[105]On the czar's handling of his encounters with William II see Hanotaux, notes, 12 October 1896, *DDF,* 1st ser., 12:781-82; Montebello to Nisard, 7 February 1896, ibid., p. 450; Lord Onslow, minute, n.d. [after 1911], G. P. Gooch and Howard Temperley, eds., *British Documents on the Origins of the War, 1898-1914,* 11 vols. (London, 1925-38), 3:382. See also Paléologue, *Guillaume II et Nicolas II,* p. 20; Szögyényi to Goluchowski, 22 December 1901, HHStA, vol. 156 (Berichte); Lord Newton, *Lord Lansdowne: A Biography* (London, 1929), p. 273.

[106]H. H. Fisher, ed., *Out of the Past: The Memoirs of Count Kokovtsov* (Stanford, Calif., 1935), p. 320.

[107]Bompard to Rouvier, 22 February and 24 February 1906, *DDF,* 2d ser., 11, no. 1, pp. 356-57, 399; Hardinge to Lansdowne, 13 June 1905, Gooch and Temperley, eds., *British Documents,* 4: 197.

and, like Alexander III, he found the kaiser's antics tiresome, pretentious, and even "mad."[108] The czar rarely traveled to the great European capitals, preferring the seclusion of his brother-in-law's miniature court in Darmstadt or the cozy family gatherings at his grandparents' palace in Copenhagen. Like his father, Nicholas tried as often as possible to slip through Germany without setting foot in Berlin or Potsdam. From his ascension in 1894 until 1910 the czar visited the German capital only once, and then for only a few hours, because the kaiser adamantly refused his suggestion that they meet at Wiesbaden, conveniently near Darmstadt.[109]

When Nicholas II had no choice but to agree to a rendezvous, he hoped that his meetings with William might be, as he once put it, "quite simple and homely."[110] This proved to be a utopian expectation. Even when the kaiser was agreeable, he took an exuberant delight in ceremony and honors, and the czar could do nothing but cater to his colleague's fancy. On the eve of a visit from the kaiser Nicholas wrote in disgust to his mother than there was no way he could avoid investing the kaiser with the insignia of an admiral of the Russian navy. The thought of what lay ahead, he declared, was enough to make him vomit.[111]

Nicholas could limit his encounters with the kaiser, but there was no escape from his letters and telegrams. Although the czar had initially encouraged the correspondence, he soon found exchanging messages with William a tiresome task and tried unsuccessfully to terminate the arrangement.[112] The czar resented the didactic tone of William's letters, the criticism which he heaped on his French allies, and the caustic barbs frequently directed at the uncle of both sovereigns, the "arch plotter," King

---

[108]On the kaiser's antics see Bing, ed., *Secret Letters,* pp. 150–51 (10 October 1901 N.S.); Bülow, *Denkwürdigkeiten,* 2:130; Radolin to Holstein, 29 September 1899, *HP,* 4:157–58. On Nicholas II's suggestion that the kaiser was "raving mad," see Mossolov, *Court of the Last Tsar,* p. 202.

[109]*GP,* 13:216; Schelking, *Recollections,* pp. 45–46, 129–30.

[110]Bernstein, ed., *Willy-Nicky Correspondence,* p. 105 (n.d. [1905]).

[111]Bing, ed., *Secret Letters,* p. 120 (4 August 1897 N.S.).

[112]Holstein to Hatzfeldt, 27–28 November 1896, Ebel ed., *Hatzfeldt Papiere,* 2:1098.

Edward VII.[113] Like many Russian ministers, the czar believed, certainly not without justification, that the real purpose of William's overtures was to involve Russia in difficulties with England or France from which Germany ultimately would be the beneficiary.[114] So deep were Nicholas's suspicions of the kaiser that his long-term minister Count Witte discovered that the easiest way to win the czar's consent to something was to inform him that William opposed it.[115]

William's advances to Nicholas were thus completely counterproductive, increasing rather than diminishing the hostility the czar felt toward his German colleague. The kaiser, typically, believed that the failure of the Willy-Nicky correspondence to contribute more to strengthening Nicholas or to improving Russo-German relations was entirely the czar's fault.[116] Nicholas, on the other hand, regarded William as the cause of many of Russia's difficulties with Germany, especially those that emerged during the Russo-Japanese war of 1904–1905. The czar was desperate to ensure the continuation of German economic aid during the conflict, and in July 1904 the kaiser took advantage of his colleague's embarrassment to force him to consent to a trade treaty very favorable to German interests. The war proved increasingly disastrous for Russia, and a year later, at a meeting at Björkö, Nicholas felt forced to yield to William's cajolery and signed a defensive

---

[113]On the kaiser's didacticism see Hanotaux, notes, 12 October 1896, *DDF,* 1st ser., 12:781–82; Bülow, *Denkwürdigkeiten,* 2:86; Witte, *Memoirs,* p. 406; Zedlitz-Trützschler, *Zwölf Jahre,* pp. 67–69 (24 May 1904); for his criticisms of Edward VII see Dillon, *Eclipse of Russia,* pp. 327–28; Bülow, *Denkwürdigkeiten,* 2:86–87; Goetz, ed., *Briefe Wilhelms II.,* p. 331 (19 November 1903), p. 377 (22 August 1905); Boutiron to Delcassé, 24 October 1904, *DDF,* 2d ser., 5:464. Nicholas also resented the uncomplimentary remarks the kaiser made about him. See Derenthall to Hohenlohe, 21 June 1899, *GP,* 13:312–14.

[114]Paléologue, *Three Critical Years,* pp. 139–40 (5 December 1904); Harold Nicolson, *Sir Arthur Nicolson, Bart., First Lord Carnock: A Study in the Old Diplomacy* (London, 1930), pp. 287–89; Jefferson, "Salisbury's Conversations with the Tsar," p. 220; Alexander Savinsky, "Guillaume II et la Russie: Ses dépêches à Nicolas II (1903–1905)," *Revue des deux mondes* 92, no. 12 (15 December 1922): 771, 787, 801–802; Witte, *Memoirs,* p. 406; Korostovets, *Graf Witte,* p. 146.

[115]Korostovets, *Graf Witte,* p. 124.

[116]Zedlitz-Trützschler, *Zwölf Jahre,* pp. 102–103 (7 December 1904).

alliance.[117] The Russian government, which was strongly opposed to the treaty, effectively sabotaged it by forcing the czar to insist that France, then embroiled with Germany in the Moroccan crisis, join the accord. The treaty thus came to nothing, and Nicholas refused thereafter to listen to any talk from the kaiser about reviving it.[118]

The support which Russia gave to France at the Algeciras conference, called to deal with the Moroccan situation provoked by the kaiser's landing at Tangier, destroyed Bülow's goal of securing the cooperation of Russia in a joint maneuver against Great Britain. William II, who had erroneously anticipated that neither England nor Russia would sustain France at the conference, was very undone and declared that Russia's hostile role at Algeciras in all probability marked the end of what remained of Russo-German friendship.[119]

After 1906, Germany directed its policy more and more toward Vienna, especially after Bethmann Hollweg succeeded Bülow as chancellor in 1909, and relations with Russia deteriorated. Bethmann believed that Germany's diplomatic future lay with Austria-Hungary rather than with Russia, which by the time he became chancellor was irreconcilably opposed to Vienna. The chancellor nevertheless attempted to restore good relations with Saint Petersburg, but he found—as had every one of his predecessors—that William's personality worked against such efforts. Bethmann complained that when he was in Russia the kaiser behaved like a parvenu, alternately bombastic and insecure, forever tactlessly talking only about himself.[120] There was a corresponding decline in William's relations with the czar, who grew increasingly suspicious of the kaiser in the last decade of peace.[121] The correspond-

---

[117]On Nicholas and Björkö see especially Savinsky, "Guillaume II et la Russie"; also Lamar Cecil, "Coal for the Fleet That Had to Die," *AHR* 69, no. 4 (1964): 990–1005.

[118]Izvolski, *Recollections*, p. 70.

[119]Winzen, *Bülows Weltmachtkonzept*, p. 420.

[120]Joachim von Winterfeldt-Menkin, *Jahreszeiten des Lebens: Das Buch meiner Erinnerungen* (Berlin, 1942), p. 156.

[121]For Nicholas II's suspicions on the eve of World War I see Buchanan to Grey, 3 April 1914, Gooch and Temperley, eds., *British Documents*, 10:781.

ence between the two rulers gradually faded away after 1905, and the letters and telegrams that continued to be exchanged were restricted almost entirely to ritualistic greetings and, by the kaiser's own admission, rarely treated political affairs.[122] Even before the debacle of Algeciras, William had realized that his correspondence with Nicholas was not a success, though he claimed that it had at least contributed in a general way to better Russo-German relations.[123]

The kaiser's relations with both Alexander III and Nicholas II thus proved uniformly unsuccessful. William's hope for an eastern monarchical constellation gradually evaporated after 1890 as Russia drew closer first to France and then, with the Anglo-Russian colonial agreement of 1907, to England as well. With a more adroit diplomat on the German throne this might not have happened, for both Alexander and his heir were profoundly mistrustful of French republicanism and resented Britain's imperial sway throughout Asia and its perversity in providing shelter to Russian anarchists. A sound Romanov-Hohenzollern relationship might have enabled the czar to resist blandishments sent his way from Paris or London and to retain some sort of treaty arrangement with Germany. Certainly Nicholas's French and British allies feared what might happen should the czar fall under the kaiser's spell.[124] Bismarck and William I had, after all, managed to preserve the tie with Saint Petersburg in spite of the decision taken in 1879 to ally with Vienna; nor had Alexander's suspicions of Germany led him to Paris as long as William I occupied the German throne.[125] But with William II's ascension Russia's relations with Germany began to fall apart.

[122]Szögyényi to Berchtold, 12 March 1914, HHStA, vol. 171 (Berichte), 21/P A-F; Izvolski, *Recollections*, p. 56; Vorres, *Last Grand Duchess*, p. 56.

[123]Szögyényi to Goluchowski, 2 February 1899, HHStA, vol. 152 (Varia).

[124]Herbette to Ricard, 5 December 1895, *DDF*, 1st ser., 12:329; Courcel, notes, 26 March 1897, ibid., 13:296; Bihourd to Delcassé, 26 March 1904, ibid., 2d ser., 3:506; Cambon to Pichon, 8 August 1907, ibid., 11:209.

[125]On the importance for Russo-German affairs of the relationship of William I and Alexander III see Kennan, *Decline of Bismarck's European Order*, pp. 368, 393, 397.

There were, to be sure, impediments in the way of Russo-German friendship at the end of the nineteenth century which the kaiser, even if he had had a more sensible and ingratiating personality, could not have overcome and for which he was not responsible. It would be wrong either to attribute the worsening of the connection between Saint Petersburg and Berlin solely to him or to argue that he might have been expected to convert Russia from an enemy to an ally singlehandedly. At the same time, he cannot be exonerated from having, by his own indiscretions and fulminations, unnecessarily made a problematical situation worse. In an era supercharged with nationalist passions, burgeoning armaments, and imperial rivalries, William's unending loquacity, his persistent obtrusiveness, his strut and braggadocio only increased the tensions that beset Europe and often made him seem to be responsible if not for their existence then at least for their intensity.

The importance of the kaiser's personality as a factor in Russo-German relations can be illustrated by briefly considering a parallel example of personal diplomacy that was exercised in Saint Petersburg by a far more talented ruler. Germany's difficulties with Russia were no thornier than the imperial rivalries that separated Russia and Britain. Yet shortly after 1900 the British and the Russians succeeded in eliminating many of their points of friction and began building the bridge that would result in their alliance against Germany in World War I. While a number of diplomatic and strategic considerations were important in bringing about the Anglo-Russian entente of 1907—not the least of which was the fear of German militarism so actively championed by the kaiser—considerable credit should be given to the assiduous cultivation which Edward VII lavished on Nicholas II.

The worldly and indulgent English king found Nicholas deplorably unsophisticated, immature, and reactionary. But he understood how with grace and tact to overcome the hostility of the czar to England, to avoid unnecessary intrusion on the privacy Nicholas so treasured, and to resist giving unsolicited advice. Edward VII knew quite well that the delicacy with which he handled the czar was in sharp contrast to the unfortunate behavior of his Hohenzollern nephew. The king saw no point in making unnecessary trips to Russia and wisely declared that he had "no desire to play the part of the German Emperor, who always meddles in other people's business. What advice could I possibly give the [Russian] Emperor as to the management of his country? What right have I to do so, even if he were to listen to me, which I much doubt."[126] Nicholas, for his part, was grateful for the perfect consideration always shown him by the English sovereign, whose behavior, he told one of the king's courtiers, "sealed and confirmed the intention and spirit of the Anglo-Russian agreement."[127] The czar's suite expressed to the king's entourage the entirely positive response that Edward VII's visit to Nicholas at Reval in 1908 had produced in their ruler, so contrary, the Russian statesmen noted, to the unfortunate impact a meeting with William several months earlier had generated.[128]

Members of European royal houses and their statesmen were also struck by the arresting difference between Edward VII and William II. Even the kaiser's mother once lamented that her son was not more like her brother, and two of William's sisters, whom he had alienated by his officiousness, were of the same opinion.[129] Edward VII was always the British Foreign Office's premier ambassador of good will, at home in Paris, Copenhagen, Saint Petersburg—indeed, even in Berlin, where the smart set considered him to be the epitome of elegance. The kaiser, on the other hand, was to his officials an imperial albatross, creating difficulties rather than contributing to their elimination. Friedrich von

[126]Sir Sidney Lee, *King Edward VII: A Biography*, 2 vols., (London, 1927), 2:565.

[127]Viscount Grey of Fallodon, *Twenty-five Years, 1892-1916*, 2 vols. (New York, 1925), 1:207-208; Nicolson, *Carnock*, pp. 274-75.

[128]Lord Hardinge of Penshurst, *Old Diplomacy* (London, 1947), p. 157; Lee, *Edward VII*, 2:593.

[129]Hardinge, *Old Diplomacy*, p. 127; Crown Princess of Prussia to Queen Victoria, 15 December 1874, RA Z28/80. For comparisons with Edward VII to the kaiser's disadvantage see Lamar Cecil, "History as Family Chronicle: Kaiser Wilhelm II and the Dynastic Roots of the Anglo-German Antagonism," John C. G. Röhl and Nicolaus Sombart, eds., *Kaiser Wilhelm II, New Interpretations: The Corfu Papers* (Cambridge, 1982), p. 105.

Holstein, the senior counselor of the Wilhelmstrasse who had observed the two sovereigns for many years, declared in 1906 that "the most talented diplomat of the day is King Edward VII. The least adept is our kaiser. He is absolutely no statesman."[130]

A year after Holstein rendered his definitive judgment, British and Russian diplomats, helped by the amicable foundation established by Edward VII and Nicholas II, signed a colonial agreement which proved to be the first step in bringing about Russia's envelopment in the Anglo-French camp. Hardly more than a decade later this coalition would destroy the German empire and force William II abjectly to appeal to Queen Wilhelmina, his one loyal colleague, to provide him with consolation and a place of refuge.[131]

[130]Holstein to Ida von Stülpnagel, 12 June 1906, Helmuth Rogge, ed., *Friedrich von Holstein: Lebensbekenntnis in Briefen an eine Frau* (Berlin, 1932); p. 258; Valentine Chirol, memorandum, 19 October 1908, Gooch and Temperley, eds., *British Documents,* 6:159.

[131]I wish to thank Her Majesty the Queen for gracious permission to use materials from the Royal Archives, Windsor.

5

European Politics and Security at the Genoa Conference of 1922

CAROLE FINK

The international economic and financial conference that met in Genoa in April and May 1922 is not readily associated with the European security problem of the 1920s. Standard interwar histories refer to Genoa (if at all) either because of its negative offspring—the Treaty of Rapallo and the alleged oil negotiations during the conference—or as a notable "failure" in regard to the main problems of the day: reparations, disarmament, and Soviet-Western detente.[1] Yet the Genoa meeting, halfway between Versailles and Locarno, brought thirty-four nations together for six weeks in an effort to establish a stable postwar order. This chapter examines one aspect of the Genoa Conference: the genesis and fate of its peace pact.

On 6 January 1922 the Allied Supreme Council, meeting in Cannes, convened the Genoa Conference, an international summit meeting called to "remedy the paralysis of the European system."[2] Invitations, issued to all the Allies and neutrals, were also sent to the United States and, for the first time, to Soviet Russia and the former enemy states Germany, Austria, Hungary,

---

[1]Carole Fink, *The Genoa Conference: European Diplomacy, 1921-1922* (Chapel Hill, N.C., 1984), is the first history of the meeting. There are two dated partisan accounts: J. Saxon Mills, *The Genoa Conference* (New York, 1922); Jean de Pierrefeu, *La saison diplomatique: Gênes (Avril-Mai 1922)* (Paris, 1928).

[2]*DBFP*, 1st ser., 19:18-29.

and Bulgaria. The main topic on the agenda was economic reconstruction. Central and Eastern Europe had been battered by seven and a half years of war, revolution, disease, and inflation, and the Western Allies were burdened with debts, sluggish trade, and unemployment. Three key issues needed to be settled: the end of Russia's four-year estrangement from the West; the establishment of a viable new reparations settlement before Germany collapsed; and the construction of a European peace that would lower tax burdens, revive prosperity, and stabilize governments. On 6 January the Supreme Council—Britain, France, Belgium, Italy, and Japan—voted to address these problems in Genoa.[3]

Britain's prime minister, David Lloyd George, was the father of the Genoa Conference. Hoping to grasp Woodrow Wilson's mantle as international peacemaker, the mercurial Liberal leader of a Tory-dominated coalition set out to satisfy domestic necessities with an ambitious policy of "European appeasement." Britain's ailing export industries and two million unemployed required a revival of investment and trade. By granting reparations moratoriums to the former enemy states Germany and Austria and promoting investment, credits, and trade with Soviet Russia, Lloyd George hoped to stimulate the British economy as well as promote peace in Europe. He also sought to set strict limits on any further commitments to enforce the Versailles peace and prod France and its allies to disarm. In return he offered France a guarantee of its eastern borders, promoted a ten-year European nonaggression pact, and called on the League of Nations to work for universal disarmament. Above all, Lloyd George hoped to draw the United States back into European affairs as a guarantor

[3]Raymond Sontag, *A Broken World, 1919–1939* (New York, 1971), pp. 61–69. Contemporary descriptions can be found in F. S. Nitti, *Peaceless Europe* (London, 1922); A. S. Zimmern, *Europe in Convalescence* (London, 1922); Gustav Cassel, *Money and Foreign Exchange After 1914* (London, 1922); John M. Keynes, *A Revision of the Treaty* (London, 1922); Arnold J. Toynbee, *The World After the Paris Peace Conference* (Oxford, 1925); and Winston S. Churchill, *The Aftermath, 1918–1928* (New York, 1929). The Supreme Council meeting is in *DBFP,* 19:1–136.

of peace and a generous creditor, willing to scale down or forgive the Allies' war debts.[4]

Lloyd George was spokesman for the many opponents of the Paris Peace Treaties in Britain and abroad who lamented a "broken Europe," America and Soviet Russia's isolation, the league's ineffectualness, Germany's critical economic situation, and the breakdown of stable markets, currencies, transport, and communication. An avowed revisionist, Lloyd George sought a new world order under London's tutelage, based on the expansion of economic and political contacts between former military and ideological adversaries and the removal of economic barriers and military controls. With success in Genoa, backed by bankers, exporters, and Labour, he hoped to win the next British elections on a platform of European pacification, enabling him to discard his Conservative partners and create a durable left-center government. Despite the vision, energy, skills, and political acumen of its initiator, this complex, politically oriented program foreshadowed both the strengths and the weaknesses of the Genoa Conference.[5]

Lloyd George's main diplomatic partner, Premier Aristide Briand, was a willing collaborator. Also an inventive politician and an astute practitioner of conference diplomacy, negotiation, and compromise, Briand welcomed Genoa as signaling France's coparticipation in European reconciliation and economic recovery. Even more important, Briand believed that France's ultimate security depended primarily upon maintaining the Anglo-French

[4]The Genoa plan is most concisely described in Lloyd George to Austen Chamberlain, London, 22 March 1922, LGP F5/7/21.

[5]Critical views of Lloyd George's diplomacy are presented in Francis Conte, "Lloyd George et le Traité de Rapallo," *Revue d'histoire moderne et contemporaine* 23 (January–March 1976): 44–67. More balanced appraisals appear in Stephen E. Fritz, "*La Politique de la Ruhr* and Lloyd Georgian Conference Diplomacy: The Tragedy of Anglo-French Relations, 1919-1923," *Proceedings of the Western Society for French History,* 1975, pp. 566–82; Kenneth O. Morgan, "Lloyd George's Premiership: A Study in Prime Ministerial Government,' " *HJ* 13, no. 1 (1970): 130–57; Christoph Stamm, *Lloyd George zwischen Innen- und Aussenpolitik: Die britische Deutschlandpolitik, 1921/1922* (Cologne, 1977); Hines Hall, III, "Lloyd George, Briand, and the Failure of the Anglo-French Entente," *JMH* 50, no. 2 (December 1978): supp. D1121–38.

Entente. By acquiescing in Lloyd George's grand program, he hoped eventually to secure a genuine alliance with Britain and increased security for France's East European allies.[6]

In Paris, however, there was strong negative reaction to Briand's concessions at Cannes: the unconditional invitations to Genoa accorded to Germany and Soviet Russia, the reparations moratorium extended to Germany, and the aura of British dominance without reciprocal consideration of France's needs (as symbolized in the notorious photograph of Lloyd George giving Briand his first golf lesson). Although a small segment of the French left and French industry appreciated the economic potential of Lloyd George's appeasement program, a large proportion of France clung to the Versailles Treaty and insisted on its enforcement. The more than two million French former Russian bondholders demanded that the Soviet state repay its debts in full and restore private property. The old Anglo-French misunderstanding rose to the surface at the specter of Lloyd George's Genoa crusade.

Rather than defend his policies, Briand returned to Paris and suddenly resigned, turning his office over to the hardliner Raymond Poincaré.[7] An outspoken partisan of the Entente, Poincaré balanced the demands of the treaty enforcers against France's limited political and economic power; he could not torpedo Genoa but had to set strict limits on Lloyd George's experiment in "international conciliation." For him French security—the maintenance of the benefits of a costly victory and the prevention of a

[6]Georges Suarez, *Briand*, vol. 7 (Paris, 1941), pp. 340–45; Ferdinand Siebert, *Aristide Briand, 1862–1932* (Zurich, 1973), pp. 244–76; cf. Ludwig Zimmermann, *Frankreichs Ruhrpolitik von Versailles bis zum Dawesplan* (Göttingen, 1971), pp. 29ff. Briand's political and strategic considerations are analyzed in Edward D. Keeton, "Briand's Locarno Policy" (Ph.D. diss., Yale University, 1975).

[7]On Briand's resignation see De Gaiffier to Jaspar, Paris, 9–13 January 1922, MAE(B) Fr. 1922: Suarez, *Briand*, pp. 390–410. On Poincaré see Pierre Miquel, *Poincaré* (Paris, 1961), pp. 428–29; Pierrefeu, *La saison diplomatique*, pp. 8–12; Richard D. Challener, "The French Foreign Office: The Era of Philippe Berthelot," G. A. Craig and F. Gilbert, eds., *The Diplomats* (New York, 1967), 1:52–57. On French politics and diplomacy see Renata Bournazel, *Rapallo: Naissance d'un mythe: La politique de la peur dans la France du bloc national* (Paris, 1974); Edouard Bonnefous, *Histoire politique de la Troisième République*, 2d ed. (Paris, 1968), 3:285–86.

resurgent Germany—took precedence over a Soviet strategy or a grand design to reintegrate the United States into Europe. From their first cool meeting after Cannes, Poincaré served notice on Lloyd George that the hopes and expectations raised by the forthcoming meeting in Genoa were in jeopardy.[8]

The Lloyd George-Poincaré dualism intensified the nervousness over Genoa in Moscow and in Berlin. In Moscow, chairman V. I. Lenin had already signaled his interest in "peaceful coexistence" with the West by signing trade agreements, offering joint companies and concessions, and developing the Soviet New Economic Policy (NEP) stressing private initiatives, Western investment, and technology. At Cannes, Lloyd George had responded to Russia's call three months earlier for an international conference. However, the prospect of the Genoa Conference—of face-to-face negotiations with capitalist leaders—kindled strong opposition by the commissar of war, Leon Trotsky and his followers, who feared Western penetration and continued to preach Soviet militancy and economic independence.[9] Lenin prevailed over his critics by arguing Russia's desperate need for foreign capital and for a peace that would protect its borders from the White armies and allow it to disarm. Drawing on his immense prestige, he denied any retreat from communism. Lenin also appealed to Europe's "progressive" forces to support Lloyd George's program and Russia's cause at Genoa. Moreover, he engineered a diplomatic campaign to thwart a unified Western camp (and a threatened multinational consortium of investors in Russia) by dangling eco-

---

[8]British Secretary's Notes of Conversation Between Lloyd George and Poincaré, 14 January 1922, Cab 29/95; Hardinge to Curzon, Paris, 15 January 1922, Curzon Papers, India Office, London.

[9]See E. M. Chossudovsky, "Genoa Revisited: Russia and Coexistence," *Foreign Affairs* 50, no. 3 (1972): 554-77; A. O. Chubaryan, "Peaceful Coexistence and the Origin of the Notion" (Paper delivered at the Fourteenth International Congress of the Historical Sciences, San Francisco, August 1975); See also E. H. Carr, *The Bolshevik Revolution of 1917-1923* vol. 3 (London, 1966), pp. 359-60; V. I. Lenin, *Collected Works* (Moscow, 1965-71), 42:390-93, 401-404, 410, 485-86; 45:443-44, 463, 469-70, 496, 506-13. The opposition is described and analyzed in Richard B. Day, *Leon Trotsky and the Politics of Economic Isolation* (Cambridge, 1973).

nomic and political lures before individual capitalist governments, particularly in isolated, harried Berlin.[10]

For the German government, a minority left-center coalition headed by Chancellor Joseph Wirth and Foreign Minister Walther Rathenau, dedicated to liberating the Reich from the shackles of Versailles, the Genoa Conference presented opportunities: to obtain an international forum for Germany's grievances against the Allies, to negotiate loans from neutral powers, to function as a bridge between the West and Russia, and, conceivably, to split the entente. Yet there were also dangers. Wirth's policy of "fulfillment," aimed at reducing reparations and easing other restrictions on the Reich, had not yet produced any benefits to bolster the government's authority before an intransigent right in the Reichstag. The current moratorium was due to expire before Genoa, and greater demands for German sacrifice were expected. Except for Lloyd George's pronouncements, Germany had little assurance that its position would improve.[11]

On 25 February 1922, Lloyd George met Poincaré at Boulogne, and the two leaders gave final shape to the Genoa Conference. Because of the cabinet crisis in Italy they agreed to a one-month postponement, until the first week in April. In another long, icy exchange the British and French leaders upheld their respective interests while maintaining their public support for Genoa. In return for France's participation Lloyd George had to agree to eliminate reparations and disarmament from the agenda and not to press the issue of recognition of Soviet Russia. The Genoa Conference had survived, in a much reduced form.[12]

A few days later, on 8 March, the United States announced its

[10]V. Buryakov, "Lenin's Diplomacy in Action," *International Affairs* [Moscow] 5 (1972): 93; see also Lenin, *Collected Works,* 45:434, 446–48.

[11]Germany's Genoa policy is seen in Cabinet Council discussion, 2 April 1922, *Akten der Reichskanzlei . . . Die Kabinette Wirth I und II* (Boppard am Rhine, 1973), 2:674–83. For the political debate see *Verhandlungen des Reichstags* 353 (1922):5562, 354 (1922):6648, 6655–56. An analysis appears in Hajo Holborn, "Diplomats and Diplomacy in the Early Weimar Republic," Craig and Gilbert, eds., *The Diplomats,* pp. 161–69.

[12]The text of the Boulogne conversations appears in *DBFP,* 19:170–92. The French version is in MAE(F) B88.

refusal to participate in the Genoa Conference. The Warren G. Harding administration, after successfully directing the Washington Conference in 1921-22, had come to the conclusion that it was better to stay away from Genoa to avoid an expectedly distasteful encounter with its European debtors and with the Bolsheviks. The Boulogne proceedings, which stripped Genoa of two of the most critical problems of postwar reconstruction, gave Washington the excuse to say no.[13]

Fearing that little would now be accomplished, Moscow castigated the West for the delays. Lenin hid his persistent hopes behind increasingly defiant statements, claiming that Russia would not cave in before capitalist pressure.[14] Disappointed and apprehensive, the Germans decided to issue a negative response to the Allies' new reparations demands, hoping for a decisive breakthrough at Genoa.[15] While Lloyd George and the new Italian government under Luigi Facta moved doggedly ahead with their preparations, an international "anti-Genoa" camp formed. It consisted of a motley camp of White Russians and ideologues of the Third International, Fascists and anti-Semites, American isolationists and anti-Bolshevik American labor, partisans of the League of Nations (who feared Lloyd George's threat to create a new world organization), and leaders of the new East European states wedged between Germany and Russia. On the eve of

---

[13]Hughes to Italian Ambassador Ricci, 8 March 1922, *FRUS* (1922), 1:392-94. Useful discussions of American foreign policy appear in Denise Artaud, "Aux origines de l'atlantisme: la recherche d'un équilibre européen au lendemain de la première guerre mondiale," *Relations internationales* 10 (1977):115-26; Melvyn Leffler, "American Policy Making and European Stability, 1921-1933," *Pacific Historical Review* 46 (May 1977):207-28; Frank Costigliola, "The United States and the Reconstruction of Germany in the 1920s," *Business History Review* 50, no. 4 (1976):477-502; Robert H. van Meter, "The United States and European Recovery, 1918-1923: A Study of Public Policy and Private Finance" (Ph.D. diss., University of Wisconsin, 1971).

[14]Lenin, *Collected Works,* 33:212-26, 546; 42:404; 45:485-86; I. Linder, "Lenin's Foreign Policy Activity (Oct. 1921-Mar. 1922)," *International Affairs* [Moscow] 12 (1969):49.

[15]Cabinet meeting, 24 March 1922, *Akten der Reichskanzlei,* 1:630, 634-35, 639; St. Quentin to [French] Ministry of Foreign Affairs, Berlin, 27 March 1922, MAE(F) B90.

Genoa the press trumpeted the debate between Genoa's partisans, who intended to revise the Versailles peace by practical arrangements with former enemies, and those like Poincaré and Czechoslovak Foreign Minister Eduard Beneš who feared the procedures and costs of conference diplomacy. Beneš argued persuasively that without American participation and a solid, well-prepared structure the conference would serve primarily as a propaganda forum for the Germans and the Russians.[16]

The international clamor not unexpectedly diminished Lloyd George's political authority at home. The Tories were able to block his efforts for a general election before Genoa, which would have given him a powerful national mandate to bolster his diplomacy. The outspoken dissidents in the cabinet chipped away at his program: the foreign secretary, Lord Curzon, objected to the prime minister's usurpation of Foreign Office prerogatives; the chancellor of the exchequer, Unionist leader Austen Chamberlain, complained about his bullying of France, and the colonial secretary, Winston Churchill, opposed any substantive dealings with the current Soviet rulers. Despite Lloyd George's vigorous efforts in the press and before Parliament, for the first time the cabinet placed specific restrictions on his conducting of business in Genoa: whatever emerged from the negotiations, he could not act alone without Britain's allies, and he could not offer government credits or de jure recognition to Moscow.[17] Thus hamstrung by Poincaré and his own cabinet, criticized by Washington,

---

[16]Samples of anti-Genoa prose appear in "Genoa or Geneva?" *Times* (London), 18 February 1922; Yves Guyot, "La Russie, L'Allemagne, et M. Lloyd George . . . ," *Journal des économistes* 81 (15 May 1922): 129–52; "Omer Kiazim," *Angora et Berlin: Le complot germano-kémaliste contre le Traité de Versailles* (Paris, 1922); Karl Radek, *Genua: Die Einheitsfront der Proletariates und die kommunistische Internationale* (Hamburg, 1922); Samuel Gompers, *A.F. of L. Information Bulletin,* 12 January 1922; see also Eduard Beneš, "Les Conférences en vue de la reconstruction de la Russie et de l'Europe," *Gazette de Prague,* 28 December 1921; "M. Beneš," *L'Europe nouvelle,* 25 February 1922. Beneš conducted an unsuccessful mediating trip between London and Paris before Boulogne; see Fink, *The Genoa Conference,* pp. 76–78.

[17]Cabinet meeting, 28 March 1922 Cab 23/29. House of Commons, *Debates,* 3 April 1922; *Times,* (London) 4 April 1922.

and goaded by the Russians and Germans, Lloyd George left for Genoa on 7 April, still hoping that a miraculous breakthrough would save his and Europe's fortunes. The Genoa Conference opened on 10 April 1922 with great fanfare. The world press flooded the Italian port, which for six weeks became an international capital. Lenin stayed away because of ill health and fear of assassination. Poincaré decided to remain in Paris. The United States was represented unofficially by its ambassador to Italy. Nevertheless, there was a colorful plenary meeting at the Palazzo San Giorgio, with chief Soviet delegate Georgi Chicherin's dramatic call for world disarmament, French delegate Louis Barthou's angry rebuttal, and Lloyd George's suave efforts at conciliation.[18] Getting down to business, the conference divided into committees to discuss the main areas of European reconstruction. To expedite the primary subject, the Allies decided to invite the Russian delegates to secret talks in Lloyd George's villa on 14 April, Good Friday. The excluded Germans occupied themselves in meetings with neutral bankers and the press and in unofficial talks with the French, British, and Russians.[19]

Although Russia was its focal point, the Genoa Conference had been advertised as a world peace conference. It therefore stimulated Europe's current hopes and fears. The new pope, Pius XI, sent a special message through the archbishop of Genoa lauding the "peacemakers" and deploring those who maintained "forests" of armaments (France) or asserted hostile ideologies (Soviet Russia).[20] During the first week the British delegation announced the vague outlines of a ten-year truce in place, which would crown Genoa's practical arrangements for economic reconstruction. This underscored the immediate threat of the repara-

[18]See Harry Kessler, *In the Twenties* (New York, 1971), pp. 159-91; Ernest Hemingway, "Genoa Conference," *Toronto Daily Star,* 13 April 1922. The text of the opening meeting appears in *DBFP,* 19:334-58.

[19]Fink, *The Genoa Conference,* pp. 155-64.

[20]Jonnart to Poincaré, Rome (Vatican), 8 and 9 April 1922, and Poincaré to Jonnart, 8 April 1922, Millerand Papers, MAE(F) 5; De Salis to Curzon, Rome (Vatican), 6 and 18 April 1922, FO 371 C5319, C5975/458/62.

tions deadline on 31 May. In the event of a German refusal to meet the Reparations Commission's demands, France was expected to invoke sanctions and possibly invade the Ruhr. Poincaré's refusal to attend the Genoa Conference reflected his unwillingness to subordinate France's rights and security to an acriminous debate with the Russians in the presence of Germans and neutrals and with Lloyd George in control. Lloyd George, unable to pry Poincaré loose from Paris for reparations talks, used his ten-year truce as a veiled warning to the "absent gentleman" against contemplating unilateral military action on 31 May.[21] Divided over the kind of European peace they desired, London and Paris suddenly lost the initiative to the other side.

On Easter Sunday, Germany and Russia signed a separate treaty at Rapallo. After the Russians divulged to the anxious Reich delegation details of their talks with the Allies (cleverly embellished to exaggerate their probable success), Rathenau accepted what he had rejected the week before the Genoa Conference. At Rapallo on 16 April the Soviets and Germans signed a bilateral treaty establishing full diplomatic and consular relations, the mutual repudiation of all claims for war costs and damages, and Russia's renunciation of reparations under the Treaty of Versailles in return for Germany's waiver of claims for the nationalization of its citizens' property in Russia. The price for relief from the alleged threat that the Allies, as part of an East-West settlement, would permit the Bolsheviks to collect reparations, was that Germany became the first major Western government to accord unconditional recognition to the Soviet state. Barred from the secret talks and facing an intransigent France, an elusive Lloyd George, and the wily, insistent Bolsheviks, Rathenau took the road to Rapallo

[21]See statement in *New York Times,* 16 April 1922, by Lloyd George's secretary, Sir Edward Grigg. See also Poincaré to Barthou, 12 April 1922, MAE(F) B83, and Barthou to Poincaré, 13 April 1922, MAE(F) Y29; Mayer to A. A., Paris, 14 April 1922, GFM 3398/1734/D733377-78; Wertheimer to A. A., Paris, 16 April 1922, BA R43, 469.

both as a defense of German interests and as an act of defiance.[22] The rapprochement of the pariahs, predicted three years earlier by Lloyd George at Fontainebleau, shook Genoa and all of Europe. With a stroke the agreement between the two foremost revisionist powers threatened the entire basis of the Paris peace settlement. There was a rumored (though nonexistent) secret military annex to the treaty that threatened Poland and Rumania as well as France itself. The truth of Rapallo was sufficiently ominous. It constituted a lopsided Soviet victory, obtained at the start of a world conference that had been convened for the purpose of mutual negotiations on credits, trade, restitution of property, and the establishment of peace. Rapallo represented not only a potential threat to the status quo but a vivid example of Soviet methods and aims. Covering its own economic weakness and internal divisions, Moscow would exploit the West's disunity for its own benefit, refuse all concessions to capitalist principles in order to accommodate the hardliners at home, but also continue to emit enough conciliatory signals after Rapallo to enable the Genoa negotiations—still con-

---

[22]There is an immense body of literature on the Rapallo treaties; see, for example, Alfred Anderle, *Rapallo und die friedliche Koexistenz* ([East] Berlin; 1963); Wipert von Blücher, *Deutschlands Weg nach Rapallo* (Wiesbaden, 1951); Karl Dietrich Erdmann, "Deutschland, Rapallo und der Westen," *VfZG* 11, no. 2 (April 1963):105–65; Walter Grottian, "Genua und Rapallo, 1922: Entstehung und Wirkung eines Vertrages," *Aus Politik und Zeitgeschichte* 25–26 (June 1962): 305–28; Herbert Helbig, *Die Träger der Rapallo-Politik* (Göttingen, 1958); Ernst Laubach, "Maltzans Aufzeichnungen über die letzten Vorgänge vor dem Abschluss des Rapallo-Vertrags," *Jahrbücher für Geschichte Osteuropas* 22, no. 4 (1975): 556–79; Horst-Günter Linke, *Deutsch-sowjetische Beziehungen bis Rapallo* (Cologne, 1970); Gordon H. Mueller, "Rapallo Re-examined: A New Look at Germany's Secret Military Collaboration with Russia in 1922," *Military Affairs* 40 (1976):109–17; Theodor Schieder, "Die Entstehungsgeschichte des Rapallo-Vertrags," *HZ* 204 (June 1967):545–609; Theodor Schieder, *Die Probleme des Rapallo-Vertrags* (Cologne, 1956); Hartmut Pogge von Strandmann, "Grossindustrie und Rapallopolitik: Deutsch-sowjetische Handelsbeziehungen in der Weimarer Republik," *HZ* 222 (April 1976): 265–341; Hartmut Pogge von Strandmann, "Rapallo-Strategy in Preventive Diplomacy: New Sources and New Interpretations," V. R. Berghahn and M. Kitchen, eds., *Germany in the Age of Total War* (London, 1981); László Zsigmond, *Zur deutschen Frage, 1918-1923* (Budapest, 1964.)

sidered crucial, though now skewed to its benefit—to continue.[23]

Rapallo heightened the distance between the European capitals and Genoa, intensifying distrust, impatience, and misunderstandings in the delegates and their governments and triggering appeals for recalls and delays. Even in Moscow days elapsed before the Politburo comprehended the importance of Rapallo. In Berlin news of the agreement, executed without the cabinet's approval, provoked controversy between the partisans of a western orientation and the easterners. In Eastern Europe the treaty dashed hopes of an independent small-power diplomacy at Genoa and raised fears about the security of Poland and the Little Entente. The most violent reaction took place in Paris. Insisting that Rapallo violated several clauses of the Versailles Treaty, Poincaré requested investigations by the Conference of Ambassadors and the Reparations Commission, called for the treaty's annulment, and called repeatedly for Barthou's return to Paris. On 24 April, in a fiery speech at Bar-le-Duc, Poincaré denounced Rapallo and raised again the specter of military sanctions should Germany default on 31 May.[24]

Rumors to the contrary, Lloyd George was not informed in advance of the Rapallo Treaty, which in fact greatly hindered his labors in Genoa.[25] For the conference to continue, Germany had to be punished to assuage Poincaré's anger. The delegates were forced into week-long, acrimonious meetings, angry letters, and press releases, which resulted in Germany's official exclusion from any future Allied-Russian talks. The Rapallo Treaty had a more serious consequence. It aborted Lloyd George's patient, year-long efforts to bring Germany into the League of Nations as

[23]Telegrams by Chicherin, 18 April 1922, and Litvinov, 20 April 1922 (intercepted by the Italian Secret Service), MAE(I) 52/4. Lenin, note to Stalin, Kamenev, and Trotsky, Moscow, 19 April 1922, note to Stalin, 21 April 1922, with draft telegrams for Chicherin, letter to Stalin for Members of Politburo, 24 February 1922, all in Lenin *Collected Works,* 45:530–34.

[24]The text of Poincaré's speech appears in *La politique française en 1922* (Paris, 1923), pp. 29–32. Reactions to Rapallo appear in GFM, L640/4783/ L203574–601; L1468/5118/L415963; 3398/1735/D739034–36, D739116–22; L996/ 5412/L286140–44; L690/4783/L203579–82, L203708–10.

[25]A. J. Sylvester, *The Real Lloyd George* (London, 1948), p. 81.

a means of counterbalancing France's control over that organization. By signing with the Russians, Germany strained the London-
Berlin connection by inserting flashes of independence into their
tutelary relationship. Reminded of the Reich's capacity to do
mischief and its potential strength, Lloyd George delivered a
ritualized hand slap and doggedly pressed on with the Genoa
Conference.[26]

The Allies resumed their talks with the Russians (who shared
none of Germany's punishment) under unpropitious circumstances.
Lloyd George urged the reluctant French and Belgians to demonstrate to their constituencies back home that they had done their
utmost to offer concessions and make peace. Chicherin made
their task more difficult. First, on 21 April he made an unauthorized
offer to recognize debts and restore nationalized property in
return for a payment moratorium and massive loans; then, one
week later, under pressure from the Kremlin to uphold the "Rapallo
precedent," he reneged and insisted on full recognition and credits
as preconditions for further negotiations. Soviet equivocations
triggered a squabble in the Allied camp. British traders were
willing to reduce loans and interest and accept ninety-nine-year
leases as a substitute for ownership, but French bondholders
demanded full debt recognition and interest, and the dispossessed Belgian property owners insisted on full property restitution.
The capitalist world was in public disarray over how to deal with
the Soviets.[27]

Hoping to revive Genoa's spirit of appeasement, and his own
leadership, Lloyd George introduced a draft nonaggression pact.[28]
The treaty contained only two articles:

1. Each of the High Contracting Parties pledges itself to refrain

---

[26]On Germany's punishment see Fink, *The Genoa Conference,* pp. 177–85; on
the setback to league membership see Slavik note to Secretary General, Genoa,
27 April 1922, League of Nations, Special Circular 177, League of Nations
Archives, Geneva; Chamberlain to Lloyd George, London, 10 May 1922, FO
800/400.

[27]*DBFP,* 19:447–702, passim; Fink, *The Genoa Conference,* pp. 185–90, 209–22.

[28]The text appears in *DBFP,* 19:570.

from any act of aggression against the territorial integrity of any other of the High Contracting Parties.

2. In the event of any act of aggression being committed in breach of Article 1, each of the High Contracting Parties pledges itself to make use of all means at its disposal, and to resort to any organization which may be available for the discussion, consideration, and adjustment by peaceful means of the dispute out of which the act of aggression arose.

Lloyd George's draft pact was an imitation of the Four Power agreement, recently signed on 13 December, 1921 in Washington, D.C., which was a similarly ambiguously worded pledge to respond to aggression solely through consultation and peaceful means. British Undersecretary of State Sir Eyre Crowe dismissed the text as "mere verbiage" that lacked any real sanctions against aggression. It was, according to former Italian Foreign Minister Vittorio Scialoja, an eloquent "moral declaration," but it lacked any reference to collective security.[29]

This was indeed Lloyd George's purpose. The draft nonaggression pact which he brought to Genoa reflected his antipathy toward the bonds created after World War I that had committed British forces to quarrels in Europe based on hastily established borders and the enforcement of controversial clauses in the peace treaties. Like the United States and the British dominions, Lloyd George now opposed Article 10 of the League of Nations Covenant, which, though clothed in vague, nonbinding terms, nevertheless assigned a specific organization, the League Council, the responsibility of "advis[ing] upon the means" by which aggression or the threat of aggression against any member's territorial integrity *or* political independence was to be handled. Although council decisions required unanimity, and were therefore unlikely to call for collective military sanctions, London, like Washington, viewed this league prerogative as damaging

---

[29]Crowe, memorandum, 20 March 1922, FO 371 C4543/458/62; Scialoja, Osservazioni, MAE(I), 52/34.

to its sovereignty and potentially threatening to its interests.[30] Lloyd George's peace pact revealed his deeply rooted commitment to appeasement. He believed that European security was unattainable through armaments and alliances and that the quest for overwhelming military superiority led inevitably to war. He also sought to prevent "wars by accident," triggered by armed reactions to aggression, when other responses might prevent a spread of war. Given the numerous possibilities for conflict in Europe after World War I, Lloyd George hoped to detach Britain from their snares. Although Britain had survived world war and the Bolshevik revolution, it had suffered considerable human and financial losses as well as political and ideological divisions. Lloyd George, at the helm of an overextended imperial power that was threatened by competition from Washington, subversion from Moscow, and revolts in its colonial lands, intended to eliminate any form of automatic collective military response to an act of aggression in Europe. According to the proposed pact, there would be no instance in which the signatories were individually or jointly obligated to take up arms to support their allies, fulfill their league obligations, or enforce the existing treaties. The treaties were intentionally omitted because Lloyd George and his entourage considered Versailles one of the primary reasons for Europe's insecurity.[31]

There was lukewarm support for Lloyd George's treaty from the neutral states, which blamed Versailles for their current economic ills. After some hesitation the Germans endorsed the nonaggression principle as a potential guarantee against French military action on 31 May. Lenin saw in the pact a means of

[30]Hurst to Crowe, London, 16 March 1922, Wigram, memorandum, 18 March 1922, Lampson, Crowe, memoranda, 20 March 1922, Crowe to Hankey, 24 March 1922, Hankey to Crowe, 25 March 1922, FO 371 C4356/458/62; Gregory to Crowe, Genoa, 23 April 1922, Leeper, Ovey, Curzon, minutes, London, 24 April 1922, Foreign Office to Gregory, London, 27 April 1922, FO 371 N3592/646/38.

[31]Philippe Millet, "Le pacte européen," L'Europe nouvelle 5 (24 April 1922): 485–86.

removing pressure on Russia's borders and facilitating the demobilization of the Red Army.[32]

There were also attempts to add substance to the document. Carlo Schanzer, Italy's foreign minister, tried futilely to add an amendment allowing the signatories to hold consultations in the event of aggression, thereby reviving the principle of collective security and the possibility of sanctions, which Lloyd George's pact was designed to avoid.[33] Beneš, self-appointed spokesman of the East European states, proposed two significant additions: a guarantee of the inviolability of the peace treaties and a structure for response to aggression that linked Britain with France and the Big Entente with the Little Entente. Beneš had three purposes. The first was to reassure France and its allies, thereby averting precipitate action and, after Rapallo, a new arms buildup. The second was to warn Germany and its former allies of the intent to enforce the status quo. Finally, Beneš aimed at splitting Russia from Germany with a conciliatory sign to Moscow. He therefore urged that the revised Genoa peace pact withhold any specific guarantee of Poland's present, "peculiar" border with Soviet Russia.

The Beneš amendments, which were mysteriously leaked in the press, were the opposite of Lloyd George's intentions. The Czech statesman reinstated the primacy of the Paris peace treaties and licensed military alliances, but he also undermined the territorial integrity of Russia's Western neighbors, whose borders had not yet been officially ratified. Beneš thus made European security subject to the enforcement of existing agreements, based on existing power alignments, a miscalculation that reflected the optimistic self-confidence of a small-power statesman.[34]

[32]Wirth to Ebert, Genoa, 28 April 1922, GFM, 3398/1734/D738578–79; Walter C. Clemens, "Origins of the Soviet Campaign for Disarmament: The Soviet Position on Peace, Security, and Revolution at the Genoa, Moscow, and Lausanne Conferences" (Ph.D. diss., Columbia University, 1961). Cf. Lenin to Chicherin, 30 April 1922, Lenin, *Collected Works,* 45:536–37.

[33]Schanzer to Lloyd George, n.d., MAE(I) 52/34; Aufzeichnung, 27 April 1922, GFM 3398/1734/D738576.

[34]A. Gajanová, "La politique extérieure tchécoslovaque et la 'question russe' à

Lloyd George, on the other hand, intended to eliminate military threats from both aggressors and treaty enforcers, dissolve the blocs, mediate and settle disputes peacefully, reestablish a balance among the powers of Europe, and achieve general disarmament to enable Britain to resume its accustomed and preferred place of leading from the edge. But first he had to hold Paris in tow to conclude successfully the Russian negotiations. He thus downplayed the nonaggression pact, pending their outcome. On 3 May the Allies sent their terms for an agreement to the Russians.[35] On the same day, however, Europe erupted with rumors of an oil scandal: the Bolsheviks had awarded concessions to British capitalists for properties confiscated from other foreign nationals.[36] Although no oil agreement was actually signed at Genoa, Britain's prolonged attempt to conduct a "moral crusade" against France for its intransigency toward the Germans and the Russians was deflated by the oil episode. The Bolsheviks, who presumably leaked the story, now controlled Genoa, and Lloyd George's fortunes.

The Germans experienced a temporary improvement in their status when a desperate Lloyd George accepted their offer to act as intermediaries with the Russians. They were asked to urge the Bolsheviks to grant the Allies what had been withheld at Rapallo: full political and economic concessions with no demands for

la Conférence de Gênes," *Historica* 8 (1964): 142–49; Masaryk to Beneš, Prague, 18 and 24 April 1922, *Dokumenty e materialy po istorii sovetsko-chekhoslovakskikh otnoshenii,* vol. 1 (Moscow, 1973), pp. 492–93, 494–95; Grigg, Notes of a Conversation with M. Beneš, 21 April 1922, Grigg Papers (microfilm, Queens University, Kingston, Ontario), roll 9; Lloyd George–Beneš conversation, 26 April 1922, *DBFP,* 19:565–71; Beneš to Lloyd George, n.d., LGP F199 3/5; Wigram, memorandum, Genoa, 1 May, Grigg Papers, roll 9.

[35]The text appears in *DBFP,* 19:694–702.

[36]Louis Fischer, *Oil Imperialism: The International Struggle for Petroleum* (New York, 1926), pp. 38–67; "The Diplomatic Smell of Oil," *Nation,* 17 May 1922; Marie-France Toinet, "La politique petrolière des États-Unis à l'égard de l'URSS, 1917–1927," *Revue française de science politique* 17 (1967):689–712. Background can be found in "Note sur les concessions de pétrole en Russie," 8 May 1922, MAE(F) B111.

reciprocity. Chicherin predictably refused. Flattered by his *Vermittler* (mediator) role, Rathenau haughtily rejected an amended Franco-Czechoslovak draft nonaggression pact. Germany supported Lloyd George's original formula: there must be no aggression, even against aggressors.[37]

Irritated by his tactless intermediaries; by the sly, dilatory Bolsheviks; and by the absent Poincaré, Lloyd George made a gaffe. In a private interview with Barthou on 6 May he allegedly vowed that if Paris blocked a Genoa treaty Britain would link up with Germany, Italy, and Russia. When the press magnified his statement as a threat to rupture the entente, Barthou gallantly denied that it had been uttered. But the damage was done. However irascible a partner, France could not be deserted for Germany. Not after the Somme. The British cabinet held to its strictures against breaking with France and forging unauthorized links with the Bolsheviks. Moreover, Lloyd George knew the limits of his power to coerce Barthou and Poincaré. The entente would have a long list of issues to settle—reparations, the Greco-Turkish conflict, Palestine, and Tangier—*after* Genoa.[38]

Increasingly weary and exasperated, Lloyd George lost control over the Genoa Conference. The Russian response of 11 May (written with the aid of the Germans) brutally rejected the Allies' terms but also appealed for further negotiations. Lloyd George grasped the suggestion of the unofficial American delegate and proposed a follow-up meeting of commissions of experts in The Hague a month later to discuss debts, credits, and property. Genoa would have a graceful burial. France reluctantly agreed but again

---

[37]Notes of Conversations, 4 and 7 May 1922, *DBFP,* 19:730–35, 777–87; Wirth to Ebert, Genoa, 4 May 1922, GFM 3398/1734/D738701-4; Rathenau-Beneš conversation, 2 May 1922, GFM D739281-82; Barrère to Poincaré, Genoa, 5 May 1922, Poincaré to Barrère, Paris, 5 May 1922, MAE(F) B97.

[38]Notes of Conversation, 6 May 1922, *DBFP,* 19:764–76; Barthou to Lloyd George, Genoa, 8 May 1922, LGP F1/3/15; Hardinge to Curzon, Paris, 10 May 1922, Curzon Papers ("The news from Genoa is that the Entente is very sick, and the poisonous Northcliffe press is making it worse"); Churchill to Derby, 8 May 1922, Derby to Churchill, 9, 13, and 22 May 1922, Winston Churchill Papers, courtesy of Martin Gilbert, London.

set limits to the agenda at The Hague and insisted on Germany's exclusion. The United States once more refused to attend, since the Russians would be present. In a face-saving finale everyone at Genoa promised not to conclude separate agreements with the Bolsheviks until the conversations at The Hague were over.[39] What became of Lloyd George's nonaggression pact? Schanzer presented a watered-down version to the final plenary session. It was to be a temporary pact, calling on all signatories to refrain from aggression and subversive propaganda until four months after the conclusion of the Hague Conference. Although frustrating hopes for a long-term solution, the pact, according to Schanzer, might lead to a general, more permanent arrangement after the Hague Conference.[40]

Summoning all his eloquence, Lloyd George announced at the final meeting of the Genoa Conference:

> We have decided to give peace a trial on our hearthstones, and when she has been there for seven months, we will not turn her out again. The psychological effects upon the peoples of the world will be electrical. The thrill of peace has gone through the veins of Europe, and you are not going to get nation lifting up hand against nation again.[41]

But eloquence could not mask Genoa's failure to make peace between Russia and the West or the reasons for that failure: Lloyd George's errors, France and its allies' anxiety about the German and Russian menace, and the negative spirit of Rapallo. Chicherin used the opportunity to ridicule the Allies' notion of "peace," complaining of Polish, Rumanian, and Japanese occupation of former czarist Russia and Western assistance to the White armies. Rathenau, barred by the French from signing even the truncated nonaggression pact (which Poincaré had reassured himself did not apply to a potential conflict on 31 May), stressed Germany's contribution to the labors of reconciling the East and West. He concluded by quoting Petrarch: "Io vo gridando: O

[39]Fink, *The Genoa Conference*, pp. 262–75.
[40]*DBFP*, 19:1019–20.
[41]Ibid., pp. 1031–32.

pace! pace! pace!" ("I go about crying: O peace! peace! peace!").[42] As expected, the conference at The Hague resulted in a stalemate, and Russia and the West decided to go their separate ways.[43] Just after the opening, on 24 June, Rathenau, attacked as a Jew and an appeaser, was assassinated by young rightist radicals. Germany, though granted another temporary moratorium, moved ineluctably toward default, hyperinflation, and confrontation with France. Lloyd George, after a final failure to obtain cabinet consent for a separate agreement with Russia, left office in October 1922, when his call for a crusade against the Turks at Chanak was rebuffed by France, Italy, and the dominions. The Genoa peace pact expired at the end of the month, and his successor made no effort to renew it. Poincaré continued to uphold the entente, in the hope of a true Anglo-French alliance; however, by the end of the year, with Britain even more aloof and Germany in massive default on its reparations payments, he reluctantly decided to enter the Ruhr.[44]

The Ruhr invasion of 1923 signaled both the failure of Lloyd George's policy and the realities that led to Locarno. France alone could not enforce Versailles in the face of British and American noncooperation. In the light of Rapallo, Paris's East European partners constituted liabilities more than aid. After an apparent victory in September 1923, France, pressed by Britain and the United States and weakened by financial exigency and political divisions, was obliged to retreat: to a junior partnership with London, to economic and political detente with Berlin, to a debt settlement with Washington, and to an implicit renunciation of its commitments in Eastern Europe. Briand, who returned to power in 1925, revived the Cannes orientation, accepting practical economic and financial arrangements as preconditions to peace and security. His new partner, British Foreign Secretary

[42]Ibid., pp. 1015, 1038.

[43]Preparations for and Proceedings of the Hague Conference, 23 May–21 July 1922, ibid., pp. 1039–1138.

[44]Sally Marks, "The Myths of Reparations," *CEH* 17, no. 3 (1978): 241–43; "Minute Respecting the 'Pact of Non-Aggression,' " 1 December 1922, FO 371 N10819/646/38.

Austen Chamberlain, who was even more adamant than Lloyd George against committing arms to European quarrels, forced France finally to substitute a simple guarantee of its eastern border for a full-scale alliance.[45]

There were some important differences between Genoa and Locarno. From its nadir during the Ruhr crisis German diplomacy revived under its capable foreign minister, Gustav Stresemann. Serving the Reich's interests by exploiting the strains in the Entente, Stresemann proposed the Rhineland pacts (a very faint echo of Lloyd George's nonaggression pact) to prevent an Anglo-French alliance. Peace was established in Western Europe by means of a nonaggression pledge by the Rhineland states, backed by a British guarantee. Germany's rewards for Stresemann's initiative were immediate and substantial: the evacuation of the Cologne zone without any evidence that Germany had completely disarmed; a guarantee against further French military sanctions, regardless of future reparation payments; a permanent seat on the League of Nations Council, which also relieved Germany of any military obligation to protect its eastern neighbors against Russia; and the prospect of substantial American investments. Stresemann successfully resisted pressure to curb Germany's ties with Moscow and, with Britain's help, refused to extend the Locarno guarantees to Eastern Europe. Germany rejoined the Great Powers at Locarno, forming a trio with Britain and France. The entente could no longer act exclusively, as at Genoa. Yet, though his gains exceeded Rathenau's three years earlier, Stresemann too was reviled by the German right as an appeaser and was hounded to an early death.[46]

Neither the United States nor Soviet Russia attended the Locarno conference. The administration in Washington, which had contributed to the Dawes Plan and to Germany's recovery, steadfastly

[45]Jon Jacobson, *Locarno Diplomacy: Germany and the West, 1925-1929* (Princeton, N.J., 1972).

[46]On Stresemann see Michael-Olaf Maxelon, *Stresemann und Frankreich* (Düsseldorf, 1972); Gordon A. Craig, *From Bismarck to Adenauer: Aspects of German Statecraft,* rev. ed (New York, 1965); Wolfgang Michalka and Marshall Lee, eds. *Gustav Stresemann* (Darmstadt, 1982).

refused to participate in Europe's political stabilization. Soviet Russia after Lenin's death turned to isolationism, seeking bilateral treaties and only limited political and economic contacts with the West.[47] Hence one of the major differences between Genoa and Locarno. In 1922, Lloyd George had hoped to establish a comprehensive European peace: wiping the war slate clean, treating victors and vanquished alike, bringing Russia and the United States back to Europe. Having failed at Genoa's grand design, Britain chose the course of partial solutions: semifulfillment of France's security needs, halfway encouragement of German revisionism, tentative (but not binding) recognition of the borders of Eastern Europe, and an armed truce with the Soviets.[48]

Both forms of appeasement—at Genoa and at Locarno—undermined the Paris peace treaties without substituting a durable structure of European security. Both arose from well-founded fears of another war and hopes for the revival of a peaceful, stable, and prosperous Europe. They nevertheless encouraged those who aimed at undoing the verdict of 1918 by force.

[47]Franklyn Griffiths, *Genoa Plus 51: Changing Soviet Objectives in Europe* (Toronto, 1972).

[48]Kenneth O. Morgan, in *Consensus and Disunity: The Lloyd George Coalition Government, 1918-1922* (Oxford, 1979), pp. 147–48, 328, praises the "active" appeasement of Cannes and Genoa over the piecemeal, passive policies of the Tories that led to Locarno and Munich.

6

Economics and Politics in Briand's German Policy, 1925-1931

EDWARD D. KEETON

Most of Aristide Briand's contemporaries hailed him as a prophet of Franco-German reconciliation, but a few damned him as a charlatan who advocated a policy later called "appeasement." Briand's record has been even more controversial in retrospect. One biographer argues that Briand could have reached a lasting accommodation with Germany had other French politicians supported him. Another considers Briand's ideas perhaps too advanced for his time, but the genesis of the Common Market. Still other historians condemn the Locarno treaties of 1925 as a first and decisive step in the destruction of the Eastern alliance system to "appease" Germany.[1] All agree only in contrasting the flexible, conciliatory policy of Briand with the unyielding, vengeful security demands of his rival Raymond Poincaré.

From the French and German diplomatic documents emerges a new Briand: the articulator of a consensus strongly backed by nearly all French politicians and industrialists—including Poincaré and such later opponents of "appeasement" as André François-Poncet and Paul Reynaud. Briand had a coherent, if flawed,

[1]Representative, though not necessarily most recent, are Georges Suarez, *Briand* (Paris, 1938-52), 6 vols.; Ferdinand Siebert, *Aristide Briand, 1862-1932: Ein Staatsmann zwischen Frankreich und Europa* (Zurich, 1973); George Grün, "Locarno: Idea and Reality," *International Affairs* 31 (1955). Themes of this article are taken from Edward Keeton, "Briand's Locarno Policy: French Economics, Politics, and Diplomacy 1925-29" (Ph.D. diss., Yale University, 1975), pp. 371-403, which examines other studies of Briand and French diplomacy in more detail.

concept of France's security. That concept has been obscured by concentration on the purely bilateral aspects of Briand's German policy. Between 1925 and 1931 he sought a diplomatic system that would compensate for an assumed French vulnerability to greater German economic and military potential. An understanding of Briand's system, and of its erosion in 1929–31, is essential to an understanding of "appeasement" in the 1930s.

To be all things to all men was the foremost political quality of Briand, cabinet minister an extraordinary number of times. He had been a compromise prime minister during the periods of ill-defined parliamentary majorities, in 1909–11, 1913, 1915–17, and again in 1921–22, 1925–26, and 1929. Character, methods, and oratory all made Briand a master of compromise. His favorite answer to insistent demands was, "We shall see." Politics was the art of the possible, and the possible might change. Except in extremis he never answered letters in writing or gave written promises. Preferring oral briefings, he refused to read government documents and often dozed ostentatiously at meetings. This "sleeper who listens," as Briand's colleagues called him, sometimes awoke to carry the decision through his native intelligence and sheer ability to grasp essentials. Unequaled in public oratory, he moved even seasoned parliamentarians with his voice, gestures, and sensitivity to his listeners' desires. Yet when his most impressive speeches were printed, they usually made no logical sense and had to be completely rewritten by his subordinates.

In domestic politics Briand adroitly maintained both a vague leftist reputation and the goodwill of economically conservative center and center-right business parties. Before 1900 he had been involved with non-Marxist Democratic Socialists and in 1905, as minister of religious affairs, had skillfully guided the left's separation of church and state. However, on the economic issues that divided left and right, he had forged much closer links with centrist groups conservative in economic policy. As wartime prime minister he enjoyed good relations with French business, and as premier in 1921–22 he collaborated with the right-oriented Bloc national. Renowned for his ability to find a balance of delicate, mutable compromises among conflicting interests and for his parliamentary wiles, Briand was a perfect candidate to gloss over the serious economic deadlock in 1925. During 1924–25 irreconcilable differences over how to stop the inflation had paralyzed the Cartel des gauches. The predominantly middle-class Radicals had agreed with their Socialist allies only in negation: against the church between 1898 and 1905 and against the nationalist right's aggressive foreign policy in 1922–23. Their electoral union in 1924 intensified their contradictions, creating a delicate ménage à quatre. The two larger parties had a majority only with the aid of Briand's and Paul Painlevé's "independent" or right-wing Socialists and of a key centrist party under the leadership of Briand's chief economic adviser, the influential industrialist Louis Loucheur. Both the inflation and the remedies—debt, tax, and budget reforms—fell unequally on the parties' electorates, thus ensuring interminable debate over precisely who must suffer for whose sake. When Radical leader Édouard Herriot fell in April 1925, no agreement on any effective counterinflationary policy seemed possible.

The most promising remedy, if in retrospect false, seemed to be a currency-stabilization loan from the United States. Such a loan could, of course, only circumvent the existing political deadlock and temporarily alleviate the worst impact of the inflation: capital flight. French cabinet ministers of that time had little economic sophistication. As practicing politicians they feared electoral retribution for budget cuts and tax increases. And they were aware that two conditions had to be met before the American government would provide its unofficial but essential support for such a loan on the New York financial market: a Franco-German rapprochement and a Franco-American debt settlement.

Briand's genius for compromise—and his lack of political enemies—made him the ideal foreign minister to attempt the Franco-German and Franco-American settlements. His attributes could have made him premier as well, had he been willing to serve the plans of Raymond Poincaré and the center-right. Poincaré and his backers wanted a *majorité de rechange,* a centrist cabinet that would shift away from the left-oriented majority elected in

1924. Briand chose to prepare his bid more carefully, under the often inattentive mathematician, professor, and now Independent Socialist premier Paul Painlevé.[2]

For Briand, statesmanship was saying first and best what others were just beginning to think. To foresee an emerging consensus and articulate it brilliantly allowed him to display a self-evident wisdom which his audience could easily share. In a series of parliamentary debates, interministerial defense-planning group meetings, and parliamentary committee hearings in 1924–25, Briand ingeniously presented ideas that were already becoming truisms, accepted by Socialist leader Léon Blum, moderate conservative Poincaré, and indeed all but the extreme left and the extreme right.[3]

In addition to overcoming France's domestic inflation, Briand hoped also to restore its foreign lending, an important instrument in its diplomacy before 1914. While Germany gradually recovered its economic and financial strength after the occupation of the Ruhr, inflation and exchange depreciation hobbled France's traditional financial arm. An American stabilization loan, revaluation of the franc, and a favorable war-debt settlement might help France regain its former economic strength abroad.[4]

Briand realized that broad currents of public opinion favored a prompt settlement of problems resulting from the Treaty of Versailles. Influential businessmen and their center-right political

[2]The major archival sources on French internal politics are Records of the Ministry of the Interior, AN, F7 12953 (e.g., "rapport," 15 April 1925); GFM 2406 (e.g., Hoesch to Stresemann, 17 April 1925, D503112-15); FO 371/11046 (e.g., Phipps to Crowe, 17 April 1925), p. 51). In addition to the *Journal officiel* and other standard printed materials, see especially the Comité des Forges, *Bulletin quotidien des informations économiques;* for U.S. financial pressure see Stephen A. Schuker, *The End of French Predominance in Europe* (Chapel Hill, N.C., 1976), Chap. 9; Denise Artaud, *La Question des dettes interalliées et la reconstruction de l'Europe (1917-1929)* (Lille and Paris, 1978), 2:740-77.

[3]The sources for this account of cabinet- and staff-level policy are the French Army Archives, Château de Vincennes, CSDNP-V, and Commission d'Études, as well as Archives of CAE 13, sess. 2, 4, 20, 26, 29, 30, 38, 46, 51.

[4]CAE 13/26, 18 March 1924, p. 14; 62, 23 November 1926, p. 215; D'Abernon to Chamberlain, 14 May 1925, FO 371/10731/185.

allies feared the destruction of French resources and the spread of bolshevism if France and Germany again went to war. Their solution was Franco-German economic cooperation, though naturally on terms that would curb Germany's superior economic and military potential. These views reinforced those of pacifists—the French Communists, Socialists, and Radical rank and file—who urged detente with the Reich.[5]

Strategic analyses based on the recent war provided a ready justification for this policy. Military planners made projections of Germany's economic and demographic superiority, supposedly demonstrating the inevitability of future German military superiority. Planners and politicians anticipated that France would stand alone against the Reich in another brutal war of attrition; they directed their concern to a number of specific economic shortcomings in industries vital to national defense. Even in peacetime, France's industrialists were convinced, Germany would dominate French coal supplies. Germany also controlled the technical processes and the mines needed to produce an admittedly costly coal-based substitute for oil.

This growing pessimism forced French politicians, diplomats, and generals to seek an unattainable balance between the United States, Great Britain, and France on the one side and Germany and the Soviet Union on the other. In both West and East the failure to achieve the balance weakened the French position and strengthened Paris's desire for a Franco-German agreement. Only the United States and Great Britain could provide France with effective economic and military aid in wartime. Yet the cost—the periodic Anglo-American financial, economic, naval, and diplomatic demands—so angered and worried Briand and his colleagues that they sought an alternative: a genuine Franco-German rapprochement, based on a defense of common European interests. France needed to limit German-Soviet cooperation, particularly

[5]See, for example, Henri Barbusse, *Clarté* (Paris, 1915); Romain Rolland, *Clerambault* (Paris, 1920); Émile Chartier, *Mars ou la guerre jugée* (Paris, 1921); Lucien Romier, *Explication de notre temps* (Paris, 1925); Lucien Romier, *Qui sera le maître? Europe ou Amérique?* (Paris, 1927); Louise Weiss, in *L'Europe nouvelle,* 18 April 1925; Aristide Briand in *Journal officiel* (Chambre: Débats, 1925), p. 359.

against its Eastern allies. Since it could little influence Soviet policies, France appealed to Germany for solidarity against the Bolsheviks' "revolutionary threat." That threat, however, grew less credible each year.

From 1919 to 1924, France had vainly tried to create formal security arrangements that would make the balance of 1919 permanent. Briand himself had failed to obtain a Franco-British alliance. He had begun the Eastern alliance system, a weak substitute for the traditional *barrière de l'est*. Even the system's advocates at the Quai d'Orsay never fully trusted it. When his successor, Raymond Poincaré, occupied the Ruhr to extract German reparations by force, the French electorate refused the necessary domestic sacrifices. Poincaré's weak and ill-prepared successor, Édouard Herriot, promptly yielded to intense Anglo-American financial pressure to conciliate Germany. Meanwhile, the impressionable Herriot read a flood of agitated warnings of German-Soviet collaboration from his ambassador in Moscow. As his colleagues cast about for a new strategy, Briand sensed what they would reluctantly choose: rapprochement with Germany.

Briand cloaked his plans in soothing rhetoric. His public speeches at Geneva were highly popular paeans to international brotherhood and cooperation. Frenchmen termed this *briandisme:* vague, idealistic statements that all would be well if France treated Germany kindly, but with European solidarity maintained against "aggression." In private Briand gave notice that Franco-German detente had a price. It included maximum concessions from the Anglo-Saxons, further estrangement between Germany and Russia, and Germany's entry into the League of Nations. The league, which had been the victors' vehicle for enforcing the Treaty of Versailles, would continue to shoulder France's burden of enforcing the status quo. When he used the term "disarmament," Briand meant only that the league would sanction the existing (Versailles) balance of power.[6]

[6]See archival sources in n. 3 above (e.g., CAE 13/30, 31 March 1925, pp. 8–10; CSDN/p–v, pp. 92–97).

Briand was determined to tackle several crucial economic problems through astute political bargaining in order to win what France needed from Germany. Uneducated in and unconcerned about economic "details," he relied heavily on his friend and political collaborator Louis Loucheur, one of a powerful group of center-right industrialists.

Germany's strength in World War I had convinced successive French governments and their strategic experts that its still-formidable industrial potential would give it overwhelming military advantage in another such war of attrition. French planners therefore battled for influence over major industrial areas on Germany's periphery. They won the iron ore and the massive steel mills of Lorraine, control over the Saar mines and metallurgy until the plebiscite scheduled for 1935, special customs provisions for steel sales in Germany, and reparations claims to Ruhr coke. Supported by the Foreign Ministry, French industrialists expanded into these border areas.[7]

In Eastern Europe, France's policy in the Upper Silesian plebiscite ensured that its ally Poland would control Germany's major prewar eastern industrial area. Here too the Foreign Ministry's financial and diplomatic support persuaded reluctant French industrialists to invest in Polish metallurgy and mining. French control over the major Czech arms firm Skoda, private French investments in Polish and Rumanian oil industries to control oil supplies, and various other smaller ventures were all part of the French government's efforts.[8]

To achieve economic independence, and to placate politically influential producers, Paris also encouraged inefficient industries. Government-financed economic reconstruction of the heavy-industry complex in northern France assured capacity rather than efficiency. The government made plans for a more indepen-

[7]Ludwig Zimmermann, *Frankreichs Ruhrpolitik* (Göttingen, 1971); Walter A. McDougall, *France's Rhineland Policy, 1914-24* (Princeton, N.J., 1978); and archival series cited in nn. 8, 9 below.

[8]CSDN/p-v, pp. 47-53, 121-24. Major archival series: French Finance Ministry F30/1033, 1034, 1060, and MAE(F), Pologne, 213 (e.g., memorandum, 8 January 1924, pp. 1-4), 214, 220.

dent oil policy, separate from that of the major Anglo-American firms, through control of oil deposits, transport, storage, refining, and distribution.

In 1924-25, French industrialists finally rebelled against this policy, declaring their preference for cooperation with Germany and their willingness, if necessary, to sacrifice their secondary East European investments. Until that time their conflicting interests (especially in a heterogeneous iron-and-steel industry notorious for its disunity) had allowed the French government to follow its own arbitrary interpretation of the country's strategic needs. However, the government's grandiose plans frequently ignored France's economic weaknesses, the continuing interdependence of French and German industry, and irreconcilable conflicts of interest with Poland and Rumania.

The most insistent voices among the French industrialists came from businessmen involved in the recovery of Lorraine and the temporary control of the Saar. The major French steel producers needed to sell Lorraine steel and surplus Lorraine iron ore on the German market and to purchase the German smelting coke that was best suited to French needs. But Germany's new steel processes and industrial restructuring had eliminated its need for Lorraine imports and coke exports. In 1925, France's use of Lorraine steel for reconstruction and the special provisions under the Treaty of Versailles for Lorraine exports terminated. New markets had to be found. To secure these markets, the French iron-and-steel industry lobby group and the French commerce ministry wanted to negotiate a steel cartel with Germany.[9]

A general European overcapacity in steel developed in 1924, worsening problems related to France's control of the Saar and the postwar French replacement of German capital in Luxembourg. A complex network of companies under the joint control of

---

[9]Major archival series: GFM, ser. K947, L1491, L1495 (e.g., Schalkau, memorandum of François-Marsal conversation, 14 January 1923, L436899–903, and June 1924, memorandum of Méry conversation, L436988) and PAM 18842, 18907 (e.g., Morin, note, 20 March 1924). For a broader treatment see the pioneering and authoritative work of Jacques Bariéty, *Les Relations Franco-Allemandes après la Première Guerre Mondiale 10.11. 1918–10.1.1925* (Paris, 1977).

French and German firms developed. Some had such prominent board members as André François-Poncet, the influential industrialist, deputy, and later ambassador to Berlin, and Carl von Schubert, secretary of state in the German Foreign Ministry. The decisions of the Paris and Berlin governments on such matters as labor costs, freight charges, and customs policy directly affected French industrialists in the Saar; long-term investment decisions depended on the continuation of France's political control of the region. In Luxembourg the metallurgical companies relied on exports for a major portion of their sales. Like France's ally Belgium, they were extremely sensitive to French and German customs and cartel agreements.[10]

Numerous other economic groups also depended on Franco-German harmony. Special cartel marketing arrangements with German producers attracted the French coal, chemical, potash, and aluminum industries. Especially eager were French agriculturalists and others whose products faced exclusion in 1925, when, under the Versailles provisions, Germany recovered its tariff freedom. The latter group included the restive small farmers of Alsace and Lorraine and the viticulturalists in the Radical party's traditional southern strongholds. Briand himself thought that the agriculturalists were somewhat naïve to support his policy of Franco-German rapprochement merely to increase their wine exports. Nevertheless, all these diverse groups and the steel industry did share one goal: to improve their weak position by having the French government establish influence over Germany's economic policies.[11]

The existing French investments in Eastern Europe did not dampen the enthusiasm of businessmen and government officials for a Franco-German settlement. Long accustomed to freedom of

[10]Principal archival sources: PAM 18907, 18962 (for François-Poncet see Cavailler to Marcel Paul, 12 April 1920; for Schubert, Laurent to Cavailler, 9 October 1924; MAE(F), Luxembourg, 29.

[11]Erwin Respondek, *Wirtschaftliche Zusammenarbeit zwischen Deutschland und Frankreich* (Berlin, 1929). Potash: AN F30/4186; aniline dyes: GFM L1492, L1495, K947; coal: GFM 2406; wine: GFM 2406 (Hoesch to Stresemann, 1 May 1925, D503193).

action in the colonies, French capitalists were surprised and disappointed by the controls exerted by the governments of Poland and Rumania over profits, exchange rates, and investment. They therefore tended to restrain the French government's attempts to counter Germany's economic expansion through new French investments in the East. Moreover, France could neither supply its needs for coal and oil from East European sources nor permanently supplant long-standing East European trade relations with Germany. Even before Locarno, French Foreign Ministry experts believed that trade and investment in Eastern Europe would remain of secondary importance.

Among the most prominent individuals involved in European trade were the heads of France's major steel producers, coal firms, and banks, such as Eugène Schneider, of Schneider-Creusot; Guy and Humbert de Wendel, politicians and leaders of the Wendel steel family; Théodore Laurent, president of the Comité des Forges; Henri de Peyerimhoff and Henry Darcy, leaders of the Comité des Houillières; Horace Finaly, president of the Banque de Paris et des Pays-Bas; Émile Moreau, later president of the Banque de France; Frédéric François-Marsal, center-right finance minister; Paul Reynaud, businessman and deputy; André François-Poncet; and Louis Loucheur.[12]

These men and their colleagues were the major force behind the French center and center-right political parties that came to favor a Franco-German diplomatic rapprochement in order to encourage Franco-German economic agreements. In 1920–21 and again in 1923 they had discussed their needs with German industrialists, first through Charles Laurent, the ambassador to Berlin, and then directly. Their support for an economic and political rapprochement with Germany meant that the most vociferous right-wing group, a band of middle-class nationalists led by

---

[12]For more on these individuals see the archives cited in nn. 7–11 above and printed lists of corporate officers in *Qui Êtes-Vous?* (Paris, annual); Société Générale Alsacienne de Banque, *Annuaire de sociétés par actions*... (Strasbourg, 1925); Roger Mennevée, ed., *Les Documents Politiques, Diplomatiques, et Financiers,* particularly the April 1928 issue; and the *Annuaires* of the Comités des Forges and the Comité des Houillières.

Louis Marin, lost most of its power to influence French foreign policy. And it meant that Briand, under the tutelage of Loucheur and dependent on the center-right's parliamentary support, considered a bargain with Gustav Stresemann vital for his political allies as well as for his country.[13]

Convinced of the political, strategic, and economic logic of a Franco-German rapprochement, Briand viewed the German proposals of February 1925 for a mutual security pact as an opportunity, not a danger. His tactic was to acquiesce in an ambiguous public agreement, with France holding out the possibility of further concessions, while Germany and the other powers met France's security needs. If the agreement was worded too precisely, there would be diplomatic complications and domestic repercussions; at home Finance Minister Joseph Caillaux was encountering difficulty winning the Socialists' support for his counterinflationary proposals. Briand's diplomatic probes revealed that France would have to offer Germany diplomatic concessions as the price for a security agreement which would, in turn, solve the economic problems so vital to radical winegrowers and center-right businessmen.

When bilateral economic negotiations reached an impasse, Stresemann, through a French intermediary, offered France help in obtaining American loans and negotiating extensive Franco-German industrial agreements, but only after a diplomatic agreement.[14] Meanwhile, Briand had learned that failure to conclude a European security agreement would halt the American loan, on

[13]*Vossische Zeitung* staff to Stresemann, 16 May 1925, GFM 2406/D503211-16, 301. See also sources cited in n. 9 above and PAM 19010; Loucheur Papers (Hoover Institution, Stanford, Calif.), box 12, folders 13, 18; Georges Soutou, "Une autre politique? Les tentatives françaises d'entente économique avec l'Allemagne," *Revue d'Allemagne* 8, no. 1 (1976):21-34.

[14]Aubert, memo, 29 July 1925, MAE(F), Grande Bretagne, 80, pp. 244-49; Hoesch to Stresemann, 6 August 1925 GFM 2945/571874-75. For the development of the Locarno negotiations see *FRUS* (1925), vol. 1, *Documents diplomatiques belges, 1920-40,* vol. 2, and the following archival series: MAE(F), Grande Bretagne,

which Caillaux's success in forging a new center majority on financial issues depended. According to Briand, two decisions could stabilize the new majority and obtain the loan: to ratify the French war debt and to negotiate the security agreement.

Except for a sharp but brief dispute with Stresemann over the evacuation of the Rhineland, Briand delayed the discussion of Franco-German security and economic issues until the Locarno Conference. Before it began, he ensured that a security pact would leave France's alliances legally intact. From detailed discussions both with British jurists and with British Foreign Secretary Sir Austen Chamberlain, he concluded that France could aid its Eastern allies and remain free to cross the Rhineland in the event of German aggression. In late August and early September, with the help of Czechoslovak Foreign Minister Eduard Beneš, he overcame strong but maladroit Polish opposition. At the same time Briand sent Finance Minister Caillaux to Great Britain and the United States for the crucial war-debt negotiations.

During the Locarno Conference itself Briand offered Stresemann future concessions—the so-called *Rückwirkungen* ("retroactions") —but demanded counterconcessions of his own. Characteristically, he made his delivery of the *Rückwirkungen* subject to future negotiation, a concept Stresemann was either too literal-minded or too eager to appreciate fully. Briand partly satisfied the British and German desires to limit his Eastern alliances and encouraged Stresemann to hope for an early evacuation of the Rhineland. But he purposely introduced ambiguities that could make these future concessions dependent on larger strategic and economic gains for France.

These French counterparts of the *Rückwirkungen* consisted of

75–85, Russie, 302; GFM, 2406, 3123, 4509, 7129, 7319; Cab, 23/50; FO 800/258 (especially Chamberlain to Crewe, 27 June 1925, p. 239); FO 371/10728–46 (esp. 10739, Chamberlain, memorandum of conversation with Briand, 11 September 1925, p. 208); CAE 13/38, 1 July 1925; CAE 13/46, 19 December 1925; CAE 13/51, 23 February 1926.

informal Anglo-American promises of support in the event of another war with Germany, progress in making long-term Franco-German economic arrangements, and the settlement of reparations payments at a level equal to war-debts payments. In the East, Briand expected Germany to repudiate German-Soviet military and economic cooperation which could threaten France's Eastern allies. As the conference records show, Briand referred to these goals as inseparable parts of the developing Franco-German rapprochement which eventually would permit delivery of the *Rückwirkungen* to Stresemann.[15]

After Locarno, Briand encountered unexpected pressures to proceed more rapidly with the bargain he had held out to Stresemann. His promises at Locarno and the offer of minor troop reductions in the Rhineland failed to elicit sufficiently strong German government pressure on its own businessmen, as the first of many temporary accords in the steel-cartel and trade negotiations revealed. At the same time the British continued to press for an early end of the Rhineland occupation, which Briand perceived as a temporary advantage that could be used as a bargaining tool.

Briand also became preoccupied with strengthening those Germans who preferred the "Western" orientation of Locarno to the Rapallo policy of closer German-Soviet relations. He feared that the German-Soviet Treaty of Berlin of 1926 and Józef Piłsudski's coup in Poland shortly thereafter would encourage an aggressive *Ostpolitik* in Berlin by those who wished to profit from the renewed Polish-Soviet tension. Meanwhile, a serious deterioration of Franco-Italian relations made Paris worry about the future of the Austro-Hungarian successor states.[16]

With the popularity he had gained from Locarno, Briand was

---

[15]See especially conference minutes, 12 October 1925, FO 371/10742, pp. 143ff; Stresemann, memoranda, 12-14 October 1925, GFM 7319/HI60019-34; conference minutes, 8 October 1925, MAE(F), Grande Bretagne, 85, pp. 83-93.

[16]Briand: CAE 13/63, 19 January 1927, pp. 210-11; East: MAE(F), Russie, 142, 302, 333-34, 359; Pologne, 75, 135; *DBFP*, ser. IA, vols. 1, 2; *ADAP*, ser. B, vol. 1, 1;

able to succeed the colorless Painlevé as premier and to continue Caillaux's movement toward center-oriented financial policies. Yet these steps alone could neither stop inflation nor resolve the war-debt and stabilization-loan questions. Caillaux's Franco-American war-debt agreement proved so unpopular that Briand shrank from submitting it to parliament. The impending naval negotiations and Austen Chamberlain's domestic concerns frustrated France's hopes for Anglo-American support. The Socialists and the Radicals expected Briand to conciliate Germany; the center-right expected him to find allies against Germany and obtain a commitment from the evasive Anglo-Americans to France's diplomatic and economic needs. Briand had to make visible progress quickly.

In June and July 1926 a final inflationary crisis forced Briand to choose conciliation with Germany. The Anglo-American refusal to offer a loan prompted Briand to make desperate, unofficial suggestions to Stresemann to settle outstanding issues in return for a lump-sum reparations payment. This would provide the foreign exchange necessary for currency stabilization through an international bond issue. Such a settlement, as Briand told German Ambassador Leopold von Hoesch, would help both France and Germany reduce American influence on their policies.[17]

In his desperation to secure Stresemann's agreement to such a lump-sum reparations settlement at Thoiry in September 1926, Briand neglected his own sine qua non: Anglo-American backing. The United States and Great Britain somewhat patronizingly regarded their financial influence as a means of ensuring a more lasting settlement than France and Germany would devise alone. The two English-speaking powers, concentrating primarily on their extra-European concerns, feared a bilateral improvisation

---

Italy: MAE(F), Italie, 97; Scialoja to Mussolini, 11 December 1926, and Avezzana to Mussolini, 22 December 1926, *DDI,* ser. 7, vol. 4, nos. 536, 556.

[17]Hoesch to Stresemann, 30 June 1926, *ADAP,* ser. B, vol. 1, 1, no. 263. See also MAE(F), Allemagne, 398; *DBFP,* ser. IA, vols. 1–2; CAE 13/51, 23 February 1926.

which might fail and thereby embroil them again in a European conflict. Neither was willing to forgive its war debtors. And the statesmen of both nations had an all-too-human suspicion of anything done without the benefit of their wisdom. Without the opening of the New York and London financial markets no French loan could be funded, and none was.

Raymond Poincaré, Briand's long-term colleague, sometime adversary, and new prime minister, rescued him. These two men had nearly come to blows in a wartime cabinet meeting over Poincaré's innuendo that Briand's penchant for Greek princesses had affected the Salonika invasion. Briand was elusive, independent, a master of intuitive oratory, never wedded to abstract principles, Bohemian in his personal life, and accustomed to hail all with the familiar *tu*. Poincaré was the opposite: formal, precise, a defender of principle, unwilling to gloss over his needs, a model of conjugal rectitude, and never known to discard the formal *vous*. Personal enmity divided them, but political interest united them. In 1926 their desire to forge a center coalition in foreign and domestic policy proved stronger than past antagonism. Indeed, Poincaré was not as bellicose nor Briand as pacific as the popular press delighted in telling its readers. No doubt Poincaré would have welcomed more deference from his colleague, but he fought loyally to protect Briand from right-wing criticism after Thoiry.[18]

Poincaré tolerated Briand's methods and agreed with his diplomatic goals, partly from conviction and partly from the need to win the support of the Radicals and Socialists who wanted Franco-German reconcilation. The Socialists' support was essential to Poincaré's Union nationale cabinet and its antiinflationary program. Poincaré's economic program succeeded through classical defla-

---

[18]See particularly telegrams 39–40, 10–12 December 1926, Cabinet to Briand and telegrams 26, 31, Briand to Cabinet, MAE(F), Allemagne, 126; Poincaré, memorandum, 12 December 1926, "Briand" folder, Berthelot Papers, in the custody of M. Langlois-Berthelot; and analysis of French politics in FO 800/260 and *DBFP*, ser. IA, vol. 2 (especially Crewe to Chamberlain, 15 December 1926, no. 360).

tionary measures and a restoration of psychological confidence and thereby relieved Briand of the immediate financial pressure for a new reparations settlement. Poincaré's center-right coalition (which Briand wanted and now served as foreign minister) stopped the inflation; Briand's foreign policy assured the continued support of the left and the industrialists.

After the stabilization of the franc, Briand, Poincaré, and the center-right pressed for a settlement with Germany despite the opposition of the Anglo-American powers. It was time to determine what Stresemann would accept and what France by itself could offer. The ending of inflation greatly strengthened those business interests and other domestic forces that advocated both a Franco-German rapprochement and the reduction of France's dependence on Britain and America. Because the revaluation of the franc outpaced reductions in domestic costs and eliminated the major industrialists' export advantages, a market agreement with Germany became all the more necessary. Revaluation also created a conflict between the industrialists, who wanted it to stop, and the middle-class supporters of the Union nationale, who wanted a full restoration of the value of their savings. The two groups agreed only on foreign policy, on Franco-German reconciliation.

French men of affairs, meanwhile, moved from disappointment over Anglo-American omissions to irritation at specific Anglo-American transgressions. After Thoiry the United States and Great Britain announced their intention to use reparations bond sales as an instrument for the settlement of the entire complex of reparations, war debts, Rhineland occupation, and French security demands, all to their own benefit. In view of the divergence between French and American attitudes on these matters, the terms angered France. Tempers rose as well over the Allies' oil policy, over the first French attempts to compete with the Anglo-Americans for loans to Eastern Europe, and over tariff negotiations. Loucheur, Commerce Minister Henri Bokanowski, and other prominent businessmen appealed for closer Franco-German cooperation against American economic competition.

In public they argued fervently for a "United States of Europe."[19] Strategic and diplomatic developments reinforced these arguments. In early 1927 politicians and generals agreed that the planned Maginot Line fortifications would make France sufficiently secure to risk a direct agreement with Germany. At the same time they doubted their ability to maintain a coalition against Germany indefinitely. Great Britain and the United States had already clashed with France during the naval negotiations. When Mussolini threatened Yugoslavia, the latter's Little Entente allies offered only tepid support. During the controversy over Lithuania, Poland and the Soviet Union exchanged thinly veiled threats of military intervention.[20]

During 1927, Briand proposed several bilateral Franco-German agreements. Limited by the Anglo-American refusal to cooperate in a reparations and Rhineland-evacuation agreement, he could not offer the comprehensive settlement that Stresemann needed. Instead, as part of the negotiations for the trade treaty in August 1927, he vainly sought to bargain a slight reduction in occupation troop strength in return for extensive German economic concessions. He revealed his larger goal by suggesting future, more substantial Franco-German industrial agreements. These were to be a step toward his associate Loucheur's proposal of May 1927 to the World Economic Conference: European industrial cartels to resist American domination.[21]

Since the arrangements Briand now sought with Germany were

[19]For example, Hoesch to Stresemann, 23 October 1927, GFM L1488/L435432–34. See also Crewe to Chamberlain, 3 January 1927, FO 371/10624, pp. 75–80; André François-Poncet, article in *Revue des Vivants* 1 (February–March 1927): 230–41; citations of Lucien Romier in n. 5 above.

[20]Maginot Line: CAE 13/63, 19 January 1927; Lithuanian crisis: MAE(F), Pologne, 75, 113, 136, Russie, 302, Allemagne, 400, as well as Herriot Papers, 12 (Guerre memorandum, 28 February 1927); Italy: MAE(F), Italie, 111–14, Yougoslavie, 70–71, FO 800/261, *DDI,* ser. 7, vol. 5; CAE 13/78, 15 November 1927.

[21]CAE 13/51, 23 February 1926, 62, 23 November 1926. Hoesch to Stresemann, 27 August 1927, GFM L1488/L434973. On the reparations-evacuation problem, see MAE(F), Herriot Papers, 12, cabinet notes, especially 19 August 1927, and the series in *DBFP,* ser. IA, vols. 3–4; *ADAP,* ser. B. vols. 4–5; and MAE(F), Allemagne, 134, 400. On Loucheur see *League of Nations Publications* 2 (1927): 52.1, pp. 129–34.

in some measure directed against Anglo-American financial and economic interests, he attempted to eliminate any possibility of retaliation. Worried about the political longevity of the Francophile Chamberlain, he paid an ostentatious visit to London in May and did his best to gloss over Anglo-French naval disagreements. Even more concerned about the continuing Franco-American conflicts over navies, war debts, and tariffs, he sought to win American public opinion by appealing to pacifist sentiment. And to forestall the worst—outright American support for a defiant Germany—he proposed a bilateral nonaggression pact, which Secretary of State Frank Kellogg transformed into an innocuous multilateral expression of peaceful intentions.[22]

In the East, Briand offered Germany an inducement for cooperating with France and renouncing German-Soviet schemes against Poland. At the League Council meeting in December 1927, he privately sought the support of Stresemann and Piłsudski for the detailed but unrealistic proposals drawn up by his diplomatic experts for the retrocession of the Polish Corridor to Germany. In exchange Germany would join a multilateral Eastern security pact, make economic concessions to Poland involving the key Polish Upper Silesian industrial complex, and renounce cooperation with the Soviet Union. For France, with its newly strengthened franc, these arrangements promised increased influence in Eastern Europe at Germany's expense.[23]

Briand's startling proposals, whose advantages were evident to numerous Frenchmen (including Poincaré), consequently posed dangers for Stresemann. By making concessions to Germany and delivering concessions from France's Eastern allies, France would win German acceptance of its plans for market agreements directed largely against the United States. By eliminating German-Soviet

[22]Chamberlain, memorandum, 18 May 1927, *DBFP,* ser. IA, vol. 3, no. 201. The Kellogg-Briand Pact: MAE(F), États-Unis, 65–66; GFM 4505; *FRUS* (1927), vol. 2; CAE 14, 14 November 1928.

[23]See especially unsigned memorandum from Seydoux's office, 23 November 1926, MAE(F), Allemagne, 400, pp. 64–79, as background for Chamberlain memorandum of conversation with Briand, 12 December 1927, *DBFP,* ser. IA, vol. 4, no. 91; Stresemann memorandum, 11 December 1927, GFM 2406/D505768–69.

collusion against Poland and ensuring the benevolent neutrality of Britain and the United States, France would maintain her Eastern and Western barriers against German military expansion. This goal of Franco-German rapprochement was the policy of the French center and center-right. But the policy had a fundamental flaw: Stresemann had little reason to make economic concessions or to renounce future alignments with extra-European powers against France. Since Germany's relative power would continue to grow, the greatest concessions France and Poland could offer were far less than those Stresemann could hope to obtain in a few years.

In 1928, Briand's inability to resolve new economic and diplomatic problems further weakened his position. The election results in August strengthened Poincaré's domestic policy and Briand's foreign policy. However, the Union nationale cabinet still exploited moderate voters' fear of another "cartel" government and hope for a Franco-German agreement as a means of uniting its disparate middle-class and industrial supporters. The formal revaluation of the franc was at a parity major exporters considered too high and thus weakened France's position in the renegotiation of the Franco-German steel cartel agreements. New developments abroad added further pressures: the American reparations agent raised the question of a settlement, a maladroit Franco-British arms compromise aroused opposition in Washington and in British public opinion, a dispute over details of the Kellogg-Briand Pact irritated French political circles, Mussolini demanded speedier progress in the Franco-Italian negotiations, and the sporadic sniping between Poland and Lithuania caused the French cabinet again to fear an imminent Polish-Soviet conflict.

In view of the delicate state of affairs Briand wanted to defer an overall reparations and evacuation settlement. But Poincaré's and Briand's private attempts to woo moderate German politicians had encouraged Stresemann. Mistaking these attempts to bypass him for subtle hints of French willingness to make concessions, the ailing Stresemann visited Paris in August 1928 with inflated expectations. As usual, Briand saw the danger and eluded him. It was the blunter Poincaré who explained realities to Stresemann, while the latter's doctor tried vainly to shorten the discussion. Evading any discussion of the Rhineland issue crucial to Stresemann, Poincaré instead offered irenic and unrealizable proposals for Franco-German cooperation against American economic hegemony and Soviet-sponsored revolution.[24]

For Stresemann, bargaining even from an expectation of Germany's future strength became increasingly taxing because of his failing health and Briand's vacillation. Yet regardless of his diminished patience and strength Stresemann's tactics soon succeeded, for an overall Western settlement could not be delayed indefinitely. In the fall of 1928 the Radicals withdrew from the French cabinet, French steel producers proved unable to resist German demands for quota increases, and Anglo-American pressure forced Briand to agree to negotiate a new reparations and evacuation plan. These developments made Franco-German rapprochement all the more urgent for Briand, Poincaré, and their business-oriented Union nationale.

Briand had attempted, first, to fashion a settlement with the United States and Great Britain and then to bargain directly with Stresemann; in the end he had to make do with what remained as the deadline for a settlement approached in the summer of 1929. His center-right supporters wanted an immediate financial settlement with the United States to head off a damaging conflict and longer-term concessions to Germany to secure Franco-German cooperation against American exports. At the League Council meeting in Madrid in June 1929, Briand made a confidential proposal to Stresemann for a European diplomatic bloc. He maintained that reparations and the evacuation question were transient issues compared with the long-term prospect of Franco-

---

[24]Schubert, memorandum, 29 August 1928, GFM 7414/H175513. Cf. brief cabinet notes, 28–29 August, 1 September 1928, MAE(F), Herriot Papers, 20. Briand and Poincaré's attempts: CAE 13/63, 19 January 1927, pp. 72, 160–61, 210–11; GFM 4502 (e.g., Hoesch to Schubert, 27 January 1928, E118815–20; Schubert memorandum, 23 June 1928, E119041–49); also K436 and 5138.

German economic cooperation against the United States and the non-European world. Like Poincaré a year before, he was voicing the anxieties of his business supporters. And as before, Stresemann was unpersuaded.[25]

This appeal to Stresemann was all the more crucial because Anglo-American support for France was at its lowest since the Ruhr occupation. The new British Labour government refused to continue even Chamberlain's highly conditional support on reparations and the Rhineland evacuation. The American position on reparations stipulated unwelcome linkages and financial conditions. To avoid a default that could threaten France's commercial credit, Poincaré deployed all his personal and parliamentary forces behind ratification of the highly unpopular Franco-American war-debt agreement. Poincaré saved the ratification but destroyed his health, leaving Briand to continue alone the reparations and evacuation negotiations. A "political truce" produced by the abstention of the Radicals allowed Briand the luxury of silence on domestic issues. Foreign-policy success would consolidate a center government around him; failure would end his extraordinary career.

At the Hague Conference in August, Briand was forced to accept Anglo-American demands for payment and linkage of the reparations and evacuation questions. He and Stresemann traded hopes: Stresemann gave guarded approval to Loucheur's now-familiar jeremiad on world "overproduction" and American competition. Briand roused Stresemann with vague proposals for immediate cession of the Saar without a plebiscite; in return German and French industrialists were to share control of private companies that would operate the Saar mines, thus protecting French metallurgical interests. Thus Briand hoped again to elude Anglo-American economic influence in the future through exten-

---

[25]Schmidt, memorandum, 11 June 1929, GFM, 3214/D702490–96. See also Poincaré's preface to Gaston Riou, *Europe, ma patrie* (Paris, 1928), and Seydoux's remarks in Hoesch to Stresemann, 1 January 1929, GFM 4502/E120280–81.

sive Franco-German economic cooperation involving new arrangements in the Saar.[26]

In September 1929, with his usual rhetorical flourish, Briand proposed a European political federation to the League of Nations Assembly. Yet his intentions had not really changed since Locarno: he still sought to limit Germany's economic and political potential, especially its ability to make future alignments with other powers, and to satisfy key French domestic groups. Anglo-American participation had fallen by the wayside; after four years of contention Briand now sought his balance exclusively through closer relations with Germany.

Briand's dramatic proposals came to a gloomy end in 1930–31. For France's Eastern allies French loans were no substitute for German markets. Germany refused the Saar scheme, and problems in Franco-German relations continued. France clashed with the United States, Great Britain, and Italy during the naval negotiations. Continued uncertainties in Eastern Europe further weakened Briand's position. Stresemann's death, the Depression, and new alignments in German politics posed deeper problems. France could offer little, and Stresemann's successors had much to gain by waiting.[27]

Like his policy, Briand lingered on for lack of an alternative. The French Chamber of Deputies in the early thirties still revolved around a center-right coalition, businessmen still needed agreements with Germany, and France still had few diplomatic alternatives. The new center-right premiers, André Tardieu and Pierre Laval, younger than Briand, took matters into their own hands, but they believed that only the foreign minister was failing, not his policy. Briand gradually yielded to his advancing age, illness,

[26]Finance Committee minutes, 14 August 1929, FO 371/13605, pp. 199–206. Imhoff, memorandum, n.d. [September 1929] GFM, 712/L503382. Saar: F30/1126/1 (e.g., interministerial conference minutes, 26 September 1929); MAE(F), Sarre, 172 (e.g., unsigned memorandum, 5 September 1929) and 186 (e.g., "rapport Coulondre," 22 October 1929).

[27]See Peter Rowe, "European Federation Projects and National Policies, 1929–1933" (Ph.D. diss., Yale University, 1960), based on GFM sources. For additional information see FO 800/281, MAE(F), Société des Nations, 1253–54.

and disappointment and became a largely honorific figure. He was already a legend at his death in March 1932, and his name evoked a passionate debate between nationalists and men of compromise.

A master of compromise and consensus, Briand helped articulate a new French view of Germany. It was a consequence both of French strategists' equation of the Reich's economic strength and its military potential and of the requirements of French domestic interests and politics. Initially he believed that French control of formerly German industrial areas, diplomatic support from the Anglo-American powers, and the prevention of German-Soviet cooperation could limit German potential.

But Briand's domestic base cut across his policy. Germany's very power was an attraction to the center-right industrial groups that needed Franco-German agreements. When their government failed to cope with inflation, business leaders and their political supporters swayed official policy after 1925 toward cooperation rather than competition with Germany and German industry. The transition from inflation to revaluation in late 1926 convinced the key center-right groups supporting Briand and Poincaré's coalition government that Franco-German economic agreements were essential. France's disappointment with its other diplomatic partners further enhanced Germany's attractiveness. Major sectors of French business viewed Franco-German rapprochement as the nucleus of a European grouping capable of resisting both Soviet and Anglo-American pressures. Because of the continued deterioration of France's position in 1929–30, Briand issued a futile call for European union, but Germany had more to gain by waiting for further concessions.

Briand's ideas did have an enduring influence on French foreign policy. In 1931 ambassador and industrialist André François-Poncet sought economic and political agreements with German conservatives. Moreover, the center-right's obsession with France's economic inferiority may well have been crucial to the defeat of Joseph Paul-Boncour's and Gaston Doumergue's plans of 1933 and 1934 for an Eastern alliance; to Léon Blum's temporization in 1936; and to Édouard Daladier's and Georges Bonnet's surrender of France's remaining advantages. Paul Reynaud and other center-right politicians and businessmen who had sought Eastern concessions and Franco-German industrial rapprochement in the 1920s heavily influenced France's diplomacy in the late 1930s. Their overestimation of German power and their preference for compromise weakened and confused France's diplomacy. Even Reynaud proved surprisingly tardy and ineffectual in abandoning "appeasement." After World War II, with a different German internal balance, these same French figures played a more positive role in creating a new European Community.

7

The Jewish Leadership in Germany and the Nazi Threat in 1933

HERBERT S. LEVINE

Jews have lived in Germany since Roman times, never precisely foreign, never entirely integrated, always a very special form of German society. After 1933 the government of the Third Reich made a determined and almost successful effort once and for all to separate Jews from German society and so to bring to an end these "two thousands years of parallel history."[1] Since the end of World War II and the full revelation of the extent of Nazi mass murder, a debate has raged in the Jewish community and among interested scholars, most of them of Jewish origin, over the role played in the catastrophe by the European Jewish leadership. In the early 1960s the debate was rekindled by the works of Hannah Arendt and Raul Hilberg, which stressed Jewish passivity and the cooperation of Jewish leaders with the Nazi authorities.[2] It was Arendt who put the issue in its baldest and perhaps most offensive form: "The whole truth was that if the Jewish people had really been unorganized and leaderless, there would have been chaos and plenty of misery but the total number of victims would hardly have been between four and a half and six million people."[3] In short, the Jews would have been better off if they had had no leaders at all.

---

[1]Therese Weiss, Lecture delivered at Ramstein Air Force Base, West Germany, December 1978.

[2]Raul Hilberg, *The Destruction of the European Jews* (Chicago, 1961, 1967); Hannah Arendt, *Eichmann in Jerusalem* (New York, 1963).

[3]Arendt, *Eichmann*, p. 111.

181

Echoes of this theme can be found in many investigations of the behavior of the European Jewish leadership.[4] It is a question that lies at the heart of the emotional, moral, and political response of the Jews to the trauma of their recent history. At war here are several understandable motives; the desire to produce an objective history of the European Jews during this crucial and almost final period of their existence runs head-on into demands to name the "guilty," to produce "heroes and martyrs," and even to drop the whole subject lest it embarrass the survivors and their fellow Jews and detract from the fight against modern anti-Semitism by reducing the guilt borne by the Nazis and their henchmen.

These inhibitions and political goals are built into the general discussion of the role played by Jewish leaders during the Holocaust.[5] Elsewhere I have pointed to the chilling effect this has had on scholarly investigation of the behavior of the Jewish leadership, both during the execution of the "final solution" itself and during the initial period of Nazi-Jewish confrontation in Germany.[6] And in a detailed examination of the career of one very exceptional German Jewish politician, Georg Kareski, of Berlin, I tried to confront the delicate question of collaboration between German Jews and Nazis before the development of the final solution.[7] In what follows, I attempt as careful a presentation as possible of what transpired in 1933, when for the first time German Jewish leaders faced the awful reality of National Social-

[4]E.g., Jacob Presser, *The Destruction of the Dutch Jews* (New York, 1969), esp. pp. 238-77; Isaiah Trunk, *Judenrat* (New York, 1972); Reuben Ainsztein, *Jewish Resistance in Nazi-occupied Eastern Europe* (New York, 1974).

[5]For a recent example see Martin Panzer, review of the novel *King of the Jews* by Leslie Epstein, *Jewish Post and Opinion,* 9 February 1979.

[6]Herbert S. Levine, "Comments [on the Holocaust]," *Societas* 2, no. 3 (1972):271-78; "German Jewish Politics and the Nazi Threat" (Paper delivered at the annual meeting of the American Historical Association, San Francisco, 1973); "Die wissenschaftliche Untersuchung des Verhaltens der Juden zur Zeit der nationalsozialistischen Verfolgungen und die Hemmungen einer unbewältigten Vergangenheit," *Tradition und Neubeginn* (Cologne, 1975), pp. 409-18.

[7]Herbert S. Levine, "A Jewish Collaborator in Nazi Germany: The Strange Career of Georg Kareski," *CEH* 8, no. 3 (1975): 251-81.

ist rule. These leaders had to respond to four major sets of problems:

1. Nazi policy toward the Jews in 1933 was in fact confused. This created the ultimately false impression that policy differences among the Nazis and with their non-Nazi partners in the elite of German society could be exploited by the Jews to their benefit.

2. The Jewish community itself was divided, between established German Jews and relatively recently arrived Eastern European immigrants ("Ostjuden"), between right- and left-wing Jewish heirs to German political traditions, and between those who saw themselves only as Jewish Germans and the Zionists who insisted on the existence of a Jewish national identity.

3. The worldwide Depression that helped the Nazis into power created additional problems for German Jews by limiting their financial resources, internal and foreign, by forcing more people to look to the Jewish community for financial assistance, and by limiting the possibilities for successful emigration.

4. The Nazi takeover of power changed the German political landscape so basically that politics in the old sense came to an end. The Jewish organizations were left with a tradition of lobbying and antidefamation activity that proved irrelevant in the Third Reich.

My goal here is some clarification of an early stage on "the twisted road to Auschwitz"[8]—clarification of developments that tragically helped prepare the way for extermination. This discussion is not simply devoted to a chapter of Jewish history. It belongs here, in this forum. If I may be permitted the liberty of quoting myself:

>...the destruction of the Jewish communities in Germany fits within the framework of German contemporary history, not only because it took place partly within Germany and because the principal destroyers were Germans, but because the Jews in

[8]Karl A. Schleunes, *The Twisted Road to Auschwitz* (Urbana, Ill., 1970).

Germany [and particularly their leaders] were themselves so tragically German.[9]

Hitler's appointment as Reich chancellor on 30 January 1933 placed the Jews of Germany under the government of a man who had vowed to expel them from the life of the German nation. But for most German Jews the first reports of anti-Semitic outrages in rural areas were dim disturbances on the horizon. In Berlin, where one-third of Germany's Jews lived, a Jewish witness reports:

> In the month of February [1933] Jews were not yet persecuted as Jews, but were arrested and put in concentration camps in their capacities as former Socialists or as members of the Reichsbanner Black-Red-Gold or the League of Republican Officials or as members of the Peace League or as Communists. Whoever did not fall into one of these categories still felt safe, since the limits were quickly established.[10]

To a few the facts were revealed relatively early, with brutal clarity. Attacks on Jews as Jews did not begin in Berlin until late March, but there were preliminary incidents elsewhere, including a widely publicized Sturmabteilung SA attack on Jewish lawyers and judges in Breslau on 11 March.[11] Many other attempts at intimidation and terror were reported from all over Germany. In late March the terror struck Berlin, and the details were reported in the foreign press.[12] Gangs of SA men roamed the streets, attacking passers-by they supposed or knew to be Jews, beating and robbing them, and pulling the beards of the orthodox Ostjuden, who were special marks in part because their distinctive appearance eliminated the possibility of error. Jews as Jews could no longer feel safe.

In the first months of 1933 the Jewish community had to respond both to the terror of the SA and to the tightening of Nazi government control, especially over the police, which together

---

[9]Levine, "Wissenschaftliche Untersuchung," p. 409.

[10]Kurt Jakob Ball-Kaduri, *Das Leben der Juden in Deutschland im Jahre 1933* (Frankfurt am Main, 1963), p. 44.

[11]Ludwig Foerder, "SA-Terror in Breslau," in Gerhard Schoenberner, ed., *Wir haben es gesehen* (Hamburg, 1962), pp. 18–22.

[12]*Manchester Guardian,* 27 March 1933.

destroyed confidence that the Jews were still living in the traditional German *Rechtsstaat* ("Constitutional State"). The immediate problem of the Jewish leadership was to determine precisely what the new rulers intended to do about the "Jewish question." The Nazis themselves faced the same difficulty from the other side. There had been no concrete Jewish question until the Nazi takeover created one.[13] Until 1933 it had been a matter of propaganda and SA rowdyism. Now the Nazis found themselves in a position to realize their anti-Semitic promises without any clear idea of how to go about it. There were important non-Nazi interests to consider, particularly those of the army and of German industry, and foreign reaction could not be ignored by a Germany that was still disarmed. Hitler's conservative allies regarded anti-Semitism as an occasionally useful political tool for reaching the masses. They themselves probably did not care much for Jews, but in the interests of Germany's fragile economy and its foreign policy they would have preferred that Hitler do nothing at all about the Jewish question.

At the same time, the great army of Nazi followers, particularly in the SA, expected that something would be done. Those who demanded practical action against the Jews were a small minority of those who had voted for the Nazis, but they were strategically placed within the party and the SA. Outbreaks of disorder by impatient Nazis disappointed with government inaction hurt the new regime at home and abroad. Hitler was busy with the details of foreign and economic policy and gave no clear guidelines on the Jewish question. In fact, the policy of the new government was unclear on many points. Before the takeover of power, for example, there was no concrete planning for the promised attack on the "Marxist" political parties and the independent trade unions, whose leaders were faced with problems similar to those of the Jewish organizations when they dealt with the new regime. But the economic and political needs of the infant Third Reich demanded that the German left and its workers' organizations be

---

[13]A major thesis of Schleunes, *Twisted Road.*

eliminated rapidly. This was Hitler's first internal priority.[14] A systematic settlement of the "Jewish question" could wait. Party and government officials had to grope uncertainly toward a Jewish policy, and the Jewish leadership came stumbling after.

By far the largest Jewish organization at the time, with about 70,000 members, was the Central Association of German Citizens of the Jewish Faith (Central-Verein deutscher Staatsbürger jüdischen Glaubens), commonly known as the CV. The CV was an individual-membership organization that had fought the antidefamation battle as a national Jewish lobby since before the turn of the century. It had been a vigorous political opponent of national socialism before 1933.[15] The general policy of the CV was based on the legal defense of the Jews as German citizens, an insistence that Jews were part of the German people, and an opposition to Zionism that would be harsh in the extreme.[16] On 30 January the change of government caught the CV with its two chief executive officers incapacitated by illness. Board Chairman Julius Brodnitz took over the organization's affairs. His first reaction was to make contact with circles around Vice-Chancellor Franz von Papen and with State Secretary Ludwig Grauert of the Prussian Interior Ministry. Grauert was in close touch with Hermann Göring, who was directing the machinery of the Prussian government and police.

The first reaction of the Zionists was no different. The Zionist group around Georg Kareski and Alfred Klee in Berlin, the leaders of an organization within the Jewish congregation (Gemeinde) known as the Jewish People's party, also cultivated Papen's friends. Rudolf Diels, the first head under Hermann Göring of the Prussian political police (soon to be called the Secret State Police, or Gestapo) had contacts both with Zionists and with the CV. Although the leaders of the Jewish organizations had long had

[14]Timothy W. Mason, *Sozialpolitik im Dritten Reich* (Opladen, 1977), pp. 81ff.

[15]The best account is in Arnold Paucker, *Der jüdische Abwehrkampf gegen Antisemitismus und Nationalsozialismus in den letzten Jahren der Weimarer Republik* (Hamburg, 1968).

[16]CV pamphlet, *Deutschtum, Judentum, Zionismus und Palästina-Aufbau* (Berlin, n.d. [ca. 1930]).

contact with major politicians as part of their position at the head of lobbying organizations in the national capital, their connections with the Nazis were understandably slim. They tried to remedy this after 30 January through non-Nazis in the government, and the information network thus established proved useful. They received word of impending actions and sometimes could transmit warnings to endangered individuals. And on 3 March, Göring himself granted an interview to Brodnitz and CV Deputy Director Alfred Wiener and assured them authoritatively that the Jews, by and large, had nothing to fear.[17]

Diels was willing to help Jews and kept open his old school friendship with Berlin Zionist Leo Plaut.[18] Göring seemed moderate and reasonable. Papen was not a Nazi and for a time was thought to be the real power in the government. The Nazis were not deliberately luring the Jews into a false sense of security. They were now bearers of unaccustomed government responsibilities and did not yet know how far and in what direction their Jewish policy would develop and to what extent they could make themselves independent of their conservative allies. Despite Nazi propaganda, the Jews were not a coherent political group and represented no objective threat to the regime. They could wait.

Since they were not a political group, they had no public political line and could respond only confusedly to the new situation. On 15 February the *Bayerische Israelitische Gemeinde-Zeitung,* the press organ of the Munich and Bavarian Jewish Gemeinden, discussed the political stance of German Jewry. Ludwig Feuchtwanger's editorial was vague and inconsistent, but it did make the point that Jews were not committed by their history or religion to liberalism or democracy. Feuchtwanger noted the support Jews had given to Italian fascism and suggested that a positive cooperation between the Jewish population and the new German government was possible if the government did not reject the Jews. But this was exceptional. Most Jewish newspa-

[17]Ball-Kaduri, *1933,* pp. 41–42, 51–52, based on Ernst Herzfeld memoir, YV, Jerusalem, 01/8.
[18]Ball-Kaduri, *1933,* based on Wolf Schoen memoir, YV, Jerusalem, 01/229.

pers did not go so far. They restricted themselves to expressions of hope that the Depression would be ended and added reminders of Jewish patriotism, Jewish membership in the German people (except for the Zionist press), and an insistence that all citizens must still enjoy the equal protection of the law.[19]

It became harder to believe in the *Rechtsstaat* after the elections of 5 March. As the Nazis moved to consolidate their exclusive power in all areas of German life, the Jews were inevitably increasingly excluded. The Nazis euphemistically labeled the process of nazification *Gleichschaltung* ("coordination"). All the cogs in German society were to mesh perfectly, moving the country toward power, prosperity, and racial purity. In this coordinated society the Jews could have no place. The moderation of the preelection period was forgotten. Göring changed his tone to the point where a bewildered Brodnitz was forced to suppose that there were really "two Görings."[20] The network of connections built up by the Jewish leaders in Berlin after 30 January retained its usefulness on a case-to-case basis but proved powerless to control or even to monitor the general direction of Nazi policy in Jewish matters. In short, the Jewish lobbying organizations could not lobby effectively.

The Jewish leadership was taught its first major lesson in the difficulty of influencing national policy in the Third Reich when it was caught unawares by the national boycott of Jewish businesses proclaimed for 1 April 1933. On 25 March, three days before the public announcement of the boycott, Göring met with Brodnitz, of the CV; Heinrich Stahl, the chairman of the Berlin Gemeinde; Max Naumann, of the small Verband nationaldeutscher Juden (VNJ, League of Patriotic German Jews); and Kurt Blumenfeld,

---

[19]Principal sources for Jewish press reaction are the *C.V.-Zeitung,* the Zionist *Jüdische Rundschau* and the Berlin *Gemeindeblatt.* Others include the *Israelitisches Familienblatt* and the *Schild,* the latter published by the veterans' organization RJF. The extreme German nationalist position is reflected in *Der nationaldeutsche Jude,* published by the VNJ. Early reactions to the Hitler regime are summarized in Hans Lamm, "Über die innere und äussere Entwicklung des deutschen Judentums im Dritten Reich" (Ph.D. diss., Erlangen, 1951), pp. 137ff.

[20]Ball-Kaduri, *1933,* p. 52.

head of the Zionistische Vereinigung für Deutschland (ZVFD, Zionist Union of Germany). Blumenfeld had originally been neglected by Göring, but he obtained an invitation at his own initiative to represent the interests of his ten thousand Zionist constituents at the highest levels of government.

Göring insisted that the Jewish leaders send a delegation to London to persuade their colleagues abroad to cease encouraging "atrocity stories" about the "new Germany." He apparently believed that international Jewry, led by the German Jews, had started the campaign and could turn it off. The representatives of the CV, the VNJ, and the Berlin Gemeinde protested that they had not been responsible for the atrocity campaign (*Greuelhetze*) and noted that, as patriotic German Jews, they had no influence abroad. There was certainly some truth to their contention. In London, Naumann would probably have been regarded as a Jewish Nazi. Brodnitz and Stahl might have had some influence with their London counterparts, but they enjoyed no real political connections. But Blumenfeld of the ZVFD leapt into the breach. He freely acknowledged that the ZVFD had influence abroad, as part of an international movement. The Zionists would send a delegation abroad to tell the truth about the German situation. They would deny exaggerated reports, provided they were permitted to discuss those incidents that had occurred. Göring grudgingly admitted that there had been excesses, and he agreed to Blumenfeld's terms.[21]

On 27 March, Blumenfeld informed Göring's office of the steps the ZVFD had taken to combat atrocity propaganda. Two Zionists had been dispatched to London and one to Prague, and telegrams had been sent to the United States and to Poland. The ZVFD had issued a general press release repeating the public stand it had already taken on 17 March against foreign atrocity propaganda. The declaration did not deny that German Jews had been mistreated or that their situation in general was difficult. It simply

[21]Martin Rosenbluth, *Go Forth and Serve* (New York, 1961), pp. 250–54; Schleunes, *Twisted Road,* pp. 77–78. On the history of German Zionism see Stephen M. Poppel, *Zionism in Germany 1897–1933* (Philadelphia, 1977).

attacked "all atrocity reports not conforming to the truth" and criticized the "misuse" of the Jewish situation by unspecified political groups (presumably Communists and Socialists) for their own purposes. And the declaration promised a continuing fight by the ZVFD in defense of Jewish rights and the Jewish "economic position" in Germany. The statement was silent on the Nazi party and the new government.[22] The ZVFD's actions were those of an independent Jewish organization defending its own and German Jewish interests, with no trace of obsequiousness or any compromise with Nazi anti-Semitism. The Zionist leaders knew that their statements and delegation would not stop the atrocity campaign against Germany. They simply hoped to gain some political capital by doing Göring a favor.

The Zionist delegation was in London on 28 March, when the plans for the 1 April boycott were announced. The timing was odd, if the Nazis actually hoped to get some results from the London mission. Foreign Jews could hardly be expected to believe that no serious harm was intended toward their German coreligionists when they read that SA and Schutzstaffel (SS) men were to be stationed in front of every Jewish business to discourage customers. Göring and Julius Streicher, head of the national boycott committee, were not coordinating their efforts. There was still no such thing as a concrete and consistent Nazi Jewish policy.

The suddenness of the boycott news demonstrated the inadequacy of the network of official contacts that had been constructed after 30 January. The Jewish leadership not only had been unable to influence government and party policy but had been unable to predict it. The Zionist response to the boycott announcement was forthright. On 31 March the ZVFD issued a press release condemning the anti-Semitic propaganda in the Nazi press and particularly a quotation falsely attributed by the boycott committee to Theodor Herzl, which actually had been lifted from the

[22]Blumenfeld to Sonnenfeldt (Prussian Interior Ministry), 27 March 1933, Klaus J. Herrmann, *Das Dritte Reich und die deutsch-jüdischen Organisationen 1933–1934* (Cologne, 1969), pp. 63–64.

anti-Semitic forgery *The Protocols of the Elders of Zion.* The ZVFD accused Streicher's committee of lying and protested solemnly against the use of this sort of tactic to justify the committee's *Vernichtungskampf* ("battle of annihilation") against German Jewry."[23] The use of this grim term is particularly striking. The declaration would certainly have undone any impression that the earlier ZVFD statement may have left abroad that the situation of German Jews was not serious.

The non-Zionist Jewish leadership reacted similarly. On 29 March the Berlin Gemeinde issued a declaration jointly with the National Agency of German Jews (Reichsvertretung der deutschen Juden), a body formed in 1932 as a loose representative agent for the German Jewish congregations. Like the Zionists, these non-Zionist leaders denied any responsibility for the foreign atrocity campaign. They noted that the boycott was unjustly threatening German Jews with "economic ruin" and "destruction." Unlike the Zionists, they insisted as always on the membership of the German Jews in the German people.[24] The general reaction of both Zionist and non-Zionist leaders was an open attack on the boycott, a rejection of Nazi charges, and a statement of determination to defend Jewish rights.

After the boycott this determination was repeated in an article by editor Robert Weltsch in the 6 April issue of the ZVFD newspaper *Jüdische Rundschau,* "Wear the Yellow Spot with Pride." The "yellow spot" had been used by the Nazis to mark Jewish homes and businesses. Weltsch's call for a positive sense of Jewishness, combined with a reiteration of Jewish rights, made the *Jüdische Rundschau* the most popular Jewish paper in Germany and at least temporarily boosted the Zionist cause among German Jews.[25] The Jewish public response evoked by the boycott

[23]"Erklärung der Zionistische Vereinigung für Deutschland," press release enclosed in G. Landauer to Reichskanzlei, 31 March 1933, Herrmann, *Organisationen,* pp. 58–59.
[24]Kleemann (Berlin Gemeinde) and Baeck (National Agency) to Hitler, 29 March 1933, with enclosed press release, ibid., pp. 60–61.
[25]Richard Lichtheim, *Die Geschichte des deutschen Zionismus* (Jerusalem, 1954), pp. 253ff.; Ball-Kaduri, *1933,* pp. 91–92.

could only be called "defiance." It was appropriate to the moment. The boycott did not work well and was abandoned after one day, lost in the confusion of Nazi policy. But the reasons for the end of the boycott were rooted in Nazi foreign-policy goals, economic concerns, internal party bickering, and the objective difficulties of determining which firms were, in fact, Jewish. They had nothing to do with the German Jewish response.

Even before the Nazi takeover several German states had passed laws forbidding the kosher slaughtering of animals on "humane" grounds. There is no doubt that the motive of these laws was anti-Semitism. But they meant little to most of Germany's Jews. Relatively few of them kept the dietary laws in any case, and Prussia, the largest German state, did not pass a ban on kosher slaughtering. Prussian kosher butchers could "export" meat to affected states. Aside from this pinprick attack, German Jews had no reason to feel themselves discriminated against by legislation until April 1933. On 7 April they were faced with the "Law for the Rehabilitation of the Professional Civil Service" and on 11 April with a law regulating permission to practice law. These were the first proofs that practical anti-Semitic discrimination was the permanent policy of Hitler's government.

It was obvious that the Nazis intended to purge the civil service. In mid-March officials in the Reich Interior Ministry drafted proposals that became the first versions of the civil-service law. They assumed that the new authorities would need a simple law that would permit them to dismiss any official, regardless of tenure. But at the end of March, Hitler personally intervened in the drafting of the new law, to turn it in a specifically anti-Semitic direction. It was to supplement the propaganda effect of the boycott and to provide proof that the government was moving against the Jews. In the new text Jews were specifically excluded from the civil service, although they might have been excluded under other, more general provisions of the law. The propaganda purpose of the legislation demanded that Jews be excluded as Jews.

Ironically, this produced an intervention by Reich President

Paul von Hindenburg, who was lobbied by the Jewish veterans' organization, the National League of Jewish Combat Soldiers (Reichsbund jüdischer Frontsoldaten, RJF). As a result of Hindenburg's intervention the law was altered to exempt those Jewish officials who had been in the civil service before 1 August 1914, who had fought at the front in World War I for Germany or its allies, or who had lost a father or son in the war. The law thus became a piece of anti-Semitic legislation in the "moderate" conservative tradition. The whole notion of exemptions on the basis of proved service to the German people was entirely foreign to Nazi racist notions and to Hitler's personal opinions.[26]

Of special interest is the lobbying effort by Captain Leo Löwenstein, head of the RJF, which apparently produced a measurable benefit for RJF members. In a letter sent to Hindenburg and Hitler on 4 April, Löwenstein pointed out that the RJF represented about 30,000 Jewish combat veterans. He reviewed the patriotic record of the RJF, including its opposition to all "elements harmful to the people" (*volksschädigende Elemente*), Jewish or not. The RJF wished only to help in German recovery and to share, if necessary, in defending the fatherland. In a letter to the American embassy of 24 March, the RJF had attacked atrocity propaganda in the United States. It had criticized the agitation of "so-called Jewish intellectuals" among the German émigrés who had "never regarded themselves as Germans" and had "deserted their coreligionists at the critical moment" in order to hurl their "barbs" from "a safe hiding place." These people had "lost their right to participate in discussion of German Jewish affairs." But the RJF stood ready to organize the positive forces within the German Jewish community in the service of national recovery. The organization therefore hoped that families long resident in Germany and combat veterans and their dependents and survivors would be exempt from anti-Semitic discrimination.[27]

[26]Uwe Dietrich Adam, *Judenpolitik im Dritten Reich* (Düsseldorf, 1972), pp. 51ff.

[27]Löwenstein to Hitler, 4 April 1933, Herrmann, *Organisationen,* pp. 66–68.

It is not clear from the sources whether RJF lobbying alone produced the Hindenburg intervention. But the effort was remarkable for reasons apart from its apparent success. The RJF declared that Jews were willing to accede in part to old anti-Semitic demands, noting its previous efforts to retrain Jews for agricultural and craft occupations. That is, the RJF was willing to accept general Jewish downward movement on the economic scale, even while requesting special exemptions for its own constituency. It clearly proposed that anti-Semitic legislation affect only recent Eastern European immigrants and political leftists. And the RJF requested for itself a special position in helping institute and execute government Jewish policy. There was some success here. Ultimately the government recognized the RJF as the official intermediary between itself and Jewish war veterans on pensions and similar matters. But the original request went much further. The RJF asked to be granted a strong role in Jewish affairs on the basis of a presumed agreement with the government on ideology and policy. Max Naumann of the VNJ made a similar attempt in late April, in the course of which he denounced all the major Jewish organizations.[28] But Nazi racial anti-Semitism had no place for patriotic German Jews. The RJF could not expand its official role, and the VNJ and Naumann had no further role to play. The police did not ban the VNJ until 1935, but in the meantime it earned itself only the ridicule of both fellow Jews and Nazis.

The RJF was the first major Jewish organization to request for itself a special position in the new Germany. Its proposals show that Captain Löwenstein was willing to sacrifice the interests of some members of the Jewish community, political leftists and Ostjuden, to secure a place for Jewish war veterans and long-established German Jews in Hitler's new Germany. There is unfortunately no way of determining to what extent Löwenstein reflected the opinions of the RJF membership, since the criterion for membership was combat service, not adherence to the leader-

[28]Documents, ibid., pp. 73–80.

ship's political notions. The initiative of the RJF leadership does bear a resemblance to the well-known efforts of "Jewish Councils" (Judenräte) and of similar bodies all over Europe during World War II to protect certain Jews from deportation and extermination by sacrificing others. To be sure, in 1933 the German Jews were not faced with mass extermination. There is no direct organizational or political connection between this RJF lobbying and later events in occupied Amsterdam or Lodz. Löwenstein acted on the basis of the vigorous, conservative German patriotism appropriate to a retired German officer and most likely hoped sincerely that the new regime, led by its more conservative elements (represented by Hindenburg), would collaborate with the RJF. But although his effort proved ultimately unsuccessful and had no long-lasting political effect, it remains as a first example of a tendency among Jewish leaders faced by the Nazi threat to divide the Jews into apparently convenient categories, helping some by betraying others.

The attempt by the ZVFD to establish a special relationship with the authorities had a greater immediate practical effect than the RJF initiative. On 21 June, relatively late in the development of the dictatorship, the Zionists issued a policy statement in which they claimed that they had always stressed the distinction between Germans and Jews and had combated the "symptoms of decay" visible among "assimilated" Jews. The statement supposed that it was possible for German-educated Zionists to partake passively of German culture, but only because "we too are against mixed marriage and for the maintenance of the purity of the Jewish race [Art] and reject border violations in the cultural sphere." Awareness and cultivation of their own Jewish culture would "prevent the Jews from becoming rootless critics of the national foundations of the German essence. The ethnic separation [völkische Distanzierung] desired by the state would in this way be created without compulsion, as the result of an organic development." An "ethnically self-aware Jewry" (artbewussten Judentum) would cooperate loyally with the German state in encouraging Jewish emigration, especially to

Palestine, and in discouraging anti-German boycott efforts abroad.[29] The statement of 21 June was intended by the Zionist leadership to serve as a basis for discussions with the government.[30] It was followed over the next months by solid achievements. The government permitted continued emigration of German Jews to Palestine under the control of the Zionists' Palestine Office. The ZVFD created two transfer companies, Paltreu in Berlin and Haavara in Palestine, that allowed former German residents to transfer the bulk of their German assets and greatly assisted the capital-starved Jewish settlement in Palestine. The transfer agreement with the German government also called for the purchase of German goods by the Jews in Palestine, and it thereby disrupted international anti-German boycott efforts more or less as proposed in the statement of 21 June.[31]

As the shock of the boycott and the civil-service legislation wore off, public statements by Jewish organizations moved away from rhetorical confrontation with Nazi anti-Semitism. The Jewish leadership was forced slowly to the sickening realization that the Nazis would not disappear overnight and that they were seriously intent on implementing an anti-Semitic program one way or another. The informational network of informal contacts had not, in the long run, proved very useful or reliable. Only the ZVFD was successful in establishing a significant formal relationship with the government, in a limited, if very important, area.

The imitation of Nazi language in the documents of the period may shock us today. Shock is an inappropriate reaction. Löwenstein acted normally, as the head of a conservative veterans' lobby with

---

[29]"Äusserung der Zionistische Vereinigung für Deutschland zur Stellung der Juden im neuen Staat," 21 June 1933, reprinted in Herrmann, *Organisationen,* pp. 15–17, and in Franz Meyer, "Zwei Denkschriften," Hans Tramer, ed., *In zwei Welten* (Tel Aviv, 1962), pp. 116–19.

[30]Blumenfeld to Franz Gürtner (Reich Justice Minister), 29 June 1933, IZ MA108/DZA/RJM/Staatsbürgerrecht 2/9.

[31]Ernst Marcus, "The German Foreign Office and the Palestine Question in the Period 1933–1939," *Yad Vashem Studies* 2 (1958):179–204; Ludwig Pinner, "Vermögenstransfer nach Palästina 1933–1939," Tramer, ed., *In Zwei Welten,* pp. 133–66; David Yisraeli, "The Third Reich and the Transfer Agreement," *JCH* 6, no. 2 (1971):129–48.

organizational and constituent interests to protect and without foreknowledge of later catastrophes. An objective modern interpretation of the Zionist language of the period is more difficult, thanks to the identification of Zionism with "racism" promoted by Arab enemies of Israel and their supporters. This is no place for a full discussion of the history and current nature of Zionist ideology. It should be sufficient to point out that Zionism is a form of nationalism. Any form of nationalism must bear at least a superficial resemblance to national socialism, which attempted to absorb the German nationalist tradition. This is as true of Czech and Polish nationalism as it is of Zionism.

In the circumstances of 1933 it is not surprising that the ZVFD sometimes expressed itself in language that approached the vocabulary of national socialism. The Zionist leadership tried to establish a relationship with the new regime by speaking its language, as did Captain Löwenstein. The documents cited above were also aimed at Jews. Jewish political organizations tried to prove to their members and potential members that they could remain relevant in the drastically changed atmosphere of German politics. There is certainly no evidence that the ZVFD ever faltered in its basic political abhorrence of national socialism. Nor is there any evidence that the rhetorical imitation of the Nazis confused Jews about the essentially anti-Jewish nature of the regime. On the contrary, the extreme anti-Semitism of the Nazis inevitably created a need for a positive sense of Jewish identity that the Zionists were ideologically equipped to fulfill. The reaction of German Jews was no different from the reaction of Jews elsewhere in the world who saw in Zionism an answer to the growing international anti-Semitic threat.

In March 1933 a committee of state officials and outside "experts" on Jewish affairs, including Rudolf Diels, met in Berlin and produced a plan for a government Jewish policy. The key to the plan was the proposed imposition of an "Association of Jews in Germany" on the German Jewish community. The organization and its involuntary members were to be under the authority of a *Volkswart* (a "guardian" of the interests of the German people) appointed by the government. Jews were to be defined on the basis of the religion of their grandparents, with provision made for part-Jews. The *Volkswart* was to have the right to excuse some Jews from membership in the association and declare them to be full Germans. All others would have to append a *J* to their names and would not be permitted to adopt "German" names. They would be able to follow economic pursuits as resident aliens, but the *Volkswart* could forbid ostentatious display of wealth. Members of the association would not be permitted to practice law, serve in the army, participate in German cultural life, work for German newspapers, or engage in a range of other activities. They would have to attend their own schools. Marriages and sexual relations between association members and Germans would be forbidden.[32]

Most elements of the anti-Jewish legislation adopted between 1933 and 1939 may be found in this plan, but the plan and the committee of minor lights that produced it had no future as such. The ideas were not especially Nazi and were in the tradition that went back to Heinrich Class and the Pan-German League.[33] The notion of an involuntary Jewish association was not realized until 1939. It became an instrument of mass expropriation, deportation, and murder—something very far from the political scene of 1933. For the time being, the Nazis produced neither a Jewish policy nor an office with jurisdiction over all Jewish affairs. The Jewish leaders had to find their own way through the jungle that sprang up and covered their once familiar country.

The immediate situation of German Jewry was beyond the control of its official leadership. About 37,000 Jews left Germany in the course of 1933, more than in any other year before the forced deportations of the war period. It is impossible to tell how many left exclusively because they were Jews and how many chose emigration because they belonged to endangered political and cultural groups. The leadership of the community recom-

[32]Adam, *Judenpolitik*, pp. 33ff.
[33]Daniel Frymann [Heinrich Class], *Das Kaiserbuch* [original title: *Wenn ich der Kaiser wär*, 1912], 7th ed. (Leipzig, 1925), pp. 69–72.

mended that its constituents stand fast. The Zionists insisted that emigration to Palestine must be carefully planned and preceded by a long period of preparation. Most of the fewer than 7,000 Jews who left for Palestine in 1933 had long been preparing to do so through the ZVFD and its affiliate organizations.[34] As late as December 1933, Executive Director Ludwig Holländer of the CV was insisting in public that Jewish emigration without pressing personal need was not merely inadvisable but also "impermissible."[35]

Holländer meant that German Jews ought not to desert their coreligionists and thereby prove the Nazi point that Jews had no real love for their German fatherland. But there was a practical as well as ideological point to be made.[36] Jews flooding out of Germany could not be assured of a warm welcome in other countries and a chance to earn a living. The situation of the many German refugees (Jewish and "Aryan" alike) in France and the Low Countries in that Depression year was particularly grim. But if German Jews were to stay in Germany, because they loved their homeland or because they could find no way to leave without losing all chance of earning a living, they had to deal with the pressing economic problems created by the Nazi victory.

Some of the most prestigious members of the Jewish community suddenly found themselves in difficulty. In 1933 approximately 2,000 academically trained Jewish civil servants lost their jobs. About 4,000 Jewish lawyers and junior legal trainees could not practice. About 1,000 Jewish physicians lost their public positions, and a further 3,000 had their incomes severely reduced by exclusion from insurance plans. Smaller numbers of professors and junior university teachers were in difficulty, along with newspapermen, writers, and artists. At the other end of the social scale, Jewish small merchants and peddlars found that they could

[34]Lucy S. Dawidowicz, *The War Against the Jews, 1933-1945* (New York, 1975), p. 173.

[35]*C.V.-Zeitung,* 29 December 1933.

[36]The following paragraphs are based primarily on "Arbeitsbericht des Zentralausschusses der deutschen Juden für Hilfe und Aufbau, 1. April-31. Dezember 1933," n.d. (Spring 1934), IZ MA727/1.

not get their licenses renewed and lost permission to sell at public markets. All of these individuals, many of whom were not eligible for unemployment assistance from public agencies, expected help from the Jewish community. They added their demands to those of the Jews who were already unemployed as a result of the Depression. Under the pressure of overwhelming need the welfare services of the Jewish community reorganized.

In April 1933 the Central Committee of German Jews for Assistance and Construction (Zentralausschuss der deutschen Juden für Hilfe und Aufbau) was created by representatives of the Gemeinden, Jewish charitable organizations, and the larger Jewish political groups. The Zionists did not take part in the initial discussions, but they determined to support the committee, thus widening its political base and creating an institution which united Zionists and non-Zionists for the sake of Jewish welfare efforts. The Central Committee served as the reception point for the funds that began to flow into Germany from Jewish groups abroad. It was hoped that its activities could establish a new basis for Jewish existence in Germany (hence *Aufbau*). For the time being, to be sure, emergency aid (*Hilfe*) was what was most needed. Of those Jews who successfully applied to the Central Committee's economic office for aid in 1933, only 21 percent were referred to the loan office for assistance in regaining their financial footing. The remaining 79 percent were considered economically hopeless cases and were granted simple welfare payments to keep them going.

The Jewish leadership still operated on the assumption that a modus vivendi could be reached with the authorities. Since individual organizations had failed, with the exception of the Zionists in a limited area, it seemed logical to apply the Central Committee's unity formula to the creation of a political body that could negotiate with the government in the name of all German Jews. The National Agency of Jewish State Associations (Reichsvertretung der jüdischen Landesverbände) already existed. It had been formed in 1932 but had done little since its founding. It represented only the Gemeinden, and most German Jews had never heard of it. But one of its cochairmen, the well-known

Berlin rabbi Leo Baeck, cosigned the Berlin Gemeinde antiboycott declaration of 29 March with his organization's name.[37] On 6 June, Baeck tried to arrange an interview with Hitler by putting forward the National Agency as a suitable partner for negotiations with the government. The initiative failed.[38]

On 17 September at a meeting in Berlin the old National Agency was replaced by a new National Agency of German Jews (Reichsvertretung der deutschen Juden) under the presidency of Leo Baeck. The new organization grew out of months of detailed negotiations in which Zionists and representatives of the CV and the RJF ironed out some of their differences and devised a formula that also allowed for the representation of the Gemeinden.[39] The new National Agency was dominated from the beginning by the CV and the ZVFD operating in uneasy partnership, with the RJF playing a secondary role. Both President Leo Baeck and his executive director, Otto Hirsch, of Stuttgart, were close to the CV and non-Zionist. By participating fully in an organization under their leadership, the ZVFD for a time resigned itself to a role suitable to its minority position within the Jewish community. Since it retained unchallenged authority over its most important concern, emigration to Palestine, the sacrifice was not great. The Berlin Gemeinde, which had tended to reject superior authority, also agreed to work within the new organization. All the founders hoped that the re-formed National Agency would serve as an effective lobby to achieve the working relationship with the government on all Jewish matters that no organization had been able to achieve alone.

In 1962, looking back on the events of the 1930s from a postwar perspective, Franz Meyer, of the National Agency, described the

---

[37]See n. 24 above.

[38]Baeck to Hitler et al., 6 June 1933, Herrmann, *Organisationen,* pp. 81–82; original in IZ MA108/DZA/RJM/Staatsbürgerrecht 2/9 shows that the "old" National Agency was operating from Kantstrasse 158, later address of the "new" agency.

[39]The problems are summarized, with the relevant primary sources and secondary literature, in Levine, "Kareski," pp. 258–59. See also Leonard Baker, *Days of Sorrow and Pain: Leo Baeck and the Berlin Jews* (New York, 1978), pp. 158–67.

situation facing German Jewish leaders as an illustration of Arnold Toynbee's principle of "challenge and response."[40] The situation was certainly a new one, and it is not unreasonable for Jewish leaders to look back and see it in Toynbee's terms. But it was impossible in 1933 for these men and women to determine what precisely was challenging them. And there was no way by which they could measure the appropriateness of their "response" on a political scale. In the absence of any other alternative the German Jewish organizations acted in a pragmatic way to defend the interests of their constituents as best they could, wherever they were threatened at any given moment. Although Jewish leaders achieved a certain degree of organizational unity, they adopted no long-range policy, nor was any possible. Their record here is no worse or better than, and no different from, that of other non-Nazi German leadership groups threatened by the Nazis, especially the Social Democrats, the trade unionists, and the church hierarchies.[41]

The Nazis clearly held all the important cards, but they could not yet decide which ones to play. Were the Jews to be attacked in the streets or permitted to live in relative peace? Did they have to fear denunciation and arbitrary arrest, or could they still rely on basic legal rights? Were they to continue to participate in the German economy, and, if so, for how long and in what way? How significant and how permanent were the Hindenburg exemptions for veterans and other "deserving" Jews? The very definition of "Jew" was still uncertain. Entirely uncertain was the role, if any, to be played by Jewish organizations or leaders in any eventual solution of the "Jewish question."

It is easy to imagine the unnerving effect this situation had as the months wore on. But the situation seemed to have stabilized by the end of 1933. It is not surprising, given what they had survived, that many Jewish leaders and their constituents were prepared to

---

[40]Meyer, "Zwei Denkschriften," p. 115.

[41]The literature on these subjects is considerable. See esp. Mason, *Sozialpolitik,* esp. chaps. 2, 3; Guenter Lewy, *The Catholic Church and Nazi Germany* (New York, 1964); John S. Conway, *The Nazi Persecution of the Churches, 1933-1934* (London, 1968).

believe that the worst had come and gone and that they would now be allowed to settle down within their somewhat circumscribed limits. A total of 37,000 Jews left Germany in 1933, but only 23,000 left in 1934. No Jewish leaders expected their problems to be solved by emigration, though selective emigration might help by relieving pressure on strained welfare services. The Zionists, of course, welcomed the new interest in emigration to Palestine, but they did not yet think in very large numbers. Jewish leaders in all organizations expected that the problems of German Jewry would have to be solved in Germany.[42] Jewish organizations abroad were also anxious that German Jews remain in Germany, rather than leave and become direct burdens on their foreign coreligionists.

Considering the magnitude of their problems, the community's leaders did not do a bad job of making the necessary readjustments. They accomplished a great deal of practical work. They helped frightened and impoverished people to emigrate or, in some cases, to return to Germany. The Palestine Office began to send larger numbers than ever before to Palestine, and other Jewish agencies did the same for emigration elsewhere. For the Jews who remained, a beginning was made with occupation retraining, since it was obvious that some Jews would have to find new ways of earning their livings. Jewish organizations provided direct welfare to soften the blow of readjustment. The community worked painfully toward a new version of itself, smaller and less ambitious than the old version but still both German and Jewish. There was even room for new, private initiative. Kurt Singer, a physician and amateur musician, founded the Jewish Cultural League in Berlin in 1933 to give work to unemployed musicians, actors, and others and to provide a new cultural center for a community suddenly forced to turn in on itself. The work of the Cultural League was even given a kind of Nazi approval as evidence that the Jews were being permitted to establish their own autonomous cultural life in Germany.[43]

[42]See n. 36 above. This attitude was universal in the Jewish press.
[43]Herbert Freeden, *Jüdisches Theater im Nazideutschland* (Tübingen, 1964).

The German Jews could strengthen the practical work of their community and struggle with the question of cultural identification within the limits set by the authorities. More difficult was the effort to take part in determining those limits. The Jewish leaders began with the assumption that they were representing readily definable interests that could be defended by lobbying in Berlin along lines already established in the pre-Nazi period. Contacts with non-Nazi politicians and officials were used to get in touch with the new holders of power. When this approach proved to have only limited usefulness, individual organizations attempted to establish more formal relations with the government. Finally a joint attempt was made through the reorganized National Agency. At all times the individual factions within German Jewry made every effort to ensure that they would be included in all contacts and that their specific interests would be represented in any future negotiations. These concerns made the new National Agency seem the most reasonable way to organize the Jewish response to the Nazis.

The National Agency was entirely a Jewish body, set up in accordance with the wishes of the leaders of the German Jewish community without any interference or encouragement from the government. It was in no sense a "puppet" or "collaborationist" organization. Although the RJF leadership represented in the agency sometimes espoused extreme German nationalist ideas, the agency's most prominent leaders were men of a politically liberal persuasion who could not be suspected of harboring sympathies toward the new regime. The method adopted by the National Agency was entirely consistent with the traditions of the Jewish leadership. If it was not intended for true collaboration with and support of the Hitler regime, neither did it aim at resistance. As a lobby (*Interessenvertretung*) the National Agency would neither oppose nor support the government, which in any case could not be overthrown with Jewish aid and certainly did not welcome Jewish support.

The apparent lack of interest by the Nazis in obtaining Jewish cooperation presented the Jewish leadership with an especially difficult problem. If the German Jews had actually been able to exert important influence abroad, the Nazis might have been more interested in talking with them, but the first experiments showed that anti-Nazi agitation abroad could not be fought effectively through the German Jews. Hitler himself always refused to meet with Jews or even to correspond directly with them. Göring was willing, but meetings with him did not prove very useful. Most contacts with the authorities were at a relatively low level. It was the Jews who pressed again and again for some sign of cooperation from the Nazis and the Nazis who hesitated. They had not yet come to terms with the necessity of actually dealing with the people whom they would shortly destroy. It took time for jurisdictional questions to be clarified and for a center to develop within the amorphous government and party bureaucracies, a center that could deal with the National Agency.

Perhaps the hardest thing for the Jews of Germany to understand was that they were not important. The country was swamped with anti-Semitic propaganda, but the Jews themselves mattered very little. Nazi anti-Semitic policy developed largely through internal ideological and political processes and continually caught the German Jews by surprise simply because it was not developed with any relevance to them, save that they were hurt by it and ultimately killed by it. This was a hopeless position for an ordinary interest group like the CV. The ZVFD, although dominated by the political ideology of Zionism, also found that political cooperation with the Nazis was ultimately impossible. It, too, could function only as an interest group, defending its control over emigration to Palestine. The leaders of these organizations were part of an informally self-co-opting Jewish elite that had been fighting anti-Semitism and seeking organizational and institutional advantages for decades in a difficult but not a crisis situation. No structure existed through which the leadership could determine the wishes of its constituency, nor was any attempt made to create one. Emergencies had to be met on a day-to-day basis, and a new structure was devised for meeting them, the Central Committee for Assistance and Construction. And if the Nazis should ever prove willing to enter into general discussions on the future of the German Jewish community, the National

Agency was there as an approved body of political representatives. For the moment that was all that could be done.

Since the Nazis were not very much interested in talking, the Central Committee and other groups with public visibility, like the Jewish Cultural League and the larger Gemeinden, seemed far more important in 1933 than the National Agency. The full implications of developments in Jewish reorganization undertaken in 1933 were not visible for years. But the trend toward centralization and internal Jewish cooperation had begun and would continue. The National Agency and the Central Committee later merged into an enlarged National Agency. Zionists and their opponents settled most of their differences within the new framework, thereby strengthening it. Out of the confusion and the fear a new structure of Jewish self-organization arose that eventually became part of the machinery of destruction. The hope had been to produce an organization with which the Nazis could and would negotiate, but they were never genuinely interested in negotiation, save on peripheral matters. Eventually the Nazis did centralize their Jewish policy, in the SS and police machinery under Heinrich Himmler. And then they were ready to give orders.

8

Class Interest and State Policy in the British Response to Hitler

CHARLES BRIGHT

Britain in the 1930s was governed by committees. The rigid class stratification of British society and the exclusivity of its ruling elites gave way at the decisive levels of government to a remarkably collegial, even clubby, charmed circle. Politicians at the top formed a closed community of power in which the main referents in decision making were other members of the community. It was here, in a dense network of formal institutions and ad hoc bodies, that power in the British state was concentrated, organized, parceled out, and used.

The structure of collective procedures that registered and absorbed events was, for all its hierarchical arrangement, genuinely deliberative. Policy flowed from discussion and reflected an ongoing consensus, however vague and implicit. Talk defined the possible grounds of action as well as the negative limits upon the field of choice; talk also produced that collection of code phrases all participants understood: "mad-dog act" and "knockout blow," "missing the bus" and "showing a tooth." Although disputes and rivalries among politicians were often personal, and hence explosive, the structure as a whole tended to defuse problems and flatten out differences in the name of preserving agreement and containing change.

When Hitler took power in Germany, his presence reverberated throughout the governing structure in Britain. The national coalition, which had come together in 1931 to contain the impact of the world Depression at home and which, at bottom, represented the political modus vivendi between the classes that Stanley Baldwin and James Ramsay MacDonald had worked out in the 1920s, found itself confronted with a new and puzzling challenge that did not conform to its habitual frames of reference. Hitler posed a serious political threat to the government. He quickly became a primary focus of press and public opinion. This made him a touchstone of domestic political calculations. He forced a reappraisal of the priorities of domestic pacification and economic recovery that had constituted the national government's "doctor's mandate" of 1931. For he raised the profoundly disturbing specter of a European leader who might not play by the established rules of the game and, worse, could not be made to do so except at a price that, in 1933 or 1934 at least, seemed appallingly out of the question. A national government responsible for the country's safety and facing another general election could not ignore the new regime in Germany and its policy of rapid rearmament. Yet it could not respond to this threat without placing severe strains upon the synapses of the ruling coalition and its authority in the country.

How adequate was Britain's response? Historians have long debated the question. Most agree that the British did not make full or effective use of the five years of peace Hitler left them. Although they began to repair military deficiencies in 1934, they did not commit themselves to full rearmament until 1936. Thereafter, the Treasury's ceilings on spending and the cabinet's injunction against disturbing normal industrial routine hampered the pace. In the end the Neville Chamberlain government tried to reach a direct settlement with Hitler, partly to square the circle of mounting danger and limited rearmament but largely because the leading "appeasers" believed that through their auspices Hitler could get what he wanted without a war. This conviction was certainly wrong. Hitler's appetite proved larger than anyone imagined, and in retrospect the collapse of Chamberlain's policy seems almost inevitable. When war began in 1939, the country was not ready, and it barely survived the summer of 1940.

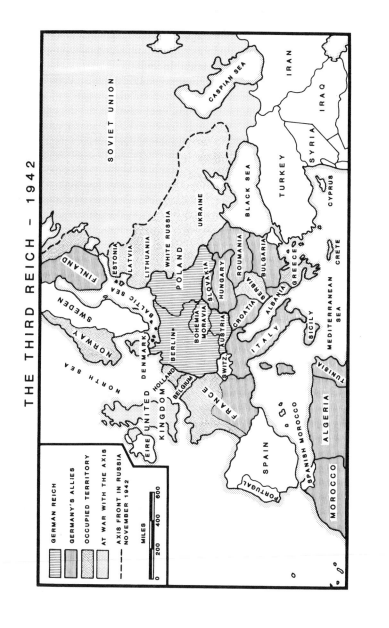

THE THIRD REICH – 1942

GERMAN REICH
GERMANY'S ALLIES
OCCUPIED TERRITORY
AT WAR WITH THE AXIS
AXIS FRONT IN RUSSIA
NOVEMBER 1942

MILES
0   200   400   600

SOVIET UNION

CASPIAN SEA

IRAN

IRAQ

SYRIA

TURKEY

CYPRUS

BLACK SEA

CRETE

MEDITERRANEAN SEA

GREECE

BULGARIA

ROUMANIA

UKRAINE

WHITE RUSSIA

POLAND

LITHUANIA

LATVIA

ESTONIA

FINLAND

SWEDEN

NORWAY

NORTH SEA

BALTIC SEA

DENMARK

UNITED KINGDOM

EIRE

HOLLAND

BELGIUM

BERLIN

BOHEMIA MORAVIA

SLOVAKIA

HUNGARY

AUSTRIA

SWITZ.

FRANCE

CROATIA

SERBIA

ALBANIA

ITALY

SICILY

TUNISIA

ALGERIA

SPANISH MOROCCO

MOROCCO

SPAIN

PORTUGAL

In explaining why the government behaved the way it did, historians have often begun with the heroism of World War II and the correct assumption that, given Hitler's ambitions, war was probably unavoidable. From this premise they have cast judgment on the competence and even on the manliness of Britain's leaders in the 1930s.[1] A few have defended Baldwin and Chamberlain. Conclusions ultimately turn on the taste and temperament of the historian, and discussion has gone in circles for many years. The opening of the archives has tended to cast the politicians who created the official record in a better light. Thus Baldwin, once regarded as complacent, lazy, indecisive, and incompetent in foreign policy, has become in recent reincarnations a pillar of strength, energetic, farsighted, and almost godlike in his comprehension of human affairs.[2] Chamberlain, always less easy to like, has also swung the circle from the provincial epigone with umbrella, sadly sure of himself, selling the pass to Hitler in the naïve belief that he was getting a settlement, to the dour schoolmarm prime minister with rational objectives and a coherent policy which he pursued courageously, if a bit obsessively.[3] Some may call this a spiral of clarification. But the outcome seems to be in the direction of smothering analysis in a mass of archival detail which emphasizes the complexity of decision making, the contrary pressures and dilemmas of choice that hemmed in Britain's leaders and precluded bold action—as though these were conditions peculiar to the 1930s—and leaves behind

[1]Standard accounts include Winston Churchill, *The Gathering Storm* (London, 1948); Paul Einzig, *Appeasement Before, During and After the War* (London, 1942); John Wheeler-Bennett, *Munich: Prologue to Tragedy* (London, 1948); Martin Gilbert and Richard Gott, *The Appeasers* (London, 1963); Martin Gilbert, *The Roots of Appeasement* (London, 1966); Christopher Thorne, *The Approach of War, 1938-39* (New York, 1967).

[2]On Baldwin see G. M. Young, *Stanley Baldwin* (London, 1952); A. W. Baldwin, *My Father: The True Story* (London, 1956); Keith Middlemas and John Barnes, *Baldwin: A Biography* (London, 1969), a lengthy defense; H. Montgomery Hyde, *Baldwin: The Unexpected Prime Minister* (London, 1973), the best study.

[3]For Neville Chamberlain see Keith Feiling, *The Life of Neville Chamberlain* (London, 1947); Ian Macleod, *Neville Chamberlain* (London, 1961); Ian Colvin, *The Chamberlain Cabinet* (London, 1971); the Earl of Birkenhead, *Halifax* (London, 1965); Maurice Cowling, *The Impact of Hitler* (Chicago, 1977), pp. 257-91.

the strong impression that things were the way they were because nothing else was possible.[4]

Another line of explanation has had less vogue. It looks not at personalities but at social interests and the structural determinants of class. This genre of historical literature has its roots in the contemporary suspicion in opposition circles that the Tory leadership was less concerned with a resolute response to Hitler than with staying in power. Baldwin's "appalling frankness" speech of November 1936, in which he apparently admitted withholding information about rearmament for fear of arousing public opinion and losing an election, produced a great debate on candor in the 1940s.[5] Curiously, his apologists, unwilling to entertain the possibility that he did not see the need for major rearmament, pitched their defense on the critics' ground by claiming that it would have been irresponsible of him to let in a Labour government at such a critical juncture and that, precisely because he grasped the urgency of the situation, it was essential "for the sake of rearmament and national security [that] the Conservatives should win the next general election."[6] This provided grist for A. L. Rowse's attack on "the class of decadence" which was

[4]See, for example, Middlemas and Barnes, *Baldwin;* Christopher Thorne, *The Limits of Foreign Policy* (Capricorn, 1973); N. H. Gibbs, *Grand Strategy,* vol. 1 (London, 1976); my own happily unpublished dissertation, "Britain's Search for Security: The Diplomacy of Naval Disarmament and Imperial Defense, 1930–36," (Yale, 1970); Telford Taylor, *Munich: The Price of Peace* (New York, 1978).

[5]Young, *Baldwin,* p. 196; Baldwin, *My Father,* chap. 17; Middlemas and Barnes, *Baldwin,* pp. 970–73; Reginald Bassett, "Telling the Truth to People," *Cambridge Journal,* November 1948; C. L. Mowat, "Baldwin Restored?" *JMH* 27, no. 2 (1955). For early versions of the Baldwin-as-liar thesis see Peter Howard, *Sunday Express,* 3 September 1939; "Cato," *Guilty Men* (London, 1940); Hamilton Fyfe, "Leadership and Democracy," *Nineteenth Century and After,* May 1941; A. L. Rowse, "Reflections on Lord Baldwin," *Political Quarterly,* July–September 1941.

[6]D. C. Somervell, *Stanley Baldwin* (London, 1953), p. 42; see also Middlemas and Barnes, *Baldwin,* p. 849. C. T. Stanage, "The East Fulham By-Election, 25 October 1933," *HJ* 14 (1971), revived the charge that Baldwin misled the public; J. P. D. Dunbabin, "British Rearmament in the Thirties: A Chronology and Review," *HJ* 18 (1975), rebutted. Martin Gilbert, *Winston Churchill,* vol. 5, *1922–39* (London, 1976), chaps. 29, 32–34, reinforces the impression that Baldwin was less than candid.

content to "lead the country, with continuous electoral success, in their illusions" rather than alert them to the true dangers of Nazi Germany.[7] For Rowse, a Labour activist in the 1930s, class interest and bias were the ultimate reason for the government's inadequate response to Hitler. The "anti-Red theme confused their minds." It "hamstrung them in dealing with the greater immediate danger to their country, Hitler's Germany." Hence, "We must blame them for being anti-Red to the extent of jeopardizing the safety of their country."

This sort of class polemic has had a modest career, despite divided views over whether the Soviet menace abroad or the Socialist peril at home most worried Britain's leaders.[8] A number of historians have concluded that the ruling elite, on the defensive in a world depression and concerned about the impact of military rearmament upon domestic stability, did not dare take risks to resist Hitler and preferred to strike a deal with him: "It was the distrust of Russia and the fear of Bolshevism . . . which made them soft on the dictators, above all Hitler, who deliberately identified himself with the struggle against Bolshevism."[9] The Russians have long insisted that Chamberlain encouraged Hitler to go east; witness Munich. Margaret George argued that it was "almost impossible to overrate" the importance of the "Conservative Red-obsession."[10] Studies of pro-German sentiment among the British elite point less categorically in the same direction.[11] Even those who cast their criticism of appeasement on the grounds of ministerial incompetence have noted that anticommunism was never far beneath the surface.[12]

But the evidence does not support the claim that fear of the

[7]A. L. Rowse, *Appeasement: A Study in Political Decline, 1933–39* (New York, 1961), pp. 12, 26–27, 116–17.

[8]For a review of the literature see Donald Lammers, *Explaining Munich: The Search for Motive in British Policy* (Stanford, Calif., 1966), pp. 1–15.

[9]Edward Crankshaw, quoted in Lammers, *Munich,* p. 5.

[10]Margaret George, *The Warped Vision* (Pittsburgh, Pa., 1965), p. 21.

[11]See D. C. Watt, *Personalities and Policies* (Notre Dame, Ind., 1965), pp. 117–35; Brigitte Granzow, *A Mirror of Nazism* (London, 1964).

[12]Gilbert and Gott, *Appeasers,* p. 25.

"Reds" determined the British response to Hitler.[13] Donald Lammers has shown convincingly that cold-war categories cannot be imposed on the 1930s and that anti-Soviet sentiment, which undoubtedly existed, was not a touchstone of British policy. That Conservative politicians routinely called their Labour opponents "Socialists" or even "Bolshevists" was the hyperbole of political combat, not a sign of fear. Violet Bonham Carter's remark of 1919, at the height of the postwar "Red scare," rang true throughout the interwar period: "When I think of Mr. [J. R.] Clynes and Mr. [Arthur] Henderson [of the Labour party], my flesh positively refuses to creep."[14] The case for class motivation cannot be founded solely upon the Red-baiting rhetoric of the hustings or upon the general and wholly predictable anti-Communist sentiment that permeated the ranks of the Conservative party. From this Lammers went on to attack the premise itself, "the fundamentally Marxian notion that foreign policy, like justice, is conducted in the interests of the class which controls the state." Since members of the same social class held "radically inconsistent ideas" about government policy, Lammers argued that it is not possible to treat policy as a simple extension of class interest. Instead, he suggested "recognizing and embracing the complex, sometimes ambivalent, often ad hoc characteristics of human activity and putting these at the center of historical explanation."[15]

Maurice Cowling took this injunction to heart in his idiosyncratic work *The Impact of Hitler.*[16] He rested his analysis of appeasement on a reductionist premise. If Britain's leaders were as narrow-minded and limited as they are often made out to be, then surely the best way to explain their actions is to focus

[13]A. J. P. Taylor dismisses it in one line: "The British were too little perturbed by the 'red peril' to desire its destruction in war" (*The Origins of the Second World War* [London, 1961], p. 228). See also his *English History, 1914–1945* (Oxford, 1965), p. 117.

[14]Trevor Wilson, *The Downfall of the Liberal Party, 1914–35* (London, 1966), p. 210.

[15]Lammers, *Munich,* pp. 12, 51.

[16](Cambridge, 1975), with full references; (Chicago, 1977), without; the book is a sequel to Cowling's *The Impact of Labour* (London, 1971).

narrowly upon the minutiae of everyday political life, reconstructing in detail the private universes of individual politicians, treating each as if he were, in Malcolm Muggeridge's words, "a separate particle of life, with eternity before and behind, coming solitary into the world, and solitary departing from it,"[17] and assuming that in the meantime everyone was so preoccupied with the immediate as to be incapable of abstracting principles or even specific interests from the whirl of daily events. Politics is not about ideas, principles, or abiding interests, class or otherwise. It is about people, maneuvering for advantage, taking chances, testing the winds, ganging up, falling out, and occasionally trotting out reasons or evoking principles to justify their activities. So absolutely does Cowling believe in the role of personality in history that he reduces everything to an interplay of personalities.

Cowling also insists upon "der Primat der Innenpolitik." A rigorous subordination of foreign affairs to domestic politics is essential to his argument. Foreign policy was the mirror of the domestic competition for power; Hitler mattered only insofar as he registered on the field of party conflict. To Cowling, Hitler's intentions in the East and elsewhere, whatever they were, were no threat to British interests or its empire and were most probably designed "to secure relations with the army and the German public." In any case, British politicians did not deal with the world on its own terms. They registered it passively. "The problem [of Hitler] was defined psephologically."[18] Thus one finds the explanation for what the British government did about Hitler in the routinized competition between political parties and among rival elements of the dominant Conservative party.

Through this back door Cowling introduces a kind of class analysis. Unlike the Marxist studies Lammers attacks, in which policy is a direct extension of ruling-class interests, Cowling treated class as a rhetorical epiphenomenon of the competition among politicians for place and position. Class was the language by which they ordered their power struggles. Like the German

[17]Malcolm Muggeridge, *The Thirties* (London, 1967), p. 161–62.
[18]Cowling, *Hitler,* pp. 9, 1.

menace, class conflict was not real, except insofar as Cowling's personages took it to be real. Class issues indirectly shaped British foreign policy by establishing the domestic terms of political combat. Thus appeasement was not primarily a policy, right or wrong, for reaching conclusions with Hitler but rather a strategy for preempting Labour and protecting Tory advantages at home. For Cowling, Halifax was "the embodiment of Conservative wisdom who decided [at some time between Munich and Prague] that Hitler must be obstructed because Labour could not otherwise be resisted."[19]

Ultimately Cowling fails to establish that the ragtag bands of Mosleyites, dissident Liberals, League of Nations enthusiasts, and Labour fragments constituted a serious threat to the government majority after 1931 or, in opposition, ever exerted much influence over government policy. Psephological pressures were weak and generally amorphous. When he turns to the factional rivalries within the ruling coalition, however, Cowling displays a surer touch. Here he is dealing not with electoral politics or conflict between classes but with government politics and arguments among elements of an established elite over competing strategies of class defense. The implicit issue in the debates and factional maneuvering among leaders and would-be leaders of the coalition was how best to orchestrate survival, how to perpetuate political control over the state and economic control over productive forces, how to protect the financial structure and the currency from political interference and popular control, and how to maintain the mechanisms of capital accumulation and social order.

Class interests were pivotal in these discussions, and Cowling rightly treats what is commonly called political history in terms of the maneuvering among rival factions of the dominant class. He fails to recognize that electoral combat alone did not define the entire political universe and that, in particular, foreign and defense policies were a function as much of bureaucratic struggles as of party politics. But his treatment of factional competition does

[19]Ibid., pp. 9, 290–91.

transcend the monolithic conception of class, and of state policy as the simple extension of solidary class interests which unimaginative Marxist analysis often employs and which Lammers criticizes in caricature. Cowling, who is certainly no Marxist, shows how the general interests of a dominant class rarely superseded the factional struggles among constituent elements whose particular interests were far from harmonious and not easily organized. Class interests were necessarily plural, with compromise formulations constantly evolving. Alliances among class fractions and strategies of class defense were always in flux, subject to review and amendment, open to challenge by rival combinations from within the same class.

To conceive of classes as internally fractious, engaged in a self-defining formulation of interests and ruling combinations through internal competition and argument, is to reformulate the problem of conflict between classes and to raise anew the problem of the relationship between classes and state policy. Here the diverse theoretical literature, both Marxist and non-Marxist, that has flourished in recent years may be of help.[20] In dismissing class analysis, Lammers was assuming an instrumentalist relationship between class and state in which the state acts as an executive arm of the dominant class, whose interests are, presumably, solidary and self-evident. Recent theoretical discussions, however, have ascribed to the modern state a certain relative autonomy from the particularist interests of the classes and class fractions of civil society. E. P. Thompson has put the central point plainly:

> Moments in which governing institutions appear as the direct, emphatic, and unmediated organs of a "ruling class" are exceedingly rare, as well as transient. More often these institutions operate with a good deal of autonomy, and sometimes with distinct

[20]Alan Wolfe, *The Limits of Legitimacy* (New York, 1977); Theda Skocpol, *States and Social Revolutions* (Cambridge, 1978); Gianfranco Poggi, *The Development of the Modern State* (Stanford, Calif., 1978); Ralph Miliband, *The State in Capitalist Society* (New York, 1969); Nicos Poulantzas, *State, Power, Socialism* (London, 1978); the exchange between Miliband and Poulantzas in Robin Blackburn, ed., *Ideology in Social Science* (London, 1972); Ernesto Laclau, "The Specificity of the Political," *Politics and Ideology in Marxist Theory* (London, 1977).

interests of their own, within a general context of class power which prescribes the limits beyond which this autonomy cannot be safely stretched.[21]

Departments of state are rarely neutral or passive agencies, and the state itself is neither an isolated control tower full of switches and levers at the command of the ruling class or class fraction nor a referee above the fray enforcing rules evenhandedly upon all factions. It is an essential participant in the process of constructing governing blocs and compiling political strategies. Bureaucracies and civil servants represent competing interests and help define the language of fractional combat and the negative constraints within which state policies are formulated.

How class power expresses itself in practice, how class interests shape or constrain policy indirectly, and how political parties, politicians, and state servants mediate between class interests and state policy are worth further exploration. The remainder of this article looks first at the role of parties in organizing class interests and in mediating tension between class interest and state policy, using the example of British politics in the 1920s. It then examines how state agencies and bureaucratic struggles reproduce fractional, often competing class interests and how the resolution of interagency conflict often serves to organize class interest and establish the parameters of state policy. A detailed analysis of the 1934–35 battle between Admiralty and Treasury that established the limits on British rearmament illustrates these themes. The final section seeks to locate Chamberlain's attempt to appease Hitler within this analytical framework.

Eckart Kehr once remarked that "the crucial precondition for the bourgeois nation state's acceptance by its inhabitants is a generally shared confidence that the state's actions are not guided by class interests."[22] Stanley Baldwin's political career rested upon his skill in organizing class interests into packages that appealed

---

[21] *The Poverty of Theory and Other Essays* (London, 1978), p. 48.

[22] Eckart Kehr, *Economic Interest, Militarism, and Foreign Policy* (Berkeley, Calif., 1977), p. 50.

to the commonweal. Although his party did try to get rid of him several times, Baldwin turned out to be a very successful party manager, a sort of secular pastor to the Conservative cause during a difficult transition. For Baldwin the party was not merely an instrument for organizing power or implementing policy but the very embodiment of English virtue. Party unity was therefore "of supreme importance," and Baldwin feared "party division on foreign policy" above all else. Baldwin, in Baron Francis-Williams's words, "was always able to put Party before Country in the sincere conviction that in so doing he was serving the permanent interests of the British people."[23]

Baldwin's experiences between 1908 and 1922 shaped his outlook on party. As a backbencher he had observed the challenge of Labour, the uproar over Ireland, and the impact of the World War on the British political system. He heard the talk of coalition which dominated bourgeois politics in those years, and he was a marginal participant in the Lloyd George coalition during the war. Aside from victory in the war, the basic appeal of coalitionism was generational.[24] It gave political voice to the "inspired and concentrated clamour" of "the last imperial bourgeoisie, the generation of the Great Depression." Coalition politics offered both a vehicle for national unity above party and class and a pathway to the top that got around the traditional clubs and party caucuses. H. G. Wells called it a "revolt of the competent" that reflected the more progressive elements derived from the pre-war Fabians and social-imperialist Co-efficients. But the insurgency had a darker side that expressed "the blank recalcitrance of ruling or aspiring elites to any further extension of democratic institutions" and aspired to "a more disciplined and regimented society based on the principles of National Efficiency." The

[23]Baron Francis-Williams, *A Pattern of Rulers* (London, 1965), p. 24. Middlemas and Barnes dispute this (*Baldwin,* pp. 96-97), but, as Barbara Malament has observed, Middlemas and Barnes also tend to equate national interest with Conservative party advantage: "Baldwin Re-restored?" *JMH* 44, no. 1 (1972).

[24]Semmel, *Imperialism and Social Reform* (New York, 1968); Goeffrey Searle, *The Quest for National Efficiency* (Berkeley, Calif., 1971); Robert Scally, *The Origins of the Lloyd George Coalition* (Princeton, N.J., 1975).

Milnerites, Tariff Reformers, Lloyd George Radicals, Liberal Imperialists, and Fabian Socialists who constructed the wartime coalition were not reactionaries or counterrevolutionaries in the Continental sense, even though they increasingly found "traditional democratic values dangerous impediments to preparing the society for modern modes of production and modern warfare."[25] Their goal was preemptive: the defense of the social order against Labour. They were convinced that failure would dissolve British society into a struggle of attrition between revolution and reaction.

Although formed to win the war, the coalition of 1916 was meant to survive the peace. Lloyd George's strategy for holding together Liberal and Conservative elements without the galvanizing effect of war combined confrontation with social reform in a rally against class challengers and economic stagnation that Robert Scally has called "a socialism of the Right, of order, hierarchy, and bureaucratic control," aimed at limiting class concessions to Labour.[26] But a rebellion of Conservative backbenchers in 1922 dashed the coalitionists' dream of an anti-Socialist Center party. The dissidents, led in the end by Bonar Law and Baldwin, disliked Lloyd George and the arrivist crassness of the coalition. They disapproved of his policies in Ireland, at Chanak, and over social reconstruction. They held quite different views on the problem of postwar recovery, preferring to restore prewar normalcy rather than construct a "land fit for heroes." Above all, they recognized that a continuation of the coalition as a centrist bloc required that "the effective hold of the parties in Parliament be broken."[27] In his effort to consolidate a bourgeois defense under his own leadership, Lloyd George became, in Baldwin's words, a "dynamic force," threatening to shatter the unity of the Conservative party and, as many saw it, weaken the party's ability to resist Labour. "Normalcy" meant first and foremost reconsolidating the Conservative party.

The break at the Carlton Club assembly in October 1922

[25]Scally, *Origins,* pp. 4–5, 10.
[26]Ibid., p. 4.
[27]Ibid., p. 369 and passim.

separated the party from its leading personalities, most of whom remained loyal to the coalition. For three years the Tory "second eleven" led the party in the wilderness. Their economic program, an orthodox mix of retrenchment, austerity, and tax reduction, appealed to the core of the party but offered no solutions to trade stagnation or unemployment. Without a patina of Liberals the government looked reactionary. Although this realignment tended to clarify the class divisions between political parties, it offered no ground for rallying Tory resistance. The one plausible party platform was protection, which Baldwin tried with disastrous results in 1923. Ultimately the party needed a language, "something to say that did not just involve resistance to working-class demands and which would save [it] being branded as an instrument of the rich against the poor."[28] It needed policies that, while serving class interests, addressed national concerns and leaders who could "talk of something—almost anything—apart from the function the party had to perform." By 1924, Baldwin had emerged, talking of pastures, rural pleasures, solid English virtues, and class cooperation and harmony. This rhetoric set him apart from Lloyd George and from the response to Labour characteristic of the coalitionists: preemptive reforms and fighting words. Baldwin's concern for party unity, his parsonlike attention to the House of Commons, and his moderate, democratic tone enabled the Conservative party to compete successfully for the votes of the political center, that middle multitude of old Liberals and new voters that constituted the swing element in British elections after the war.[29]

[28]Cowling, *Impact of Labour,* pp. 421-23. For other accounts of the period see Trevor Wilson, *Downfall,* pp. 265ff.; Middlemas and Barnes, *Baldwin,* pp. 125-249.

[29]Perhaps the outstanding social change of the interwar years was the growth of the service, or tertiary, sector of the British economy: white-collar workers, civil servants, bureaucrats, retailers, and those involved in consumer services and entertainment. Many were women, many were of working class or petty bourgeois backgrounds, and most got the vote under the postwar franchise reform. See Sidney Pollard, *The Development of the British Economy, 1914-50* (London, 1962) p. 267; Arthur Marwick, "The British Elite in the Interwar Years," in Gerhard Weinberg, ed., *Transformation of a Continent* (Minneapolis, Minn., 1975); David Butler, *The Electoral System in Britain, 1918-1951* (Oxford, 1953), chap. 2.

There was, in fact, considerable tactical collusion between Conservatives and Labour after 1924. A common desire to appear harmless brought Baldwin and MacDonald together, the one a temperamental Conservative, the other a temperamental Socialist, both woolly and platitudinous. They shared a suspicion of Lloyd George, an anxiety about the revival of centrist alternatives, and a common interest in grinding the remnants of liberalism to bits. They vied for the center vote with competitive moderation. They both needed a revival of prosperity, Baldwin because the legitimacy of success was the best defense of the economic order, MacDonald because prosperity would reestablish the economic context in which his party's Socialist theories would work.[30] Their strategies for recovery were not materially different. The intellectual universe in which they both operated was defined by the orthodox economics of the governor of the Bank of England ("Mr. Norman's Line"), and this ensured a certain uninventive collaboration. The return to the gold standard in 1925 defined the political map for the remainder of the decade and beyond. Labour occupied the terrain of responsible opposition, absorbing in exchange lower wages and high rates of unemployment, especially in the export industries. The Conservatives accepted continued industrial stagnation and derived a certain backhanded unity from the rigors of gold, discovering in austerity new opportunities to extend their political base and organize key interests. The shadow boxing between MacDonald and Baldwin and their common rejection of economic experiments expressed the political stalemate that had developed between the two parties and the classes they tried to represent.

Both leaders faced dissent within their own parties over economic policy, usually from the younger generation, whose thinking ran toward greater state intervention in economic activity and greater priority for the domestic economy.[31] The Liberal

---

[30]The best discussion of economic theories and the political parties is Robert Skidelsky, *Politicians and the Slump* (London, 1967).

[31]On the dissidents see Donald Winch, *Economics and Policy* (Fontana ed., 1972), p. 199; Skidelsky, *Politicians,* chap. 2; Hyde, *Baldwin,* pp. 274–75, 311–12;

"Yellow Book" of 1928, called *Britain's Industrial Future,* captured the drift of radical thinking in suggesting that the decline of export industries was permanent, that the only solution to unemployment was to divert "to home development . . . capital normally devoted to foreign investment." As a necessary corollary the state would have to exercise closer supervision over investment decisions and the Bank of England.[32] Such ideas were not welcome to the political leaders of either party, if only because Lloyd George had a hand in devising them. His efforts to revive Liberal fortunes in 1929 with an economic blueprint for managed capitalism proved attractive to dissidents in all parties, and in this Baldwin felt the undertow of coalitionist thinking in the center. The economic crisis of 1930–31 momentarily opened avenues of access for the economic radicals which formation of the National Coalition and its massive electoral victory in the fall of 1931 then slammed shut. The gap between Socialist Philip Snowden and Chamberlain was smaller than that separating them both from Oswald Mosley or Harold Macmillan. Orthodoxy closed ranks in the emergency to exclude innovation. This was a watershed in what Robert Skidelsky has called "the real story of the domestic politics of the interwar period, . . . the defeat of the economic radicals by the economic conservatives."[33]

Within Conservative ranks the deepest structural split during the 1920s ran along the old divide between finance and industry

---

Middlemas and Barnes, *Baldwin,* pp. 522–23; Gilbert, *Churchill,* 5:320–21. Harold Macmillan's writings were representative of young Tory thinking: *Industry and the State* (London, 1927) and *Reconstruction* (London, 1933). See also Arthur Marwick, "Middle Opinion in the Thirties: Planning, Progress, and Political Agreement," *EHR* 79 (1964); L. P. Carpenter, "Corporatism in Britain, 1930–45," *JCH* 11, no. 1 (1976).

[32]John Campbell, "The Renewal of Liberalism: Liberalism Without Liberals," in Gillian Peele and Chris Cook, eds., *The Politics of Reappraisal, 1918–1939* (London, 1975), pp. 88–113, esp. pp. 102–104. The sequel, the so-called "Orange Book," *We Can Conquer Unemployment,* appeared in 1929.

[33]Skidelsky, *Politicians,* p. 11; see also N. Thompson, *The Anti-Appeasers* (Oxford, 1971), pp. 11–13.

which had once found expression in the division between Liberal and Conservative, free trade versus protection, but which had migrated into Tory ranks with the demise of the Liberal party.[34] After the defeat of protection in 1923, tariff agitation subsided. But the City-Bank of England-Treasury axis continued to exert enormous influence within the party and among those Liberal remnants the party leadership wished to cultivate. The great aim of this financial interest was to restore the international banking and currency system, including the gold standard at fixed parity, the prewar rates of exchange, and the free movement of capital within the world economy. This required state action. It also provoked dissension within the Conservative party. Industrial and protectionist interests opposed the return to gold because it meant higher export prices, tighter overseas markets, scarcer investment capital owing to the need to maintain high interest rates, and a general setback for the cause of empire consolidation based on tariffs and imperial preference. But manufacturing interests had no alternative except protection, already defeated. They eventually acquiesced in the decision to restore gold at prewar parity because they shared the assumptions of the City and the Treasury that financial dislocation was the cause of trade stagnation and that the period of readjustment, while painful, would be brief.[35]

The government helped industry by coating the bitter pill with budget cuts, derating schemes, safeguards for vulnerable industries, and consistent support for industrialists as they passed the pain of readjustment to their workers in the form of wage cuts. For all of Baldwin's modernist talk about economies through reorganization and industrial efficiency, the government never pushed this upon the owners, even in the notoriously disorganized coal industry. When industry took the simpler expedient of slashing wages to bring down costs, the government backed it, not without hesitation,

---

[34]See especially Semmel, *Imperialism*, pp. 136–50.

[35]See Winch, *Economics and Policy*, pp. 75–92; Skidelsky, *Politicians*, pp. 25–32; Robert Rhodes James, *Churchill: A Study in Failure* (London, 1970), pp. 177–79; Middlemas and Barnes, *Baldwin*, on his faith in orthodoxy, pp. 86–87, 129–48, 155–57, 286–88, and on the return to gold, pp. 302–307.

even to the point of a general strike. This was the price of assuring party solidarity on a crucial aspect of economic policy. One faction absorbed the priorities of another and, in exchange, called upon the state for assistance in fobbing off the consequences of that policy upon a more vulnerable segment of society. Baldwin's handling of the General Strike of 1926 was a masterpiece of political maneuver that successfully converted tradeunion resistance to wage cuts into a threat to "the community," and the strike into an unconstitutional assault upon the state.[36] He emerged from the crisis with a unified party, the allegiance of industrialists, and broad popular acclaim.

The successful restoration of the gold standard created an external barrier against domestic social change. The beauty of the system in Tory eyes was its automatic operation, its immunity from Socialist tampering.[37] The Conservative government effectively reestablished British overseas finance as an "offshore island," linked to the City and the Bank of England, which could be called upon to discipline the domestic economy and to restrict social and political options.[38] The gold standard and the economic policies required to defend it tied prosperity and social welfare to external forces—the condition of world trade or international relations, the workings of world finance, or the movement of capital in overseas money markets—and disassociated economic conditions at home from what a government could do or its electors wanted done. The government's role became one of absorbing and distributing the consequences of this overseas priority.

[36]On the General Strike see Patrick Renshaw, *Nine Days That Shook Britain* (Garden City, N.Y., 1976); Julian Symons, *The General Strike* (London, 1957); Christopher Farman, "The Defeat of the General Strike," in Peel and Cook, eds., *Politics of Reappraisal,* pp. 64–87. Middlemas and Barnes, *Baldwin,* chap. 15, is a clumsy defense.

[37]"The implications . . . were that democratically elected governments in a highly-developed political system should not be trusted with matters involving currency; they were best left to a small dedicated elite, working *outside the political arena*" [emphasis added] (Winch, *Economics and Policy,* p. 92).

[38]See the story of the May Committee of 1931 in Skidelsky, *Politicians,* pp. 374–88.

The economic policies of the Baldwin government in support of the pound served in turn to consolidate the Conservative party's political base. Protecting the value of money, which was the effect of pegging gold at prewar parity, proved extremely reassuring to ordinary creditors and bondholders whose debts and interest would be paid off at prewar values. Similarly, the careful, almost obsessive handling of the national debt, necessary to inspire confidence in the pound, may have been a heavy burden on the budget and may have transferred wealth from the active to the inactive sectors of the economy, but it did much to consolidate Conservative support, especially with the rentier class so important in the constituency organizations.[39] Tory tax policies worked in the same direction. Not only were income taxes steadily reduced, but the lightest burden of general taxation fell upon that middling segment of modest means who were salaried and fully employed, politically reliable if protected, and prone elsewhere to study "fascist" alternatives.[40] This is not to suggest that fiscal policies foiled the development of "fascism" in interwar Britain, or to dismiss the importance of image, mood, and rhetoric in winning votes. It is to illustrate the continuous transaction between party and state in organizing and protecting class interests and to suggest that Baldwin's principal image, "Safety First," was grounded in his party's recovery strategy and the economic policies it permitted and was thus a vital element in the process of organizing and articulating class interest. Even when the strategy collapsed along with the gold standard in 1931, the political image of reliability and the social foundations of the party remained secure. Baldwin could thus turn disaster into the triumph of the "doctor's mandate."

MacDonald's position was far less tenable. The restoration of the gold standard constituted a political trap for his party. Like everyone else, Labour wanted recovery, and, like everyone else, it had no original ideas about how to achieve it. Consequently, when the Treasury and the Tory government charted the road to

[39]Winch, *Economics and Policy,* pp. 97ff.; Marwick, "British Elite," p. 160.
[40]Pollard, *British Economy,* pp. 206, 254–60.

recovery, Labour's only strategy was to resist. Resistance to lower wages involved the labor movement in a series of grinding strikes and a confrontation with the state, which it lost. In defeat Labour politicians accepted unemployment rates of 10 to 20 percent and the palliative of state support for the jobless as the price of political respectability and their own failure to devise alternative solutions.[41] In effect Labour accepted the terms of political combat its opponents had established. In the tactical collusion between the parties that Labour's moderation fostered, the Tories always enjoyed the upper hand. Especially with respect to unemployment the policies that Labour's constituency required were beyond the pale of orthodoxy. MacDonald and his colleagues, playing by Conservative rules, progressively lost touch with their popular base. In the crisis of 1931 the Labour Party split, as had the Tories in 1922, along the divide between leaders and led. MacDonald's forlorn visits to Lady Londonderry's parties and his imprisonment at the head of the National Coalition only made obvious what had been a long-standing condition. Labour had no alternative to a plan of recovery that precluded experiments, conformed to the class requirements of the Conservative party's constituency, and embedded the labor movement in a sterile strategy of endless anticipation, waiting for prosperity to return. It was the political equivalent of the trenches. It was the "war of position" Antonio Gramsci proposed as a metaphor for class conflict in Western societies in this period. A war of position required not brilliant thrusts at the enemy but long-term containment. It brought out the unimaginative generals. Holding out involved the continuous mobilization of power, the control of key salients over long periods, and the cultivation of important allies and resources. The operation of the system as a whole became more important than direct action against the actual class enemy, for the strategic object in a war of position was not only to win engagements or

---

[41]Eric Hobsbawm, *Industry and Empire* (Pelican ed., 1969), p. 208; see also Pollard, *British Economy,* pp. 272–79; Taylor, *English History,* pp. 236–38; Skidelsky, *Politicians.*

retain power but to cultivate and husband the sources of power themselves.

The department closest to those sources of power, the most powerful department of state in the interwar period, was the Treasury. Its control over the budget was virtually absolute, its ties with the City and the Bank of England intimate, and its orthodoxy common wisdom throughout the political system. All three Conservative prime ministers in this period saw service at the Exchequer.[42] Although the collapse of the gold standard in September 1931 destroyed the official strategy of trade revival and tore a great hole in the web of international finance, it did not diminish the Treasury's influence over policy. The Treasury's antidote for depression was the traditional medicine of retrenchment and balanced budgets, to which the national government added a dose of protection. As usual, policymakers were preoccupied with the export sector and with Britain's place in the world economy, and, as usual, the domestic economy absorbed the brunt of this external priority. The largest parliamentary majority in modern history smothered dissent and bore the government along its unremarkable course. The grinding struggle over the principles governing the distribution of assistance to the long-term unemployed, (centered on the Means Test) and the dismal stagnation of the export industries, redubbed "special areas," bore witness to the government's fragmented and ineffective response to the economic crisis. Recovery, when it came, had little to do with government initiatives.[43]

The Treasury exercised an equally determinant voice in rearmament policy. Recent research has made it plain that there was no more powerful check upon the rate or extent of British rearma-

---

[42]Bonar Law under Lloyd George, Baldwin under Bonar Law, and Neville Chamberlain (as well as Winston Churchill) under Baldwin.

[43]See Winch, *Economics and Policy,* p. 208; Noreen Branson and Margot Heinemann, *Britain in the Thirties* (New York, 1971); Skidelsky, *Politicians;* Harry Richardson, *Economic Recovery in Britain, 1932-39* (London, 1967), and his essay in Richardson and Derek Aldcroft, eds., *The British Economy, 1870-1939* (London, 1969).

ment in the 1930s than ministerial concern about public finance.[44] Everyone feared that heavy expenditure on weapons or serious deficits in the budget would generate inflation, raise taxes, diminish exports, disrupt balances of payment, weaken confidence, and in general upset the recovery they all believed, incorrectly, was the consequence of government action. Depression finance cut deeply into defense spending, which reached an all-time low in 1932. In the same year the so-called ten-year rule, which had governed military budgets for over a decade, collapsed. This rule assumed for the purpose of framing service estimates that there would be no major war for ten years. It was less an exercise in prophecy than a highly convenient political device for holding down service demands without arguing over strategic assumptions. The Japanese invasion of Manchuria and the Shanghai crisis of 1932 made the rule untenable. But, in abandoning it, the Treasury left behind a trail of caveats, insisting that Britain was not in a position "financially or economically to wage a major war" and that such a contingency, being "beyond the financial capacity of the country to provide against," could not be accepted.[45]

In 1933, when the Admiralty requested additional provision for a Far Eastern emergency, the Treasury countered that economic risks were "by far the most serious and urgent that the country has to face and . . . other risks must run until the country has had time and opportunity to recuperate."[46] When the Defence Requirements Committee (DRC), a high-level panel of experts appointed to review the defense situation, recommended spending £71 million in five years on service deficiencies, Chamberlain retorted: " . . . to put it bluntly . . . we are presented with proposals impossible to carry out."[47] In discussions of defense policy during the spring and summer of 1934, Chamberlain led

[44]The best accounts are Robert Shay, *British Rearmament in the Thirties: Politics and Profits* (Princeton, N.J., 1977) and Gibbs, *Strategy,* vol. 1, esp. pp. 279–319. See also F. Coghlan, "Armaments, Economic Policy and Appeasement: Background to British Foreign Policy, 1931–37," *History* 57 (1972: 204–16.

[45]Chamberlain, memorandum, 11 March 1932, CID 1087-B [CP 104(32)].

[46]Chamberlain, memorandum, 15 February 1933, CP 25(33).

[47]Chamberlain, memorandum, 20 June 1934, DC(M)(32)120.

the search for political alternatives that would limit liabilities. In the end he blocked expenditure on an army expeditionary force and the navy's £67 million building program. Throughout Chamberlain believed that his role was "to hold the balance between rigid orthodoxy and a fatal disregard for sound principles."[48] As the pressure of German rearmament continued to force British expansion, he and his Treasury advisers stood their ground, questioning expenditures, pressing for diplomatic initiatives to neutralize potential enemies, delaying resort to defense loans, imposing and defending ceilings on defense spending, and upholding a ban on interference with private industry. Until 1939 the Treasury "inspired and directed" the main lines of rearmament policy and "made it virtually impossible to insure that the resources available for defence were put to optimal use."[49]

The Treasury case rested on several assumptions. Economic stability was allegedly as important as planes, ships, and cannon—a claim Hitler would have laughed at. Britain's finances and credit rating, based on the stability of its export economy and balance of payments, would in theory allow Britain to outlast its enemies and supply its allies in a long war. The drawback of this strategy was that Britain could fall victim to a "knockout blow" before its "latent strength" could affect the outcome. Some military preparedness was thus necessary. But it was essential that the strain that preparedness imposed not weaken the nation's capacity actually to wage war. To run up great debts, neglect the balance of payments, increase taxation, or otherwise disturb the financial order through rearmament would destroy that "fourth arm of defence . . . without which purely military effort would be of no avail." The problem, then, was to strike a balance between fighting power and staying power. "If we were to interrupt and break down the process of the industry of peace-time," declared Minister for the Coordination of Defence Sir Thomas Inskip in 1936, "we should run the risk of destroying the financial fabric of the nation." Diverting industrial capacity to rearmament might inter-

---

[48]Keith Middlemas, *Diplomacy of Illusion* (London, 1972), p. 57.
[49]Shay, *British Rearmament,* pp. 3–4; see also Gibbs, *Strategy,* pp. 275–77.

fere with exports, upset the balance of payments, and weaken the pound. Similar logic ruled out heavy taxation, which the Treasury feared would impede recovery.[50] Defense loans were equally taboo. They increased the national debt and weakened credit. The Treasury was particularly anxious not to build up a military establishment on loans and special taxes that could not then be maintained out of ordinary revenues. Treasury logic was circular: the object of preparation for war was to avoid war. Therefore, assuming that war would not happen, it was important in preparing for war not to stray too far from the paths of peacetime normalcy. The conclusion was paradoxical: limitation on defense spending was essential to full preparedness.

The incompatibility of preparedness and financial stability—as the Treasury understood it—produced a major Admiralty-Treasury confrontation in 1934. Chancellor of the Exchequer Neville Chamberlain challenged the navy's building program and the strategic premise behind it, namely, the Admiralty's ambition to establish a Far Eastern capability. The issue was not new. The two departments had been sparring over it for years: the Admiralty "always had a 'bee in its bonnet' about Japan."[51] From the time of Admiral John Jellicoe's tour of the Pacific in 1919, naval planners had considered it "accepted policy that we must be prepared for a war with Japan."[52] Jellicoe's initial plan for a two-ocean imperial navy proved prohibitively expensive, and in 1921 the Admiralty settled for the Washington Treaty structure and the so-called

[50]See Gibbs, *Strategy,* pp. 282ff., 302; R. A. C. Parker, "Economics, Rearmament, and Foreign Policy: The United Kingdom Before 1939—A Preliminary Study," *JCH* 10, no. 4 (1975).

[51]Stanhope, minute, 14 March 1934, FO 371/17596, A2176. The basic work on the interwar navy is Stephen Roskill, *Naval Policy Between the Wars,* 2 vols. (London, 1968, 1976); for the Treasury-Admiralty controversy of 1925 see Middlemas and Barnes, *Baldwin,* pp. 317–41; for the 1934 conflict my dissertation, "Search for Security." Gibbs, *Strategy,* is the best treatment of naval rearmament.

[52]Director of Plans, minute, 3 November 1921, Adm 116/3604. On Jellicoe's mission see Roskill, *Naval Policy,* 1:275–88; D. C. Watt, "Imperial Defence Policy and Imperial Foreign Policy, 1911–1939: A Neglected Paradox?" *Journal of Commonwealth Studies* 1 (1963): 226–81; Frederick Dreyer, *The Sea Heritage* (London, 1955), pp. 240–41.

one-power standard, the principle of parity with the United States. This standard, according to the Committee of Imperial Defence,

> was satisfied if our fleet, wherever situated, is equal to the fleet of any other nation, wherever situated, provided that arrangements are made from time to time in different parts of the world, according as the international situation requires, to enable the local forces to maintain the situation against vital and irreparable damage, pending the arrival of the Main Fleet, and to give the Main Fleet on arrival sufficient mobility.[53]

Since "the most probable opponent [was] assumed, unofficially, to be Japan rather than the United States," the formula left ample margin to meet the Japanese contingency, and the Admiralty made its strategic dispositions accordingly.[54] By 1924 the navy had perfected a master plan for sending the main fleet from home waters to the Far East in the event of an emergency. This plan became an article of faith in the navy, a strategy as firmly fixed, as untested, and ultimately as unrealistic as the air force's devotion to the strategic-bombing deterrent.[55]

Sending the fleet east meant securing the naval position in Europe. For the Admiralty this required "a sufficient deterrent to keep France in her proper place when our Fleet is away."[56] The official one-power standard became in practice a de facto two-power standard keyed to the combined fleets of Japan and France. On this basis the Admiralty computed its minimum requirement for seventy cruisers. Churchill tried unsuccessfully to overturn this figure in 1925. In 1930 a Labour government, determined to reach agreement with the United States, imposed upon the navy a flat reduction in its cruiser minimum, from seventy to fifty. The

[53]CID Meeting no. 198, 30 March 1925, Cab 2/4; see also CID Paper 900-B, July 1928; Gibbs, *Strategy,* pp. 19–31.

[54]Captain Barry Domville (Deputy Director of Plans), in Arthur Marder, *From Dreadnought to Scapa Flow,* vol. 5 (London, 1970), p. 238; Roskill, *Naval Policy,* vol. 1, chap. 9, and files 2405, 2757, Adm 116/3195, 116/3311.

[55]Gibbs, *Strategy,* pp. 50–51.

[56]The Admiralty's fear of France is an often overlooked aspect of the Far Eastern priority; see, for example, Plans Memorandum, October 1931, Adm 1/8748/139; Hankey, memorandum, 29 November 1931, MO(31)8, Cab 63/44; Little, minute, 14 March 1934, Adm 116/2999.

Admiralty never reconciled itself to this defeat. After barely preserving the balance of power in the Pacific at the price of serious British concessions in cruiser strength, the Admiralty insisted that the French-Italian rivalry in the Mediterranean now jeopardized British supremacy in European waters, the essential precondition for maintaining the imperial position in the Far East. In 1932 the Admiralty declared its cruiser force "inadequate" for a "Locarno war" against France.[57] Two years later Admiral Sir Alfred Chatfield, the new first sea lord, warned that the French cruiser fleet was now Britain's numerical equal and that if the main fleet were sent to Singapore "we should have a mere handful of cruisers to meet the onslaughts of the vast French cruiser force on our Atlantic and Mediterranean trade."[58]

Chatfield was determined to achieve a two-ocean capability. To do this, he had to overturn the London Treaty limits and secure a reformulation of the treaty structure to permit a general expansion of the British fleet, especially cruisers. These goals he pursued at every opportunity.[59] He claimed that a two-ocean, two-power standard was necessary to provide a "force of sufficient strength to ensure security for the Empire and its essential interests," while maintaining supremacy in home waters.[60] As precedent he invoked the two-power standard of 1889; not for nothing has Stephen Roskill, the navy's sympathetic historian, noted a "nineteenth-century ring" to the Admiralty's Far Eastern strategy. But precedents were misleading. For the classic two-power standard had involved only European naval powers. In the nineteenth century Britain had commanded the seas of the world through its absolute supremacy in European waters. The appearance of the American and Japanese navies in the early twentieth century had revolutionized naval strategy. To secure "the Empire and its essential interests" now required a shield in the Far East as

---

[57]Roskill, *Naval Policy,* 2:80.

[58]Chatfield, memorandum, 8 February 1934, Adm 116/3373.

[59]See Roskill, *Naval Policy,* 2:170, 286–89, 326–27, 346; Gibbs, *Strategy,* chap. 9; Minutes of the Defense Requirements Committee, 1934, Cab 16/109; Report of the Defence Requirements Committee, 28 February 1934, CP 64(34), Cab 24/247.

[60]Roskill, *Naval Policy,* 2:286.

well as in Europe. Thus application of the two-power standard in the interwar years constituted a new departure which the invocation of traditional principles barely concealed. A global two-power standard was possible only within a treaty structure of some kind. Even then, construction and maintenance of a fleet of that size entailed expenditures far beyond what either a Conservative or a Labour government was prepared to sustain.[61]

The Treasury never had much sympathy for the Admiralty's Far Eastern priorities. It repeatedly challenged them during the 1920s, and by the end of the decade it had neatly trussed up naval ambitions with the ten-year rule and the London Treaty limits. These political barriers collapsed in the early 1930s. The Admiralty pointed to Japanese expansionism and renewed its pressure for more ships. The Defence Requirements Committee inclined to the Admiralty view: Germany was "the ultimate potential enemy against whom our 'long range' defence policy must be directed," but Japan remained the most immediate and acute threat.[62] Sir Maurice Hankey, the influential secretary of the cabinet and chairman of the DRC, was determined to play down the urgency of the German threat in favor of a balanced rearmament effort for overall imperial defense. But when the DRC report went to the cabinet in the spring of 1934 with the Admiralty building program attached as an appendix, Chamberlain was no more disposed to approve than his predecessors had been. The Disarmament Conference was collapsing. German rearmament had clearly begun. The air menace alarmed public and parliamentary opinion. The government, in some disarray, faced an imminent general election. Chamberlain concluded that his first priority was to restore the salary cuts imposed on government employees and to remit the special taxes levied during the 1931 emergency. His second priority was to assuage popular anxiety about aerial bombardment with a provision for the air

---

[61]See Gerald Graham, *Politics of Naval Supremacy* (New York, 1965); Arthur Marder, *The Anatomy of Sea Power* (Hamden, Conn., 1964); Gibbs, *Strategy,* pp. 14–15, 23–24, 117–20; Richard Koebner and S. H. Schmidt, *Imperialism* (Cambridge, 1964), p. 189.

[62]Report of the DRC, 28 February 1934, CP 64(34), Cab 24/247.

force larger than the DRC's request. Beyond that he could offer
no guarantee of funds. Choices were necessary. Therefore, Chamberlain concluded, "we must postpone the idea of sending out
to-day a Fleet of capital ships capable of containing the Japanese
Fleet or meeting it in battle."[63]

Elaborating this position, the Treasury argued that an essential
precondition of imperial defense was the security of the home
islands, now menaced from the air. Unless Britain were first
engaged in a European war, Japan was not likely to attack imperial interests. Yet Chamberlain observed, "The division of our
forces so as to protect our Far Eastern interests, while prosecuting
a war in Europe, [would mean] that not only India, Hong-Kong
and Australasia would be in dire peril, but that we ourselves
would stand in far greater danger of destruction by a fully armed
and organized Germany."[64] Consequently, the essential task was
to prevent a European war. This required not preparations for a
two-front war but a major air program to deter Germany and
bring Hitler to terms. Britain needed to concentrate its imperial
resources in Europe. As in 1902 this meant reaching a settlement
with Japan in the Far East:

> We should say to Japan: "What do you want in China? Is it trade?
> If so, is there not enough for us both? We want you to do nothing
> detrimental to our trade in China. What China needs is development.
> Can we not leave you free to supply capital in one area while we
> are free in another?"[65]

Chamberlain believed that the Japanese menace was overrated
and, in any case, subject to elimination through political means.
To him the German menace was far more pressing, in part
because it was geographically closer, in part because "public
opinion is already alive ... to our deficiencies in air defence,"
and in part because provision against Germany promised to be

[63]Chamberlain, memorandum, 20 June 1934, DC(M) (32)120. For Warren
Fisher's thinking see DRC Paper no. 12, 29 January 1934, Cab 16/109; Fisher to
Chatfield, 11 July 1934, Cab 21/404.

[64]Feiling, *Chamberlain*, p. 253. The autumn 1934 letters from Fisher in the
Chatfield Papers are illuminating.

[65]NCM(35), 1st Meeting, 16 April 1934, Cab 29/147.

considerably cheaper than the Admiralty's Far Eastern program.[66]

For nearly a year Chamberlain and his colleagues at the Treasury pressed his demand for a diplomatic solution in the Far East based on a political rapprochement with Japan. In the end a powerful coalition of domestic opponents blocked the initiative. Not surprisingly, the Admiralty—which needed the Far Eastern commitment to justify its building plans—led the opposition. Eyres Monsell, the first lord, denounced Chamberlain's proposal as "shameful" and "revolutionary," a course "which was not advocated even by the Communists in this country." It meant "the virtual abandonment of the whole naval position, . . . the end of the sea power of the British Empire." Lord Hailsham (Douglas Hogg), the war minister, dismissed the Treasury case as "a policy of despair and defeatism." Hankey, writing to Baldwin, could not "conceive any alternative system of Defence . . . that is not based on our centuries-old assumption of sea-power."[67] In the autumn Jan Smuts and Lord Lothian (Phillip Kerr), backed editorially by Geoffrey Dawson at the *Times* and J. L. Garvin at the *Observer,* intervened against Chamberlain because they feared that his pro-Japanese line would disrupt Anglo-American relations and weaken the bond with the white dominions.[68] A policy that offended Canada and South Africa and promised to leave Australia and New Zealand without naval protection did not commend itself to most ministers. Walter Runciman, president of the Board of Trade, added a commercial note to the opposition; reviewing the fruitless talks between the Japanese and Lancashire textile manufacturers, he concluded that "the future finances of the country was [*sic*] largely dependent on the general trend of

[66]See NCM(35), Cab 29/148, 149; Chamberlain, memorandum, 1 September 1934, FO 371/18184, F6190; Cab 32(34)2, 25 September 1934; Simon and Chamberlain, memorandum, 16 October 1934, CP 223(34). *Foreign Relations of the United States, 1934,* 1:358-59, provides an American view of Chamberlain's initiative. See also Stephen Endicott, *Diplomacy and Enterprise: British China Policy, 1933-37.* (Manchester, B.C., 1975), pp. 70-75; Watt, *Personalities and Policies,* pp. 95-99.

[67]DC(M) (32), 50th Meeting, 25 June 1934, Cab 27/507; Hankey to Baldwin, 30 July 1934, Cab 21/398.

[68]Watt, *Personalities and Policies,* pp. 83-99.

world trade and naval strength was one factor which allowed us to negotiate with success."[69] George Sansom, the commercial counselor at the Tokyo Embassy and a recognized expert on Japan, agreed: "When I hear business men in Shanghai say, 'If we back Japan she will pull the chestnuts out of the fire for us,' my only answer is that when the operation is complete there will be no British chestnuts left."[70] This seems to have persuaded Sir John Simon, the foreign secretary, who was at first sorely tempted by the prospect of becoming the architect of Anglo-Japanese rapprochement.[71] Sansom's views also echoed those of the larger commercial interests in China outside the treaty ports, which early in 1935 urged the Treasury to "keep the flag flying in the Far East."[72] This lobbying, together with Sansom's letters, effectively neutralized the extremely pro-Japanese opinions which a mission of the Federation of British Industries brought back from a visit to Manchukuo and Japan at the end of the year and which Chamberlain circulated in support of his initiative. Gradually the Foreign Office, which was always "irrevocably opposed to any deal *a deux* with Japan," was able to reassert its more cautious line.[73] Sir Robert Vansittart, undersecretary of state for foreign affairs and the member of the Defence Requirements Committee with the darkest forebodings about Germany, always supported Hankey in "showing a tooth" to Japan in the Far East, and Anthony Eden, a rising voice in British foreign policy, declared at the beginning of the ministerial controversy that "it would be fatal to British interests to ignore the paramount claims of the Far

[69]DC(M) (32), 51st Meeting, 26 June 1934, Cab 27/507.

[70]Sansom, memorandum, 10 November 1934, FO 371/18184, F7162; see also Sansom's letter, 3 November 1934, F6577.

[71]Simon, minute, August 1934, FO 371/17598, A7695; see also Endicott, *Diplomacy and Enterprise,* pp. 65ff.

[72]Endicott, *Diplomacy and Enterprise,* pp. 89ff. The interests that made representations in London in early 1935 are listed in William Roger Louis, *British Strategy in the Far East, 1919-1939* (Oxford, 1971), pp. 228-29. The outlook of these larger capital interests was distinct from that of both the Residence Association in Shanghai and the Federation of British Industries mission to Japan in the fall of 1934, both of which were enthusiastically pro-Japanese (ibid., pp. 222-24).

[73]Vansittart, minute, 28 December 1934, FO 371/18731, A127.

East, interpreted in terms of British naval power & a defensible Singapore."[74] Hankey spelled out the implications of this remark when he wrote Baldwin that, "in my opinion . . . the Cabinet are overrating the *imminence* of the German peril. The peril is there all right but will take much more than 5 years to develop. . . . Meanwhile, I hope nothing is done to let down the Navy."[75] The record of ministerial discussions clearly indicates that the overwhelming majority of the cabinet shared this opinion. In Baldwin's words, "Both Germany and Japan are political mad dogs, but the scope for a mad dog was wider in the Far East than it was in Europe."[76] The cabinet, not for the last time, underestimated Hitler.

It was one thing for Chamberlain to refuse appropriations or delay construction of a ship in the name of finance; it was quite another to suggest withholding the fleet from the Far East and depriving the whole imperial estate of its protective shield. The empire was still at the core of Britain's political culture in the 1930s, part of the existing order of things. The navy, as its symbol, struck powerful chords of communal pride in faintly remembered childhood stories of Nelson and Barham, Anson and Hood—names still of battleships. The Admiralty could thus approach the cabinet knowing that popular opinion, especially in the Conservative party, was behind it. Sentiment and interest blurred around imperial issues, but under attack the navy became a rallying point for a cluster of interests well represented within the governing elite. The navy held this position because, in the last analysis, domestic power had always rested heavily upon external success—upon the creation and defense of strategic advantages and of access to markets and resources in the world at large.

In the twentieth century this external success, such as it was, had retreated into "the underdeveloped world, especially [that] sector of it which was under effective economic and political

---

[74]Eden, minute, 9 May 1934, FO 371/18099, F3508.
[75]Middlemas and Barnes, *Baldwin,* pp. 780–81.
[76]DC(M) (32), 50th Meeting, 25 June 1934, Cab 27/507.

control by Britain: the formal and informal Empire."[77] For nearly fifty years British trade and investment had been evading European and American competition by falling back upon imperial reserves to exploit the remaining advantages of Britain's nineteenth-century commercial hegemony. What had been true of the export trades before 1914 was true of overseas investment after the war. British capital flowed increasingly into Britain's dependencies; by 1930 nearly 60 percent of British overseas assets were invested in the formal empire, while Latin America accounted for half of the remainder. In the same period, as the British share of world trade and production continued to decline, Britain maintained substantial trade surpluses with Australia, Malaya, Ceylon, Brazil, China, and India.[78] The triumph of imperial protection in 1932 symbolized the extent to which finance had joined industry in hiding out among the dominions, colonies, and other dependencies of the empire.

During the Depression, as world trade and overseas investment dried up, the imperial connection proved important in other ways. It provided a basis upon which the national government could patch together a plausible recovery strategy built around the twin pillars of domestic austerity and imperial preference. British trade gravitated steadily into imperial channels.[79] Britain's ability to impose tariffs on its colonies, if not on its dominions, ensured protected markets for British goods. More important, the overseas dependencies proved invaluable sources of cheap food and commodity imports. The fall in food prices and Britain's ability as an imperial power to exploit the impoverishment of primary producers in the underdeveloped world underwrote the domestic consumer boom that carried the country out of the slump.[80] The Depression also brought a renewed interest in

[77]Hobsbawm, *Industry and Empire,* pp. 146, 191. For the importance of "external success" to the survival of the British elite see Tom Nairn, "The Twilight of the British State," New Left Review 101–102 (1977).

[78]Aldcroft and Richardson, *British Economy,* pp. 62–97, esp. pp. 84ff.

[79]See Charles Kindleberger, *The World in Depression 1929–39* (Berkeley, Calif., 1973), p. 282.

[80]See Aldcroft and Richardson, *The British Economy,* p. 246; Pollard, *British Economy,* pp. 289–90.

certain old preserves, especially in the Far East. As textile exports to China collapsed in the 1930s, larger capital interests in China found cause for optimism in a perceived shift in the nature of British exports to that market; increasingly, they felt, China would need to buy capital goods, iron and steel products, electrical hardware, power plants, waterworks, railways, and road equipment—precisely the items which Britain had exported so successfully in the past.[81]

In view of all of this, and in spite of the manifest failure of British commerce generally between the wars, few cabinet ministers were prepared to entertain Chamberlain's proposal to cease defending these external, imperial advantages. In a profound sense the empire and domestic economy were linked, their future success interlocked; positions of power at home rested upon imperial foundations. In this way the empire was a crucial asset in the domestic war of position—a "national" interest above party which nevertheless provided important external bastions for the domestic elite and the Conservative party. Chamberlain's initiative in the name of finance thus ran into a powerful ministerial consensus that it was a vital interest to protect the imperial connection overseas. No one disputed his economic assumptions or denied his argument that, "whilst . . . it might be comparatively simple to get an air defence programme accepted, it would be far more difficult to get a programme accepted which dealt with defence measures in the Far East."[82] The cabinet went along with him in bolstering the air force provision in Europe and in postponing a decision about the navy's building program, but this represented a political hedge, not the clear choice that Chamberlain wanted. As Baldwin said, "From the political point of view, it was necessary to do something to satisfy the semi-panic conditions which now existed about the air." But this was not the preference of ministers. The air program was "a gesture to Europe," but, again in Baldwin's words, "It would be necessary to take

[81]On the China market see Endicott, *Diplomacy and Enterprise,* chap. 4; Louis, *British Strategy,* chap. 7. Between 1929 and 1936 textile exports to China fell from £7 million to less than £300,000.

[82]DC(M) (32), 50th Meeting, 25 June 1934, Cab 27/507.

especial care that by our actions we did not encourage Japan to believe that we had abdicated our position in the east."[83]

Thus Chamberlain failed to win approval for a new departure in Far Eastern policy. He was unable to draw from this confrontation with the Admiralty any permanent political device for holding down naval spending. He did not deprive the Admiralty of its Far Eastern enemy or its claim to more ships. If anything, Chamberlain's opposition strengthened the navy's influence in ministerial circles during 1935. The cabinet's decision to sign the Anglo-German Naval Agreement, which the Admiralty strongly supported,[84] and its extreme sensitivity to the Admiralty's concerns about the

---

[83]DC(M) (32), 52d Meeting, 2 July 1934, Cab 27/507.

[84]Chatfield was the most forceful proponent of the naval agreement. It was, as Michael Howard observed, "the vital need to maintain a favorable naval balance in Europe" that accounted for the Admiralty's great interest in the agreement (*Continental Commitment* [Penguin ed., 1974], p. 102). This naval balance was the sine qua non of a Far Eastern capability. Unable to limit the French navy by treaty or to maintain the necessary strategic superiority over the French fleet without cutting into the margin of ships required for the Far East, the Admiralty neatly switched European enemies. By replacing France with Germany and binding Germany to a 35 percent ratio, the Admiralty greatly improved its global strategic position (Plans memorandum, 27 May 1935, NCM (35)50, 5 June 1935, Adm 116/3373]. It was thus in order to preserve the Far Eastern priority and the building program that went with it that the Admiralty supported the agreement. Because of this preoccupation with the Far East, moreover, the Admiralty was prepared to allow Germany full parity in submarines within the overall 35 percent ratio; the Admiralty believed that the U-boat threat was containable, but, in any case, the containing would be done by destroyers, while the Far Eastern strategy turned upon having battleships and cruisers available. What remained crucial to Admiralty thinking was Japan, the naval balance in the Pacific, and the commitment to send a battlefleet to Singapore; without agreement in Europe, the navy could not cope in the Far East. As late as 1938 the director of plans felt that the pact was "probably the most valuable factor that we have today in the whole realm of defence, and what our naval problem would be if it did not exist or is denounced is difficult to contemplate" (Roskill, *Naval Policy,* 2:355). On the agreement itself see D. C. Watt, "The Anglo-German Naval Agreement of 1935: An Interim Judgment," *JMH* 28 (1955); Charles Bloch, "Great Britain, German Rearmament, and the Naval Agreement of 1935," in Hans W. Gatzke, ed., *European Diplomacy Between Two Wars, 1919–1939* (Chicago, 1972); Hines Hall III, "The Foreign Policy-making Process in Britain, 1934–1935, and the Origins of the Anglo-German Naval Agreement," *HJ* 19, no. 2 (1976).

navy's liabilities during the Abyssinian crisis,[85] were in effect political compensations which the cabinet offered in lieu of funding. In November 1935, with the third Defence Requirements Committee report, the Admiralty returned to the charge, accepting Chamberlain's strategic assumptions and turning them back upon him:

> If there is danger from Japan at all, it reaches its maximum from the point of view both of probability and extent when we are preoccupied in Europe. Unless we can provide a sufficient defence for that emergency, Australia, New Zealand, India, Burma, the rich Colonies East of Suez and a vast trade will be at their mercy, and the Eastern half of the British Empire might well be doomed.[86]

To meet this contingency, the Admiralty proposed the "DRC standard," which was, in fact, the same program that Chamberlain had rejected the year before. Moreover, the Admiralty argued that the rapid development of the German fleet under the naval agreement which it had so recently championed made a more expansive two-power standard necessary in the near future.[87] The cabinet accepted the "DRC standard" in early 1936. Almost immediately it allowed accelerated construction under that standard, so that between 1937 and 1939 the navy was receiving ships as if the full two-power standard were in effect. The Admiralty pressed for a formal commitment to the so-called "New Standard of Naval Strength," but in deference to Treasury objections the cabinet refused. Yet at no time did it deny the Admiralty funds for additional construction under the accelerated "DRC standard."[88]

The confrontation between the Admiralty and the Treasury in 1934 thus established fundamental limits upon British rearmament. Chamberlain's failure to win a new departure in Far Eastern policy and the continuing necessity to provide for imperial defense

---

[85]See Arthur Marder, "The Royal Navy and the Ethiopian Crisis of 1935-6," *AHR* 25; no. 5 (1970); Gibbs, *Strategy,* pp. 187-226.

[86]DRC 37, 21 November 1935, circulated as CP 26(36).

[87]See Gibbs, *Strategy,* pp. 340-41.

[88]Ibid., pp. 323-74. Navy expenditure ran ahead of both army and air force expenditures in 1937-39.

established sharp limits upon British efforts in Europe. Thereafter the Cabinet's problem was to devise viable policies that expressed the parameters of limited defense spending and standing imperial commitments. The notion of a "balanced" rearmament which the government pursued for the next two years was a product of these constraints. And from this same context sprang the last version of British appeasement between the wars.

The cabinet finally opted for a threadbare strategy of deterrence. By postponing decision on the navy and beefing up the air force at home, Baldwin and Chamberlain hoped to deflect domestic criticism. The air program would be substantial enough to reassure those anxious about the bombing menace and Britain's vulnerability, yet sufficiently restrained to ensure that British finances were not put to a full test. The program would also present Hitler with a British effort in the air formidable enough to encourage him to negotiate a general arms treaty rather than risk an arms race. This combination of reassurance at home and deterrence abroad was the basis of Sir John Simon's winter 1934–35 pursuit of a "general settlement," an abrogation of the Treaty of Versailles in concert with France. His aim was to limit German rearmament by agreement. This would enable the government to keep the lid on spending and maintain the conditions of balance between Europe and the Far East and between defense requirements and the Treasury's fiscal limits. But in November 1934, the pace of German rearmament was already threatening to upset the symmetry. Baldwin was able to hold onto the balance only by announcing an acceleration of the air program and fudging comparative figures in the big debate of 28 November.[89] In March 1935, Hitler killed the whole effort. His unilateral denunciation of the Versailles Treaty thwarted the Anglo-French attempt to negotiate its demise, and his claim that Germany had achieved parity with Britain in the air mocked deterrence. It made little difference whether or not Hitler was lying. If he was telling the truth, the British had made a poor measure of the power they were

[89]Gilbert, *Churchill,* 5:572–80.

trying to contain; their air effort was obsolete, and German rearmament was surging ahead without restraint. If Hitler was merely boasting, it meant that the British air program had made no impression on him; the deterrent, far from moderating his policies or persuading him to negotiate, had only spurred him into more headlong measures. Either way British policy had collapsed. For the remainder of the year the cabinet wobbled between efforts at collective resistance alongside France, Italy, and the League of Nations and direct bilateral deals with the dictators. The Stresa Front gave way to the Anglo-German Naval Agreement, and in the autumn the government rallied to the league over Abyssinia, only to fall into the temptations of the Hoare-Laval Pact.

During the autumn of 1935 these developments in Europe indeed registered psephologically. In June, Baldwin had again become prime minister in order to prepare the party for elections. He needed a platform and an occasion to go to the country. At home continued unemployment, stagnating exports, and the Means Test controversy had brought out what Chamberlain called a "continual nagging and carping of the young intellectuals."[90] This, together with Lloyd George's proposals for a "new deal" during the first half of the year, made domestic issues poor ground on which to fight an election.[91] Abroad the traditional platitudes about disarmament and multilateral guarantees had worn thin, and the Peace Ballot that the League of Nations Union used to rally flagging faith in collective security cut across the logic of British defense policy. That logic, and the limited and balanced rearmament the cabinet proposed, had also come undone. Without agreed limitations on German armaments Britain could not limit its armaments against Germany. Yet given the balance of opinion in the cabinet, the Far Eastern program remained in effect. European and Far Eastern threats required full rearmament, a policy the DRC finally recommended in November 1935. This was precisely what Chamberlain feared would break the back of

[90]Middlemas and Barnes, *Baldwin,* p. 807.
[91]Cowling, *Hitler,* pp. 33-62.

his finances and what Baldwin assumed would rouse public opinion against the government.

Privately Chamberlain advocated "the bold course," a campaign to rally support for additional defense expenditure, but Baldwin hedged.[92] By coming out for the league over Abyssinia and tying this to a moderate rearmament program—"there will be no great armaments"—he tried to reassert a balance. It may be, as Michael Howard has said, that Conservative leaders felt at their necks "the heavy and ominous breathing of a parsimonious and pacific electorate,"[93] but this, it is important to recognize, was less an obstacle to timely preparation against Hitler, whom the public feared, than it was to the sort of balanced rearmament, with full provision for the empire, which the cabinet preferred. If anything, public opinion and parliamentary criticism pulled the government toward a larger air force than it wanted. Baldwin's misleading statements on air parity during the winter of 1934–35 were part of his attempt to protect a balanced defense program against the pressure of German rearmament. His fear of full disclosure during the election of 1935 was a fear of popular opposition not to the air program but to the general rearmament program made necessary by the cabinet's reluctance to jettison the Far East. In this sense popular anxiety about the German air menace pulled against elite concerns for the security of the empire. Insofar as the momentum of German rearmament raised general apprehension and animated ministerial decisions, it threatened either to draw off resources from the defense of the Empire or to upset Chamberlain's carefully balanced budget. Either way the necessity of choice brought into direct conflict two vital interests of the dominant class, economic recovery by orthodox means and maintenance of the overseas empire. A resolution of this conflict could be found only in Europe.

Baldwin's electoral gambit succeeded on the hustings but proved bad policy. The link between collective security and limited rearmament enabled him to revive the old rhetoric of league

---

[92]Feiling, *Chamberlain,* p. 266.
[93]Howard, *Continental Commitment,* p. 79.

solidarity one last time. The target, however, was Mussolini's imperialism in Africa, not Hitler's ambitions in Europe, and this merely increased pressure on the government for additional rearmament. The Hoare-Laval Pact and the failure of sanctions deprived the policy of its popular appeal and hence its political utility. Chamberlain finally broke with the approach in June 1936, attacking league sanctions as "the very midsummer of madness" and demanding a new departure. This was his second major intervention into foreign affairs in as many years. This time Chamberlain wanted direct settlements with the dictators. The Anglo-German Naval Agreement was his model; Munich was to be his showpiece. He believed that "the double policy of rearmament and better relations with Germany and Italy [would] carry us safely through the danger period."[94] It would also control the most volatile area of defense spending.

In this new initiative Chamberlain encountered almost no opposition from within governing circles. The financial interest, anxious to limit overall spending on armaments, could combine with the imperial interest, anxious to protect its Far Eastern priority, in urging bilateral approaches to Hitler and greater "realism" in dealing with the dictators. This helped to heal a breach in ministerial ranks. It made Chamberlain's economic priorities and budgetary ceilings appear practical, by coupling them to a political strategy for controlling military claims upon the Exchequer. By holding out the promise of agreement with Hitler and the maintenance of a balanced program of rearmament for imperial defense, Chamberlain helped protect two vital bastions of domestic class hegemony, finance and empire. This consolidated Chamberlain's authority within the Conservative party. As direct appeasement developed into the preferred policy for dealing with Germany, moreover, the government presented it to the public as a diplomacy of peace in the interests of the whole nation. This underwrote Chamberlain's image as a peacemaker which served so well as a breakwater against Labour. Indeed, appeasement not only rallied opinion but also effectively neutralized opposition. Labour's

---

[94]Feiling, *Chamberlain,* p. 319, adding, "if only the Foreign Office will play up."

complaint against Chamberlain was not that he wanted peace, or even that he wanted direct dealings with Hitler, but that in pursuing these ends he repudiated collective means. Success was, of course, Chamberlain's rebuttal. But by the same token, when the bilateral strategy collapsed in 1939, conciliation of the dictators had to stop. Only then did the Treasury's economic ceilings fall away and the cabinet decide that it must sacrifice the Far Eastern priority and risk the empire to resist Hitler. But the decision was a hard one, for the defense of domestic positions and external foundations of power so crucial to the long-term survival of the governing elite required the pacification of Europe which, in the 1930s, meant binding Hitler to the established rules of international conduct. All the structural determinants of British policy supported Chamberlain's conviction that Hitler must get what he wanted without war—until Hitler's ambitions proved too immense and implacable to allow a deal. Comprehending this, and resolving, however reluctantly, to fight, was for Britain's leaders all the more difficult because it cut across the familiar and finely balanced imperatives of class interest.

9

The Sources of Italy's Defeat in 1940: Bluff or Institutionalized Incompetence?

MACGREGOR KNOX

Italy's leaders went to war on 10 June 1940 under a serious misapprehension. Mussolini's generals, as their memoirs tell us at some length, thought that Mussolini was promising them a seat at the negotiations once Germany's crushing victory in France and Flanders compelled the Western Allies to sue for peace.[1] The dictator himself assumed that his armed forces, once they had no choice, would find the strength and will to drive the British from the Mediterranean by force of arms.[2] The misapprehension soon dissolved: the military gradually realized that peace was not at hand, and Mussolini heatedly complained that the generals refused to fight and awaited resolution of their problems "on the political plane."[3] Then Mussolini's decision to attack Greece in October 1940, which he took partly as a way of compelling the army to fight someone, produced disaster at the hands of a

---

[1]See particularly Pietro Badoglio, *L'Italia nella seconda guerra mondiale* (Verona, 1946), p. 37; Quirino Armellini, *Diario di guerra: Nove mesi al Comando Supremo* (Milan, 1946), p. 24; Mario Roatta, *Otto milioni di baionette* (Milan, 1946), pp. 94–95.

[2]See Filippo Anfuso, *Dal Palazzo Venezia al Lago di Garda* (Bologna, 1957), p. 133; for a detailed account see MacGregor Knox, *Mussolini Unleashed, 1939–1941: Politics and Strategy in Fascist Italy's Last War* (Cambridge, 1982), chap. 3.

[3]Giuseppe Bottai, *Vent'anni e un giorno (24 luglio 1943)* (Milan, 1949), p. 192 (19 October 1940).

third-rate power. British thrusts in the Mediterranean and North Africa turned disaster into catastrophe, and by early 1941 the only remedy was German rescue: the Luftwaffe to Sicily, Rommel to Africa, and a German Balkan campaign. Italy ceased to be a great power even in name. Given the consequences, the sources of the misapprehension and of military failure are worth investigation, not least as a test of the most popular interpretation of Mussolini's expansionism, the claim that he consistently preferred bluff to force.

Mussolini's side of the misunderstanding, and of military failure, is quickly dealt with.[4] He was well aware that many of his generals were less than brilliant. By early 1939 he had taken to complaining to his ministers about the army administration's bumbling. The organizational fiasco of the partial mobilization in August and September 1939 convinced him that General Alberto Pariani, his army chief of staff since 1936, was a grandiloquent incompetent.[5] Mussolini also concluded that General Giuseppe Valle, the air force chief of staff, had systematically claimed more combat-ready modern aircraft than his service in fact possessed. The dictator could and did sack both generals, but he was unable either to diagnose or to cure the serious structural and professional problems of his armed forces. Unlike Hitler, Mussolini had little understanding of modern warfare. Until the German armored successes of 1940 he was under the impression that offensive action on land was excessively costly except against small powers. The major European states would face one another as "walled nations" from behind their bunker firing slits. Only independent air operations à la Giulio Douhet, sea battles, and colonial forays would relieve the 1914–18–style monotony.[6]

[4]For a fuller discussion see Knox, *Mussolini Unleashed.*

[5]For Pariani and Valle see, above all, Galeazzo Ciano, *Diario, 1937–1943* (Milan, 1980), August–October 1939, passim; additional evidence in Knox, *Mussolini Unleashed,* chaps. 1, 2.

[6]For this conception see Mussolini's remarks in 1937 about the impregnability of the defense in Leslie Hore-Belisha, *The Private Papers of Hore-Belisha,* ed.

Since Mussolini did not understand war himself, he could scarcely teach it to his generals, to whose judgment in professional questions he felt compelled to defer despite his intermittent distrust of their competence.[7] The dictator therefore normally confined his interventions in military affairs to "questions of form,"[8] such as imposing the goosestep in 1938 to prussianize the Italians, whom he aspired to mold into a warrior race while fearing that they did not want to be one. One of his major complaints about the army was not its inefficiency but its loyalty to the House of Savoy, with which Mussolini uneasily coexisted on the basis of the compromise through which he had come to power in 1922. The military, the most vital and powerful surviving element of the pre-Fascist state, remained essentially a preserve of the monarchy, despite Mussolini's insistence on serving as minister of each of the three services. The king jealously guarded his constitutional prerogatives, especially the right to declare war and to exercise nominal wartime high command. Only veiled threats by the dictator and the apparent prostration of Italy's enemies induced the king to agree to war and to delegate command partially in June 1940.[9] Even had Mussolini possessed the specialized knowledge required to supervise the peacetime reorganization of his military instrument, he would have faced strong resistance from Victor Emmanuel III; the senior generals who stood in the way of military modernization were for the most part those whose loyalty to the monarchy was most pronounced. Finally, the structural requirements of personal rule got in the

---

R. J. Minney (London, 1960), p. 115; Mussolini, "Relazione per il Gran Consiglio," undated but 4 February 1939, NARS T-586/405/000045-46. Mussolini to Hitler, 30 May 1939, *DDI,* 8th ser., vol. 12, doc. 59; Mussolini, in Commissione Suprema di Difesa, "Verbali della XVII Sessione (8-14 febbraio 1940-XVIII)," p. 134, NARS T-586/461; Mussolini, memorandum, 31 March 1940, *DDI,* 9th ser., vol. 3, doc. 669.

[7]For Mussolini's diffidence in dealing with the generals, see Alessandro Lessona, *Memorie* (Florence, 1958), pp. 325-36; Alessandro Lessona, *Un ministro di Mussolini racconta* (Milan, 1973), p. 171.

[8]Ciano, *Diario, 1937-1943* (2 May 1939).

[9]See Paolo Puntoni, *Parla Vittorio Emanuele III* (Milan, 1958), pp. 11-13, 144; Armellini, *Diario di guerra,* pp. 5, 9-10; Knox, *Mussolini Unleashed,* chap. 3.

way of military efficiency. Mussolini could not permit centralization or coordination of the armed forces except through his own
person. He lacked the skills to settle many of the technical
disputes between the services; acute and long-running interservice
feuds left the fleet without effective air cover in 1940 and prevented
any serious study of amphibious warfare.

Despite these problems, and inflated service intelligence estimates of enemy strength, Mussolini had good reason to assume in
June 1940 that his military could and would fight. In the Mediterranean and North Africa the impending collapse of the French
gave Italy superiority over Britain by land and air, and parity or
better at sea. A total of 167,000 Italian and Italian colonial troops
in Libya faced 36,000 British, Indians, and New Zealanders in
Egypt. An Italian air force of well over 1,000 reasonably modern
combat aircraft faced 3 biplane fighters on Malta and 200 largely
obsolete RAF aircraft based in Egypt. Two recently modernized
Italian battleships in line, two brand-new battleships near the end
of their training, and two modernized battleships in training
faced one modernized British battleship, four slow and cranky
unmodernized battleships, and two aircraft carriers divided between
Gibraltar and Alexandria. The Italians had a crushing superiority
in cruisers, destroyers, submarines, and light units.[10] While Germany kept the British busy at home, Italy could conduct a short,
victorious war before industrial power, which Mussolini by this
point deferred to without understanding, could exert its long-
term effect. The Italian army was admittedly disorganized and

---

[10]See Stato Maggiore dell'Esercito, Ufficio Storico, *In Africa Settentrionale:
La preparazione al conflitto: L'avanzata su Sidi el Barrani* (Rome, 1955), p. 192; I.
S. O. Playfair, *The Mediterranean and Middle East,* vol. 1 (London, 1954), pp.
91–98; Giuseppe Santoro, *L'aeronautica italiana nella seconda guerra mondiale,*
vol. 1 (Rome, 1957), p. 88; Ufficio Storico della Marina Militare, *L'organizzazione
della marina durante il conflitto,* vol. 1 (Rome, 1972), pp. 338–45. For more on
order of battle and Italian intelligence failure, see Carlo De Risio, *Generali,
servizi segreti e fascismo* (Milan, 1978), Chap. 1; MacGregor Knox, "Fascist Italy
Assesses its Enemies, 1935–1940," in Ernest R. May, ed., *Knowing One's Enemies*
(Princeton, N.J., 1984); and, despite eccentricities, Franco Bandini, *Tecnica della
sconfitta* (Milan, 1964).

sketchily equipped, but Mussolini was not unreasonably convinced that "our boys will pass, over mountains of bodies."[11] He
was right about the bodies.

The nature of the Italian military's misapprehension, and of its
responsibility for failure, are less easy to analyze. Works on the
subject have generally taken one of two positions. In the immediate postwar period the generals belabored one another and
Mussolini for failure to prepare seriously for war. Titles like
Why We Lost the War: Mussolini and War Production[12] alternated with the accusations of ineptitude and treason that the
dictator's surviving generals and marshals flung at one another.
By the 1960s the death of most senior figures of the regime had
cooled the dispute, and another kind of interpretation emerged.
Giorgio Rochat, the foremost Marxist historian of Fascist military
and colonial policy, has argued that the ineptitude of individuals
was not the answer. The armed forces' failure was a consequence
of deliberate policy. Their principal mission had not been "the
real military preparedness of the nation" but class defense of
Italy's fragile bourgeois state and support of the Fascist regime's
efforts to promote internal stability through bellicose propaganda. When it came to war in 1940, both generals and regime
acted "without counting on [their] armed forces." Bluff and
diplomacy, not war, were fascism's instruments of "imperialistic
conquest."[13] Italy's belligerence was merely a claim to share
Germany's booty.

The second of the two interpretations is a seductive one. It fits
with the generals' view and with the most common postwar
interpretation of Italy's purposes in going to war. It offers a
modern-seeming structural interpretation of events. Finally, it

---

[11] Quotation: Luigi Federzoni, *L'Italia di ieri per la storia di domani* (Milan,
1967), p. 191.

[12] Carlo Favagrossa, *Perché perdemmo la guerra: Mussolini e la produzione
bellica* (Milan, 1946).

[13] Giorgio Rochat, "Mussolini e le forze armate," *Il Movimento di liberazione
in Italia,* no. 95 (1969), p. 12; Giorgio Rochat and Piero Pieri, *Pietro Badoglio*
(Turin, 1974), p. 742; Giorgio Rochat, "L'esercito e il fascismo," Guido Quazza,
ed., *Fascismo e società italiana* (Turin, 1973), p. 119.

appears to provide a firm linkage between the military's performance and its social role. But like the incompetence-and-treason-of-individuals theory, it too has problems. First, as already suggested, Mussolini entertained more bellicose purposes in 1940 than generally assumed. Second, the evidence of ineptitude is widespread enough that bluff does not convincingly explain it. Failure is embarrassing, and no institution tolerates it on a large scale unless it cannot help itself. Third, the linkage Rochat proposed between society, politics, and military policy is simplistic. A monopoly of violence within one's own borders is the mark of sovereignty. All armies are their government's internal weapon of last resort—but not all armies fail against external enemies. Italy's fragility in the eyes of its rulers and the army's role in holding the country together were in any case not unique. In Prussia-Germany the army's domestic role was if anything greater than it was in Italy, but the consequences for military efficiency were hardly crippling. Rochat's linkage of the Fascist regime's undeniable concentration on propaganda with the military's alleged failure to prepare seriously for war is more persuasive. But it fails to explain Mussolini's insistence on fighting, and Italy's military expenditures between 1935 and 1938–39, which were twice as great in relation to national income as Britain's.[14]

Prevailing interpretations also do not fully explain either the spectacular failure of Italian arms or the military's misapprehension about Mussolini's purposes in 1940. The first problem is complex and is unlike the questions historians traditionally ask when dealing with military institutions. Evaluating military effectiveness is a neglected art. War is abhorrent; if studied, it tends to become "war and society." But given the centrality of the role of force in history, a military establishment's social role is hardly more important than how it accomplishes its ostensible purpose: to close with and destroy the enemy.

In the Italian case, given the catastrophic failures, a reverse

[14]Aggregate Italian military expenditures (including those in Ethiopia, Spain, and Albania) for 1935–36 through 1938–39 were 11.8 percent of national income; Britain's expenditures for 1935–38 were only 5.5 percent of national income (Knox, *Mussolini Unleashed*, app. 2).

approach to the problem is appropriate. What conditions and policies made failure in 1940 likely? One suggestion that can be eliminated at once is the frequently heard claim that fascism took over the military establishment after 1922 and substituted political subservience for technical competence.[15] Subservience certainly existed. Mussolini fostered an atmosphere in which flexible opportunism flourished and those who voiced too many uncomfortable truths found themselves out of favor and power. But the record of dramatic military failure at Custoza, Lissa, Adua, and Caporetto antedated fascism, and some of the more forward-looking of Italy's military figures, generals like Federico Baistrocchi or critics like Emilio Canevari, were convinced and even fanatical Fascists.[16] The suggestion that "fascistization" was preeminently responsible for the military's failures is no more convincing than its civilian counterpart, Benedetto Croce's well-worn thesis that fascism was a parenthesis in Italian history or a mysterious disease that attacked an otherwise sound body politic.

A second popular interpretation for the disaster in 1940 is one already hinted at: the disparity in equipment and industrial resources between Italy and its principal adversary, Great Britain. In his spring 1939 alliance conversations with the Germans, Mussolini had emphasized the need to postpone the Axis blow against the West until 1943 to give Italy time to consolidate its hold on Ethiopia, strengthen its defenses in Libya, bring new battleships into line, and modernize the army's artillery.[17] By 1940, Italy's forces were still far from ready for a general war against both Britain and France. But against Britain alone Italy had momentary preponderance. The Italian ground forces were short on armor and motor transport, but the small British force in Egypt also faced serious problems of equipment and supply. Finally, German efforts in the north initially kept the British from sending major reinforcements to the Middle East. Industrial infe-

[15]See, above all, Quirino Armellini, *La crisi dell'esercito* (Rome, 1945).

[16]For Baistrocchi and Canevari, see particularly the latter's biased but indispensable *La guerra italiana: Retroscena della disfatta* (Rome, 1948–49), vol. 1.

[17]See Mario Toscano, *The Origins of the Pact of Steel* (Baltimore, Md., 1967), pp. 227-28, 248, 289-90, 377-78.

riority and shortages of raw material were only a handicap in the long run; the failure of Mussolini's 1940 foray had other sources. In the search for explanations two general approaches to the problem of military performance are worth mention: that of Norman F. Dixon, an officer of the Royal Engineers turned professional psychologist, and that of Karl von Clausewitz, Friedrich Engels, and Karl Marx. The basic argument of Dixon's *On the Psychology of Military Incompetence* is that peacetime military organizations, with their emphasis on button polishing, sterile authoritarianism, and bureaucratic neatness, stifle originality, initiative, and the taste for risk—all essential in war. Dixon maintains that military establishments inevitably recruit a high proportion of officers suited to peacetime service: authoritarian personalities who suffer from "need for approval," "fear of failure," and a catastrophic deafness to unpalatable information. "Ego-weakness and authoritarianism," not stupidity, are thus the source of military incompetence.[18] The theory is seductively neat, and its extrapolation from the British army, from which Dixon has drawn his examples, is tempting. The Italian "barracks army" was indeed addicted to a rigidly authoritarian bureaucratic routine and a predilection for form before substance.[19]

But Dixon's hypothesis clearly will not bear too heavy a weight. If peacetime routine inevitably nurtures failure-prone personalities, how many military organizations can be saved? The record of Reichswehr and Wehrmacht alone demonstrates that peace—and some degree of authoritarianism—do not make ineptitude in war inevitable. It is at this point that the wider theoretical perspectives of Clausewitz, Engels, and Marx are useful. One implicit corollary to Clausewitz's insistence that war is policy "by other means" is that a military institution's style of war, of leadership, and of organization is closely related to the character of the

[18]Norman F. Dixon, *On the Psychology of Military Incompetence,* (London, 1976), pp. 394–95.

[19]For the "esercito di caserma" see Giorgio Rochat, *L'esercito italiano da Vittorio Veneto a Mussolini (1919–1925)* (Bari, 1967), pp. 295–325; for Piedmontese officers "[m]olto ligi alla forma, che, talvolta, sovrapponevano alla sostanza," see Emilio De Bono, *Nell'esercito nostro prima della guerra* (Milan, 1931), p. 21.

society that produced it.[20] Recruitment patterns, methods of warfare, and degree of military expertise are at least partly a consequence of a society's intellectual and economic conditions. Marx, and, above all, Friedrich Engels, "der General" of the Marxist tradition, further developed this insight.[21]

The problem, as with social interpretations of any sort, lies in assessing the nature and degree of social influence and in coping with what Marxists would call the element of dialectical interaction between institutions and society. In the German case, for instance, one can argue with some force that the Prussian army had as much effect on Prussian and Prusso-German society as society had on the army. From the "feudalized" bourgeoisie to the Social Democratic party—in the words of one of its leaders a "preparatory school for militarism"—the army was that society's preeminent model of organization and conduct.[22]

Despite this caution, the social interpretation has considerable merit in explaining events in Italy. The Piedmontese-Italian army did not have the central role of the Prusso-German army. Society influenced army far more than vice versa, and the consequences for military effectiveness were unfortunate. The society itself was fragmented and unmanageable. Italy, despite 1861, 1866, and 1870, remained a geographical notion. Sicilians and Piedmontese —or even Venetians and Lombards—literally did not speak the same language. Even in the thin educated elites, consciousness of

---

[20]Clausewitz unfortunately did not develop his insight (*On War,* bk. 1, chap. 3) that "military genius" depends on the *general intellectual development* of a given society" (emphasis in original).

[21]See particularly Engels on "Army" (1857) for the *New American Cyclopaedia,* in Karl Marx and Friedrich Engels, *Werke,* vol. 14 (East Berlin, 1964), pp. 5–48; see also Sigmund Neumann's essay in E. M. Earle, ed., *Makers of Modern Strategy* (Princeton, N.J., 1941); Bernard Semmel, ed., *Marxism and the Science of War* (New York, 1981).

[22]For the remark, by August Bebel, see A. J. P. Taylor, *The Struggle for Mastery in Europe, 1848-1918* (London, 1954), pp. xxxiii–iv; for the Prussian army's effect on society see, above all (for the eighteenth century), Otto Büsch, *Militärsystem und Sozialleben in alten Preussen* (Berlin, 1962); Eckart Kehr, "Zur Genesis des Königlich Preussischen Reserveoffiziers," in his *Der Primat der Innenpolitik* (Berlin, 1965).

regional and even parochial divisions ran deep. Socially the lines of division were equally complex, both in the cities and in the countryside; the endemic disaffection of the increasingly numerous industrial workers and the resigned apathy of the peasant recruits scarcely made the officer's task easier. Literacy was relatively low, and in addition the educated strata for the most part received a formalistic literary training that hardly fitted them to understand the twentieth century and to direct or even adapt to technological change. The small modern sector of the economy in the north absorbed what technical and financial talent existed. Finally, foreign rule and home-grown despotisms had prevented the formation of an adequate military tradition, as well as the creation of a national civic consciousness.[23]

Piedmont's army, a stolid nineteenth-century professional force on the French model, gave the post-1861 Esercito Italiano its style of leadership and its cadres. The apparent political radicalism of the only rival tradition, that of Garibaldi's freebooters, allowed the Piedmontese officer corps to retain control of the new army and the support of the new nation's political elite. But the Piedmontese army's poor performance in the wars of unification, which was above all a consequence of the incompetence of its higher commanders and staffs, and the absence of any Italian equivalent of the military-agrarian Junker aristocracy, left it at a disadvantage in recruitment. Relatively low pay, a consequence of Italy's attempt to maintain force levels out of all proportion to its economic strength, was a further disincentive to the recruitment of talent. The same problems, repeated at a lower social level, made it difficult to recruit first-class noncommissioned officers. The officer corps's marked predilection for first safeguarding its own size and perquisites before considering the needs of the other ranks only intensified that tendency.[24]

[23]On Italian political culture see the depressing summary of Joseph La Palombara, "Italy: Fragmentation, Isolation, Alienation," in Lucian C. Pye and Sidney Verba, eds., *Political Culture and Political Development* (Princeton, N.J., 1965), pp. 282–329.

[24]For what little is known of the post-1870 army and officer corps, see Lucio

By the turn of the century Piedmont had lost its numerical dominance of all except the highest ranks. Statistical evidence is unavailable at present, but the south and the islands—areas that offered no other escape route than military or state bureaucracy, where a parallel shift in recruitment was taking place—apparently furnished a considerable proportion of officers and NCOs.[25] The consequences of this development were depressing. The most retrograde and clientelistic areas of Italy simply did not produce people with the attitudes, much less skills, needed to run a modern military or state machine efficiently. Those who joined the officer corps did so out of family tradition, a strong consideration in the Piedmontese elite, or a desire to escape suffocating small-town or rural antecedents. Dullards joined because the military offered a career open even to those without talent. Giovanni Giolitti, the dominant figure in Italian politics before World War I, described his generals as products of an age in which Italian families sent to the military "only boys they didn't know what to do with—black sheep and half-wits."[26] The remark is an exaggeration, but one with an element of truth. Many nineteenth- and twentieth-century European military institutions had a similar problem but developed more effective means than did the Italians for keeping the inept from command positions.

The interrelated problems of lack of social prestige, of a military leadership tradition, and of an adequate pool of high-quality officer and NCO recruits explain many of the Italian military's problems in 1940. The army's inability to learn from the later phases of World War I, the ironbound mule-and-mountain-gun conservatism of its senior figures, was at least partly a product of

---

Ceva, *Le forze armate* (Turin, 1981); Giorgio Rochat and Giulio Massobrio, *Breve storia dell'esercito italiano dal 1861 al 1943* (Turin, 1978); see also John Whittam, *The Politics of the Italian Army, 1861-1918* (London 1977).

[25]For discussion of the regional and social composition of the late-nineteenth-century officer corps, see Rochat and Massobrio, *Breve storia dell' esercito italiano,* pp. 97-100; and Ceva, *Le forze armate,* pp. 63-70.

[26]Olindo Malagodi, *Conversazioni della guerra, 1914-1919* (Milan, Naples, 1960), 1:200.

the origins and intellectual level of the officer corps. Military intellectualism, the serious study of war in the manner of Clausewitz or Helmuth von Moltke, never became fashionable, despite attempts after 1866 to imitate the Prussian general-staff system. The resulting Corpo di Stato Maggiore was a closed corps of smug bureaucrats rather than an intellectual elite selected through a ruthless series of competitive examinations.[27] Appointment to the Scuola di Guerra and later promotions depended disproportionately on contacts and *raccomandazioni;* the generals' memoirs are full of references to favoritism and to struggles between cliques. Loyalty to one's patrons was more important for advancement than brains or strength of character, a situation that hardly encouraged the development or expression of independent judgment. Nor was the training at the Scuola di Guerra a stimulant to study or thought about war. By all accounts it was abstract, theoretical, and not terribly exciting.[28] The tests of individual judgment and of teamwork that an incessant round of map exercises and war games imposed on Kriegsakademie trainees and German unit staffs had no counterpart in the Italian army. Finally, the Italian army's staff tradition and machinery was overcentralized. The German concept of the mission-type order (*Auftragsbefehl*)—the revolutionary idea of telling a subordinate to do something but leaving the choice of methods to him—had little place in Italian doctrine or practice. Higher staffs customarily supervised their dependent units with obsessive attention to minor detail.

The army that this system of recruitment and training produced was scarcely suited for carving out the empire to which Mussolini aspired. Equipment deficiencies further reduced its effectiveness. The budgetary drain of Ethiopia and Spain, raw-material shortages, industrial bottlenecks, and Mussolini's decision in 1936–37 to give priority to navy and air force prevented the army from mass-producing in time for war the family of modern artillery pieces it had produced in prototype. The army

---

[27]The history of the Italian command and staff system remains to be written; Lucio Ceva is working on a volume on the interwar period.

[28]See the brief remarks in Whittam, *Politics of the Italian Army,* p. 149; Luigi Marchesi, *Come siamo arrivati a Brindisi* (Milan, 1969), pp. 5–7.

therefore fought much of World War II with artillery taken from Austria-Hungary in 1918.[29] But the other major gap in the army's arsenal, adequate medium and heavy tanks, resulted from deliberate choice. Tanks and armored cars were allegedly cumbersome in the Alps; the army hence saw little need of them until the late 1930s.[30] Only the German triumphs in the spring of 1940 and a direct order from Mussolini compelled the army to begin development of a 75-mm-gun tank.[31] But by 1940 it was too late, though Italy's industrial capacity and raw-material resources, employed in intelligent and timely fashion, could almost certainly have equipped and supported a solidly organized armored and motorized fifteen- to twenty-division army—a striking force powerful enough to dispatch Yugoslavia swiftly and drive the British from the Middle East.

The army's attempts to conform to Mussolini's aspirations took another direction entirely. Neither Mussolini nor General Pariani nor the army's conservative establishment could envisage a land war without masses of foot soldiers. In the aftermath of the Ethiopian conquest Pariani developed an eccentric theory of blitzkrieg Italian style, the *guerra di rapido corso,* which relied for its punch not on armor and dive bombers but on floods of truck-borne infantry. Neither the regime's admitted propaganda need for as many divisions as possible nor its alleged political interest in a mass army as a means of political mobilization[32] was decisive in preventing the army from using its resources intelligently. The dogged belief of the generals themselves that masses, not

[29]See Fortunato Minniti, "Il problema degli armamenti nella preparazione militare italiana dal 1935 al 1943," *Storia Contemporanea* 9 (1978); Lucio Ceva, "Un intervento di Badoglio e il mancato rinnovo delle artiglierie italiane," *Il Risorgimento* 28, no. 2 (1976).

[30]For tank development see Minniti, "Il problema degli armamenti," pp. 20–23; for Italian doctrine on the eve of the war see Stato Maggiore dell'Esercito, Ufficio Storico, *L'esercito italiano tra la 1ª e la 2ª guerra mondiale (novembre 1918–giugno 1940)* (Rome, 1954), pp. 151–59.

[31]Mario Caracciolo di Feroleto, *E Poi? La tragedia dell'esercito italiano* (Rome, 1946), pp. 63–64.

[32]See Massimo Mazzetti, *La politica militare italiana fra le due guerre mondiali (1918–1940)* (Salerno, 1974), pp. 139–40.

machines, were decisive in war was the vital doctrinal ingredient in the failures of 1940 in North Africa and Greece. Intellectual rigidity and doctrinal backwardness were not peculiar to the army. The navy, which had a much smaller officer corps than the army's and remained an elite technical service, was able to recruit talent more easily than its land-bound counterpart. But it suffered in the interwar period from a disastrous inability to envisage war except as a Mediterranean Jutland, a cataclysmic clash of battle fleets.[33] It also carried overcentralization to extremes unheard of until worldwide satellite communication became available in the 1970s. In 1940 the commander of the Italian fleet at sea had almost no scope for independent judgment except when he was actually in contact with the enemy. The navy staff war room in Rome, with its banks of teleprinters and chairborne admirals on duty around the clock, directed the fleet's activities—although with communications delays. Respect of the instincts of the man on the spot, a time-honored tradition in the British Royal Navy which had effects similar to that of the German Auftragsbefehl, was unheard of.

Doctrinally, the navy was correspondingly uninspired. The navy staff ruled out night action between major units, despite the emphasis other navies, such as the Japanese, placed on that difficult but rewarding art. The navy's complacent assumption that the Anglo-Saxon powers "could not be appreciably ahead of us" in radar development was as important as Italy's industrial and technological weaknesses in ensuring the British a decisive advantage by 1941.[34] Italian submarine construction and tactics were equally, and equally unwittingly, backward. Throughout the interwar period the navy staff also showed remarkably little interest in Italy's area of special expertise in World War I, attack by infernal machines on capital ships in harbor. Only the devotion of a small band of enthusiasts from the La Spezia submarine flotilla

---

[33]For the navy's doctrine, organization, and strategy in 1940, see Ufficio Storico della Marina Militare, *L'organizzazione della marina,* and *Le azioni navali in Mediterraneo dal 10 giugno 1940 al 31 marzo 1941* (Rome, 1970).

[34]Ufficio Storico della Marina Militare, *L'organizzazione della marina,* pp. 168–69.

provided the navy with the frogman-guided torpedoes that sank the battleships *Valiant* and *Queen Elizabeth* at Alexandria in 1941.[35]

Finally, the navy chief of staff from 1934, Admiral Domenico Cavagnari, virtually nullified his service's preparations for a decisive fleet action by refusing to fight one. The admiral's "fleet in being" strategy was at least in part an inheritance from World War I, but Cavagnari carried it to unfortunate extremes. His systematic evasion of action in the summer and fall of 1940, when the prerequisites for decisive victory over the British Mediterranean Fleet existed, ultimately presented the British with lucrative targets for the torpedo bombers that sank three Italian battleships in Taranto harbor in November.[36]

The air force was little better off. Its strategic myth, General Giulio Douhet's theory of absolute air warfare, helped inspire Mussolini's vision of a war of position on the ground and of movement in the air and at sea.[37] But the air force staff, while proclaiming the dogma, failed to explore its practical application. Wars in Ethiopia and Spain, where Douhet-style independent air action against the enemy industrial base was impossible, encouraged little rethinking. One unconventional general, Amedeo Mecozzi, steadfastly maintained that the air force's primary mission should be ground support, but to no avail.[38] Quality of personnel—a function of recruitment—also contributed to the air force's relatively ineffectual performance in 1940.[39]

[35]The navy staff's file on the development of the weapons (Archivio Storico della Marina Militare, Rome, bundle "Mezzi d'assalto: Documentazione varia 1935-1940") makes clear the crucial role of initiative from below.

[36]For a detailed if reticent account of Taranto, see Ufficio Storico della Marina Militare, *Le azioni navali*, chap. 9; for Cavagnari's avoidance of action see Knox, *Mussolini Unleashed*, chap. 4.

[37]For Douhet's views see his *Il dominio dell'aria* (Milan, 1932).

[38]See particularly Amedeo Mecozzi, "I quattro compiti delle ali armate," *Rivista aeronautica*, 13, nos. 9-11 (1937).

[39]See the summer 1940 correspondence, much of it lamenting a shortage of officers "fully up to their tasks," between the chief of staff of the air force and his chief subordinate in North Africa: Archivio Centrale dello Stato (Rome), Ministero dell'Aeronautica, Gabinetto, bundle "A.S.—1940. Ispezione Generale Pricolo—Relazioni," folder "Corr. con il Generale Porro."

Besides intellectual and doctrinal rigidity, the services' officer corps suffered from a further woe: a narrow-minded interest-group mentality that placed excessive value on corporate prestige and perquisites. Self-interest coincided with doctrine in the army's insistence on maintaining the premobilization skeletons of two to three times as many divisions as it could fill out with solidly trained cadres or Italian industry could equip with modern weapons. The army's overblown structure meant that peacetime field training was almost unheard of; during most of the year the units were too weak to permit it. Reserve officers and NCOs, on whose skill and experience the war-strength army depended for its cohesion, rarely received more than sterile classroom instruction and practice in military paperwork. The conscripts did their time amid barrack square, guardhouse, cookhouse, and billets and learned little of terrain use, tactics, or even their weapons. The army failed dramatically in training the reserve junior officers and NCOs on whose competence the effectiveness of the war-strength line units rested. In the words of a senior general, writing to Chief of Staff Pietro Badoglio in August 1940 as one Piedmontese to another:

> As long as it is a question of risking one's skin, [the junior leaders] are admirable; when, instead, they have to open their eyes, think, decide in cold blood, they are hopeless. In terms of reconnaisance, security, movement to contact, preparatory fire, coordinated movement and so on, they are practically illiterate.[40]

When the junior leaders failed to learn their jobs under fire, units degenerated into armed mobs.

Structural megalomania at the expense of training and equipment was at least partly a legacy of post-1870 attempts to back Italy's great-power claims with imposing force levels. But the persistence of the dogma of mass warfare in the interwar period, when technology was rapidly changing the bases of the military art, was an indication of its convenience to the army hierarchy's corporate interest: the larger the army's structure, the more senior officer slots. The consequences appear to have troubled

---

[40]Trezzani to Badoglio, 1212, 25 August 1940, NARS T-821/139/000312-16.

few in the bureaucracy. Nor did many senior generals object to Pariani's organizational revolution of 1938–39, the transformation of the thirty-odd preexisting three-regiment divisions into sixty-three (later seventy-three) two-regiment "binary" divisions. Ethiopia and Spain, Pariani claimed, had shown that the three-regiment division was too cumbersome for rapid maneuver. Maintenance of Italy's international status and competition with a rapidly rearming Germany were additional rationales for the multiplication of paper division strength.[41] But Pariani's invention was also a method of generating additional command positions and staff slots. It encountered little resistance from his colleagues and successors until the attack on Greece, which revealed the "binary" division's dramatic lack of staying power.

Defense of vested interests also inhibited interservice cooperation to a degree remarkable even by international standards. From 1935 on, air force and navy quarreled over air support for the fleet and the development of torpedo bombers. The air force, pursuant to Douhet's crackpot air-warfare theories, and with Mussolini's approval, blocked the navy's insufficiently resolute proposals for building aircraft carriers. The navy ultimately had to do without; only after the disaster at Matapan in March 1941 did the two services make adequate arrangements for air support to the fleet.[42] Army requests for more ground support met with only slightly less resistance. Similarly, army and navy hardly discussed and never practiced amphibious operations, despite their obvious necessity in a Mediterranean war. The three service staffs implicitly agreed on one fundamental point: cooperation with the other services led to the sacrifice of one's own budget in the interest of joint missions. What made interservice rivalry so acute, apart from Mussolini's failure to coordinate the armed forces, was the intellectual narrowness of the services themselves. Recruitment, leadership style, doctrine, and narrow-minded

[41]See the delightfully frank minutes of a November 1937 meeting between Pariani and the army's senior generals, in Stato Maggiore dell'Esercito, Ufficio Storico, *L'esercito italiano,* pp. 240–59.

[42]See particularly the navy account in Ufficio Storico della Marina Militare, *L'organizzazione della marina,* pp. 35–51.

interest-group behavior made military failure in 1940 hard to avoid.

What made it almost inevitable was the military's already-mentioned misapprehension about what the regime expected of it. This misapprehension was not a product of that alleged "gradual renunciation of the armed forces as an instrument of imperialistic conquest" that Rochat has detected in Italy's military policies.[43] Cavagnari, for all his limitations, did his best to prepare the fleet for a major war, even if he refused to fight one when the time came. The navy's massive building program and even more grandiose paper expansion projects in the late 1930s testify to a serious attempt to create an instrument adequate to Mussolini's imperial ambitions, a navy capable of dominating the Mediterranean and striking far outside it into the Atlantic and Indian oceans.[44] The air force overvalued the easy combat experience gained in Ethiopia and Spain and seriously thought it was preparing for general war. Its expansion programs produced indifferent results but were too expensive to be deliberate bluff. From 1935 to 1939 the air force ordered more than 8,700 warplanes and nearly 3,000 trainers, notable figures by international standards.[45] Valle's inability to count aircraft in 1939 was less a cynical exercise in long-term deceit than a desperate attempt to cover up confusion in procurement and temporary bottlenecks in the aircraft industry.[46] The army comes closest to confirming Rochat's interpretation. Under Pariani it attempted to maintain its traditional position as the first of the armed forces by advocating the *guerra di rapido corso* as the solution to Italy's strategic problems. This slogan indeed contained an element of bluff, given army deficiencies in motor transport, armor, and artillery. Pariani's

---

[43]Rochat, "L'esercito e il fascismo," p. 119.

[44]For details see Minniti, "Il problema degli armamenti," pp. 42-43.

[45]Ibid., p. 35; the first serious British air rearmament plan, "Scheme F," of February 1936, provided for production of 8,000 aircraft in three years.

[46]For the air force's initial "rejection" of the monoplane fighter and consequent procurement debacle, see Lucio Ceva, "Lo sviluppo degli aerei militari in Italia (1938-1940)," *Il Risorgimento* 35, no. 1 (1983). Valle in any case aimed his deceit primarily at the political leaders, not—in connivance with them—at the public, as the bluff thesis requires.

admonition to a subordinate in 1937 not to do "too much training"[47] hardly says much for the general's sense of urgency. One of his successors, Undersecretary of War General Ubaldo Soddu, gave an even more open profession of charlatanism when he allegedly urged one of his staff not to worry: " . . . when you have a fine plate of *pasta* guaranteed for life, and a little music, you don't need anything more."[48] But the operatic side of Pariani's army was not its only one. When it was under the gun in September 1938 and August 1939, Pariani proclaimed the army ready for war with the West.[49] If Pariani was bluffing, he was in imminent danger of merciless comeuppance. More probably he thought he was telling the truth.

Deception of a sort nevertheless did figure in Italian policy in 1940: Mussolini tricked his military and the Italian monarchy into war. Privately he seethed to prove himself as "*condottiere* of the nation at war" in a swift, decisive conflict. But to his high command he gave the reassuring impression that Italian belligerence was "a colossal bluff . . . played out coolly, with the mentality of a poker player."[50] Italy's aim, the generals concluded, was to seize booty not on the field of battle but at the peace table; military and king stifled their last doubts and took the bait at the end of May 1940. Their misapprehension is not evidence that Italy's military policy rested on bluff. The error of Mussolini's military associates and their reluctance to fight once committed demonstrate rather the success of Mussolini's deception and the military's own lack of strategic imagination.[51] In initially resisting war, generals and admirals started from the correct assumption that, until at least 1943, Italy's armaments would be unequal to an

[47]Caracciolo, *E Poi?* p. 43.

[48]Giacomo Carboni, *Memorie segrete (1935-1948)* (Florence, 1955), p. 61.

[49]See Ciano, *Diario, 1937-1943* (25 September 1938, 23 and 26 August 1939).

[50]Ibid. (29 May 1940); Armellini, *Diario di guerra,* p. 24; Anfuso, *Dal Palazzo Venezia,* p. 128: "[Badoglio], like all marshals, evidently doesn't like the word war. Fine! We won't call it war." See also Knox, *Mussolini Unleashed,* chap. 3.

[51]Even the semiofficial work of General Emilio Faldella (*L'Italia e la seconda guerra mondiale: Revisione di giudizi,* 2d ed. [Bologna, 1960], p. 149) expresses dismay over the military leaders' "supine acceptance of the situation of the moment" in the spring of 1940.

offensive Mediterranean war against *both* Western powers combined, even if Germany helped by distracting the French in the north. The military's antiquated notions of warfare prevented it from anticipating the collapse of France, and until the French actually sued for peace in mid-June, those who counted in the Italian high command persisted in judging that Italy's prospects were poor.[52] The pretense of bluff was thus the only way Mussolini —his freedom of action constricted by the monarchy and by his military advisers—could get action.

Subsequently the military proved unable to abandon its defensive mentality. Mussolini's sudden about-face after 10 June, from promising a seat at the peace table to demanding victory, met at first incredulous resistance and then a reluctant advance in the hope that some "hidden political rationale" (in the words of Marshal Rodolfo Graziani, commander in North Africa) would save the day.[53] The one thing the military did not do was make intelligent use of the resources it did have to achieve a swift decision over the British. Failure was a consequence not of bluff but of the built-in deficiencies in the recruitment, tradition, and training of the military.

[52]Ciano, *Diario, 1937–1943* (9, 18, 29 May and 9 June 1940); Badoglio to Mussolini, 1 June 1940, Stato Maggiore dell'Esercito, Ufficio Storico, *La preparazione al conflitto,* pp. 190–91.

[53]Graziani, diary (7 September 1940), ACS, Carte Graziani, bundle 70, "Appendice."

Hans W. Gatzke, Germany, and the United States

ANNELISE THIMME AND CAROLE FINK

As a scholar and teacher Hans W. Gatzke epitomizes the rare combination of intellectual independence, rigorous standards, tolerance of divergent opinions, and shrewd good judgment. He has contributed substantially to the historical profession and also to the links between Germany and the United States. This book represents an expression of his students' esteem and affection and, we trust, demonstrates the influence of his training, guidance, and breadth.

Gatzke is one of the many Germans who immigrated to the United States in the 1930s. His intimate experience with both countries and the choices he made formed his life and work. He grew up in the Weimar Republic and became politically conscious in the early 1930s. The seizure of power by the National Socialists was the fundamental political experience of his generation. Much has been written about his contemporaries who chose political radicalism as well as those who were forced into exile by the Third Reich's racial persecution. There were also some young Germans like Gatzke, neither Communists, Socialists, nor Jews, who rejected national socialism and acted according to their convictions.

The young opponents of the Third Reich faced difficult decisions. Some stayed in Germany, some joined the resistance movement, and some left the country. Those who immigrated to the United

267

States confronted a number of choices, which were affected by their ages, their educational backgrounds, and the circumstances of their departure. Some refugees and expatriates never identified with their new home and retained their language, culture, and German loyalty. Others, like Gatzke, became thoroughly committed to their adopted country but, though preferring the latter, never renounced their ties to and critical perspective on the country of their birth.[1]

Hans Gatzke was born on 10 December 1915 in Dülken, a small town near the Dutch border. His early childhood took place against the backdrop of World War I and the tumultuous early years of the Weimar Republic; he lost both his parents before he reached his teens. Originally conservative in his political tastes, Gatzke during his adolescence became a local leader of the independent youth group Deutsche Freischar. In 1933 he had his first brush with the new regime when it began incorporating the independent youth organizations into the Hitler Youth. Gatzke refused to make the change.

In 1934 he graduated from the Oberrealschule in Wuppertal and applied for a scholarship to study abroad. Tall, blond, and blue-eyed, Gatzke seemed the model "Aryan" representative of the Third Reich; the German Exchange Service awarded him a year's study in the United States. With few family ties in Germany and little sympathy for national socialism, Gatzke at eighteen was immediately attracted to his new environment. He attended Williams College, where his student and faculty friends urged him to remain in the United States. He chose, however, to adhere to the stipulations of his scholarship and return to Germany.

Gatzke studied law at the universities of Bonn and Munich. His reputation as a less than wholehearted supporter of the Third Reich began to cause difficulties. The Gestapo searched his

---

[1]See Hans W. Gatzke, *Germany and the United States: A Special Relationship?* (Cambridge, Mass., 1980), p. xi. Gatzke's identification with the political emigrés from Nazi Germany is also subtly expressed in his review of Anthony Heilbut, *Exiled in Paradise: German Artists and Intellectuals in America from the 1930s to the Present* (Boston, 1983), *PSQ* (Summer 1984): 386–87.

rooms, and the Exchange Service called him to Berlin for an "interview." Realizing that neither he nor the kind of legal career he envisaged fitted into the National Socialist system, Gatzke decided to return to the United States. Helped by friends at Williams, he left in early 1937 without informing the German authorities of his intention not to return.

After obtaining his bachelor's degree at Williams, Gatzke entered the Graduate School of Harvard University in 1938. He received his training in history from the late William Langer, whose seminar in those years produced many distinguished scholars, including Klemens von Klemperer, H. Stuart Hughes, and Carl Schorske. Later, when Gatzke became a teacher, he adopted Langer's seminar method: an hour-long student report, followed by unsparing criticism by the other seminar members and then by Langer himself. The critical judgment developed in these sessions gave Langer's protégés invaluable guidance in their future careers.[2]

The outbreak of World War II stirred patriotism among the emigrés, who were committed to the struggle against nazism. Gatzke had applied for United States citizenship in 1937 and thus was liable for military service. Like all other German emigrés, however, he was also classified as an "enemy alien" after Pearl Harbor and as such was subject to suspicion and various restrictions. In 1942 he translated and edited Karl von Clausewitz's *Principles of War.*[3] It was intended as a contribution to the war effort but instead brought him an intensive investigation by the FBI. He was finally cleared and drafted in 1943. After infantry training he was attached to the Psychological Warfare Division of Staff Headquarters, American Expeditionary Force, and became a member of a small group that operated a top-secret radio station ("Operation Annie") out of Luxembourg. In recognition of his services he was awarded a direct commission in 1945 and reentered Germany with the Third Army. When the war ended,

---

[2]William Langer, *In and Out of the Ivory Tower* (New York, 1977).

[3]Karl von Clausewitz, *Principles of War,* trans. and ed. Hans W. Gatzke (Harrisburg, Pa., 1942; English ed., 1943; Portuguese ed., 1947).

Gatzke served as information control officer in military government until 1946. In that capacity he helped rebuild Radio Frankfurt (now Hessischer Rundfunk) and was active in the reconstruction of the German Rundfunk and its transfer from Allied to German hands.

After his release from service Gatzke returned for one year to Harvard, where he served as tutor in the History Department while completing work for his doctorate. In 1947 he left Cambridge for his first real teaching position, on the history faculty of Johns Hopkins University, in Baltimore, where he remained for seventeen years.

In 1950, Gatzke's dissertation appeared as a book under the title *Germany's Drive to the West: A Study of Germany's War Aims During the First World War.*[4] Awarded the Herbert Baxter Adams prize of the American Historical Association for the best work in modern European history that year, it at once established Gatzke's scholarly reputation. In the context of German historiography since 1919, *Germany's Drive to the West* is a remarkable work. It signaled a new approach to the historiography of the Second Reich with a detachment and objectivity rarely achieved by even mature German scholars. The young German-American army veteran reflected neither the German preoccupation with the *Bewältigung der Vergangenheit* ("the surmounting of the past") nor the tendency of non-Germans to interpret the entire German past as preparation for the Nazi period.

Germany's Drive to the West analyzed the economic and political bases of the *Drang nach Westen,* the conservative, anti-British alignment between 1914 and 1918. Long before it became fashionable, Gatzke demonstrated the links forged between industry and politics in the Kaiserreich and the manipulation of public opinion toward nationalist ends. Written from contemporary published sources before the release of German archival documents, the book anticipated the work produced eleven years later by Fritz

---

[4]Baltimore, Md., 1950; paperback ed., 1966; latest ed., 1978.

Fischer and others who had access to government records.[5] Fischer and his followers stirred a bitter debate in Germany over German expansionism and responsibility for World War I and also stimulated investigations of other countries' wartime policies. Gatzke's first work was never translated into German. Like Étienne Mantoux's critical dissection of John M. Keynes's *Economic Consequences of the Peace* and Luigi Albertini's *Origins of the First World War, Germany's Drive to the West* has been available to the postwar generation of Germans only in the English-language edition. It nevertheless made a substantial contribution to the debate over war aims, the politics of Wilhelmian Germany, and the question of continuity in German foreign policy in the twentieth century.

Gatzke's personality and style were reflected in his first book, which treated large, controversial questions without polemics. It applied American standards of scholarship to the heated arguments about his former country's history. In its unusual restraint *Germany's Drive to the West* expresses Gatzke's controlled and disciplined political passion and his moral force. It does not shy away from forthright statements and uncomfortable truths but does avoid emotional or moralistic judgments. The absence of an apologetic or inquisitorial tone makes this book, after thirty years, as fresh and useful today as when it was written. Gatzke's concise style, thorough presentation, and consistently shrewd interpretation make it a model of political history.

In 1952 the American government made available to scholars the captured German records which had been microfilmed after the war. Gatzke embarked on a critical reinterpretation of Germany's leading statesman under the Weimar Republic, Gustav Stresemann, whose wartime orientation as a proannexationist he

[5]See Gatzke's reviews of Imanuel Geiss, *Der polnische Grenzstreifen, 1914–1918: Ein Beitrag zur deutschen Kriegszielpolitik im Ersten Weltkrieg* (Lübeck and Hamburg, 1960), *JMH* 34, no. 2 (1962):216–17; Fritz Fischer, *Griff nach der Weltmacht: Die Kriegszielpolitik des kaiserlichen Deutschland, 1914/1918* (Düsseldorf, 1961), *AHR* 68; no. 2 (1963): 443–45; Fritz Fischer, *World Power or Decline: The Controversy over German War Aims in the First World War,* trans. Lancelot L. Farrar et. al. (New York, 1974), *AHR* 81, no. 1 (1976): 167.

had noted in *Germany's Drive to the West.* After examining the bulk of Stresemann's papers, Gatzke published invaluable bibliographical articles guiding scholars through hundreds of rolls of microfilm, pointing out the major characteristics of the material, and suggesting areas of research.[6]

In 1954 he published his second book, *Stresemann and the Rearmament of Germany.* Considerably more than a monograph on Weimar Germany's secret rearmament, the book revised the prevailing, largely hagiographic view of Stresemann that had presented him as a precursor of Bonn's democratic leaders. Gatzke offered a sober, realistic, yet also fair description of a German statesman who liked to compare himself with Metternich and Bismarck. Gatzke saw in the negotiator of the Locarno treaties and the Young Plan of 1929, which reduced Germany's reparations payments and led to an early evacuation of the Rhineland, "not the good European, the honest dreamer of peace and apostle of reconciliation as he appeared to many of his contemporaries and most of his biographers." Instead he characterized Stresemann as a "great German statesman, the greater perhaps for the two-faced policy which devotion to his country and the belief in its future made him pursue, and which at the same time was so at variance with his upright character as an individual."[7] Gatzke's balanced discussion of Stresemann's realpolitik was labeled negative by supporters of Weimar's illustrious foreign minister, and it has continued to produce heated debate among scholars. Nevertheless, specialized monographs on German foreign policy based on German but also French, English, Italian, Belgian, Russian, and American documentation have little altered Gatzke's appraisal of Stresemann's diplomacy.[8]

[6]Hans W. Gatzke, "The Stresemann Papers," *JMH* 26, no. 1 (1954): 49–59; "Gustav Stresemann: A Bibliographical Article," *JMH* 36; no. 1 (1964): 1–13.

[7]Hans W. Gatzke, *Stresemann and the Rearmament of Germany* (Baltimore, Md., 1954; paperback ed., New York, 1969). The quotation is from the 1969 edition, p. 115.

[8]Gatzke is still considered the foremost authority on Stresemann; see his reviews of Manfred Enssle, *Stresemann's Territorial Revisionism* (Wiesbaden, 1980); Wolfgang Michalka and Marshall Lee. eds., *Gustav Stresemann* (Darmstadt, 1982), *Militärgeschichtliche Mitteilungen* (1982):152–53, (1984): 195–96.

Gatzke became one of the leading writers on Russo-German political and military relations in the 1920s.[9] He also penned terse critical reviews in the major historical journals of works on World War I and the Weimar Republic and its leaders.[10] In 1952 he was invited by William Langer to contribute to his *Encyclopedia of World History,* and in 1960 by Golo Mann to write an extended chapter for the monumental *Propyläen Weltgeschichte.*[11]He has written articles for *Collier's Year Book* and *Encyclopedia Americana,* and from 1955 through the mid-sixties he reviewed books on German and European history for the *Baltimore Sunday Sun.*

In 1964, Hans Gatzke was appointed to Yale University, where he joined another emigré German historian, Hajo Holborn, as a colleague and friend. At Johns Hopkins and at Yale, Gatzke has been a popular teacher, known for his informative and scintillating lectures, as well as his interest in undergraduate education.

[9]See especially Hans W. Gatzke, "Dokumentation zu den deutsch-russischen Beziehungen im Sommer 1918," *VFZG* 3, no. 1 (1955): 67–98; "Von Rapallo nach Berlin: Stresemann und die deutsche Russlandpolitik," *VfZG,* no. 1 (1956): 1–29; "Stresemann und Litwin," *VFZG* 5, no. 1 (1957): 76–90; "Stresemann and Russia," *World Affairs Quarterly* 27 (1957): 344–55; "Russo-German Military Collaboration During the Weimar Republic," *AHR* 63, no. 3 (1958): 565–97.

[10]See, for example, Gatzke's reviews of Ludwig Dehio, *Deutschland und die Weltpolitik im 20. Jahrhundert* (Frankfurt-am-Main, 1955), *JCEA* 16 (1956): 302–303; Klemens von Klemperer, *Germany's New Conservatism* (Princeton, 1957), *AHR* 63 (1958): 124–25; Ludwig Zimmermann, *Deutsche Aussenpolitik in der Ära der Weimarer Republik* (Göttingen, 1958), *JCEA* 19 (1959): 458; Herbert Helbig, *Die Träger der Rapallo-Politik* (Göttingen, 1958), *AHR* (1960): 590–91; Erich Matthias and Rudolf Morsey, eds., *Das Ende der Parteien* (Düsseldorf, 1960), *AHR* 66 (1961):1036–37; Edward Bennett, *Germany and the Diplomacy of the Financial Crisis 1931* (Cambridge, Mass., 1962), *JCEA* 23 (1963): 118–19; Walther Hubatsch, *Germany and the Central Powers in the World War, 1914–1919* (Lawrence, Kans., 1963), *JMH* 36 (1964): 101; Andreas Dorpalen, *Hindenburg and the Weimar Republic* (Princeton, 1974), *AHR* 70 (1965): 774–76; Walter Laqueur, *Russia and Germany* (London, 1965), *Jahrbücher für Geschichte Osteuropas* 14 (1966): 607–608; Gerald Feldman, *Army, Industry, and Labor in Germany* (Princeton, 1966), *AHR* 72 (1967): 622.

[11]William L. Langer, *An Encyclopedia of World History,* rev. with the assistance of Hans W. Gatzke. (Boston, 1952); Hans W. Gatzke, "Europa und der Völkerbund," *Propyläen Weltgeschichte* (Berlin, 1960), 9:311–50.

As a graduate teacher Gatzke has upheld the highest standards of the profession. His seminars are stimulating laboratories of historical investigation in which German history and European diplomacy are cast in a truly international perspective. Sharing his judgment and scholarly experience, he cites works of quality and urges his students to master their subject by exhaustive research and analysis. He has directed his doctoral students in a broad range of subjects, encouraging their independence, providing generous assistance when necessary, and taking pride in their original, creative work.

Two major texts evolved from his undergraduate lectures. The first, published in 1957, is *The Present in Perspective,* a topical study of world history since 1945.[12] The second is a collaborative work on the history of Western civilization, first published in 1961.[13] Despite the remarkable inflation in numbers of textbooks of the 1960s and 1970s and their dramatically rapid demise, Gatzke's *Mainstream of Civilization,* periodically revised and updated, remains a popular and highly respected work.[14] Its objective presentation, excellent organization and illustrations, and attention to the student's perspective make it a valuable teaching tool and a sound beginning for the serious student of history.

When Hajo Holborn died in 1969, Gatzke succeeded him as American coeditor of the "Quadripartite Project," an international commission of American, French, British, and German historians established in 1960 with headquarters in Bonn, charged with editing and publishing the German diplomatic documents of the period 1918 to 1945. Gatzke has provided an account of the difficulties that beset the project: geographical distances, personnel changes, financial limitations, personality

[12]Chicago; 1957; 2d ed., 1961; 3d ed., 1965.
[13]Joseph Strayer, Hans W. Gatzke, and E. Harris Harbison, *The Course of Civilization* (New York, 1961).
[14]J. R. Strayer, Hans W. Gatzke, E. H. Harbison, and E. L. Dunbaugh, *The Mainstream of Civilization* (New York, 1969; 2d ed., with Strayer and Harbison, 1974; 3d and 4th eds., with Strayer, 1979, 1984).

clashes, and other obstacles.[15] This account reflects Gatzke's approach to historical problems. He weighed the difficulties, praised those who tried to surmount them, but did not shrink from judging candidly the unpleasantness and failures which dogged the project from the beginning. Despite the frustrations the volumes in the *Akten zur deutschen auswärtigen Politik* are notable for their meticulous selection, editing, and organization, and the project represented the fruition of international collaboration in what once was "a major battle-ground for nationalist passions and prejudices."[16]

Primarily a traditional political and diplomatic historian, Gatzke possesses a special sensitivity that ferrets out problems, weaknesses, and concealments. In his introduction to the collection *European Diplomacy Between Two Wars, 1919–1939,* he stated bluntly that Weimar Germany's revisionist policy, despite the sympathy it stimulated abroad, was a major cause of postwar instability.[17] His interests in biography and in the Third Reich led to his investigation of psychohistory and to his forceful, undoubtedly painful critique of the study of Adolf Hitler in wartime by Langer's psychiatrist brother.[18] Gatzke insisted that, whatever its merits, psychohistory must not stray from the facts or embellish its data.

---

[15]"The Quadripartite Project: *Akten zur deutschen auswärtigen Politik, 1918–1945:* Experiment in International Historiography," in Alexander Fischer, Gunter Moltmann, and Klaus Schwabe, eds., *Russland-Deutschland-Amerika: Festschrift für Fritz T. Epstein zum 80. Geburtstag* (Wiesbaden, 1978), pp. 333–41.

[16]Ibid., p. 341.

[17]Hans W. Gatzke, ed., *European Diplomacy Between Two Wars, 1919–1939* (Chicago, 1971), pp. 7–12.

[18]Hans W. Gatzke, "Hitler and Psychohistory," review of Walter Langer, *The Mind of Adolf Hitler: The Secret Wartime Report* (New York, 1972), and Reply, *AHR* 78, nos. 2, 4 (1974): 394–401, 1161–63. Gatzke's views of Hitler and the Nazi period can be traced in his reviews of H. R. Trevor-Roper, *The Last Days of Hitler* (New York, 1947), *AHR* 53; no. 3 (1948):606–607; Albert Speer, *Inside the Third Reich: Memoirs,* trans. Richard and Clara Winston (New York, 1970), *AHR* 76, no. 5 (1971): 1562–63; Norman Rich, *Hitler's War Aims: Ideology, the Nazi State, and the Course of Expansion* (New York, 1973), *PSQ* 88, no. 4 (1973): 765–66; Robert Payne, *The Life and Death of Adolf Hitler* (New York, 1973), *AHR* 79; no. 1 (1974): 178–79; Werner Maser, *Hitler: Legend, Myth, and Reality,* trans. Peter

While Clio's couch was filled in the 1970s with compelling subjects like Hitler, Gatzke steadfastly maintained his methodological principles, working primarily from documentary sources, rarely appropriating theories from other disciplines, and continuing to offer new information and new interpretations based on solid, painstaking research and written in clear, precise language. His book reviews, models of cogent analysis, contribute unbiased appraisals of new work and encouragement to young and mature scholars alike.[19]

Inevitably Gatzke turned his scholarly attention to German-American relations.[20] In *Germany and the United States: A Special Relationship?* published in 1980, he completed a long-standing commission from Harvard University Press for its American Foreign Policy series. In this book, written for the general reader as well as for the scholar, Gatzke reviewed his own roots as well as the ties between the two nations and drew on his scholarship, experiences, and years of reflection. His thorough investigation of German history, politics, and culture complements an original study of over two centuries of German-American relations. *Germany and the United States* displays those qualities that have marked Gatzke's work from the beginning: political acumen tempered by restraint and witty common sense.

---

and Betty Ross (New York, 1973), *AHR* 79; no. 4 (1974): 1205–1206; Joachim C. Fest, *Hitler: Eine Biographie* (Berlin, 1973), *AHR* 80, no. 4 (1975): 1001–1002; Dietrich Orlow, *The History of the Nazi Party: 1933–1945* (Pittsburgh, Pa., 1973), *AHR* 79; no. 2 (1974): 525–26; Jens Peterson, *Hitler-Mussolini: Die Entstehung der Achse Berlin-Rom, 1933–36* (Tübingen, 1973), *AHR* 79, no. 3 (1974): 779.

[19]See especially the reviews of Wilhelm Deist, ed., *Militär und Innenpolitik im Weltkrieg, 1914–1918* (Düsseldorf, 1970), *CEH* 5 (September 1972): 278–83; Hans Mommsen et al., eds., *Industrielles System und politische Entwicklung in der Weimarer Republik* (Düsseldorf, 1974), *AHR* 81, no. 5 (December 1976): 1149–50; Roland Stromberg, *Redemption by War: The Intellectuals and 1914* (Lawrence, Kans., 1982), *Historian* 46, no. 1 (November, 1983): 110–11.

[20]See Hans W. Gatzke, "The United States and Germany," *Current History* 38 (1960): 6–10; Hans W. Gatzke, "The United States and Germany on the Eve of World War I," in Imanuel Geiss and Bernd J. Wendt, eds., *Deutschland in der Weltpolitik des 19. Jahrhunderts* (Düsseldorf, 1973), pp. 271–86.

Readers of his latest book will find objective analysis of all the major historiographical debates in German history; fine pen portraits of German and American leaders; excellent balance in political, social, economic, and cultural history; and an exceptionally useful survey of the German Democratic Republic, the "other Germany," since 1945. Gatzke treats such contemporary issues as West Germany's foreign workers, its political radicals, and its evolving policy toward the Soviet bloc with the skill and acuity of a close observer of Bonn's past and present.[21]

From imperial Germany in 1915 to the Nazi state, from America in Depression and war to the expanding, occasionally violent sixties and seventies, from defeated and occupied Germany to a stable and prosperous West German Republic, Hans Gatzke has experienced the achievements and conflicts of two great nations in the twentieth century. With his work and ideals he serves as eloquent witness to his age. As an individual he radiates courage, critical discernment, and unselfish giving in his teaching and scholarship, which have been an inspiration to his friends, students, and colleagues.

[21]In his reviews of Hans-Jürgen Grabbe, *Unionsparteien, Sozialdemokratie und Vereinigte Staaten von Amerika, 1945-1966* (Düsseldorf, 1983); and Gordon D. Drummond, *The German Social Democratic Party in Opposition, 1949-1960: The Case Against Rearmament* (Norman, Okla., 1982), *JMH* 56 (September 1984): 562-64, Gatzke comments on the formative years of the West German Federal Republic as well as Bonn's place in the Western alliance.

The Contributors

CHARLES BRIGHT (Associate Professor, University of Michigan, Ann Arbor) is a diplomatic historian with a special interest in theories of the state, the subject of a book he recently coedited (with Susan Harding), *Statemaking and Social Movements: Essays in History and Theory.*

LAMAR CECIL (Professor, Washington and Lee University, Lexington, Virginia) is a leading scholar of the Wilhelmian period, author of *Albert Ballin: Business and Politics in Imperial Germany, 1888–1918* and *The German Diplomatic Service, 1871–1914.* He is currently working on a biography of Kaiser William II.

CAROLE FINK (Professor, University of North Carolina—Wilmington) is a European diplomatic historian specializing in the interwar years. She has published *The Genoa Conference: European Diplomacy, 1921–1922,* and translated and written the introduction to Marc Bloch's *Memoirs of War, 1914–15.*

ERICH J. C. HAHN (Associate Professor, University of Western Ontario, London, Ontario), for a number of years assistant editor of *Akten zur deutschen auswärtigen Politik,* has published several articles on nineteenth- and twentieth-century Germany in the *American Historical Review, Journal of Modern History,* and *Central European History.*

ISABEL V. HULL (Associate Professor, Cornell University, Ithaca, New York,) is a specialist in modern German history and the author of a study of pre–World War I decision making, *The Entourage of Kaiser Wilhelm II.*

EDWARD D. KEETON, author of a much-cited Yale dissertation on Aristide Briand, is a diplomat, currently attached to NATO in Brussels.

MACGREGOR KNOX (Associate Professor, University of Rochester) is a comparative historian of modern Italy and Germany who specializes in political and military affairs and the author of *Mussolini Unleashed, 1939–1941: Politics and Strategy in Fascist Italy's Last War.*

HERBERT S. LEVINE (Professor, Freie Universität-Berlin), writes on German-Jewish history and is the author of *Hitler's Free City: A History of the Nazi Party in Danzig, 1925–39.*

WILLIAMSON MURRAY (Associate Professor, Ohio State University, Columbus) specializes in strategic studies of pre–World War II Europe. He is the author of *Strategy for Defeat: The Luftwaffe 1933–1945* and *The Change in the European Balance of Power, 1938–1939: The Path to Ruin.*

ANNELISE THIMME (Professor, University of Alberta, Edmonton), a historian of modern German politics and culture, is known for her research on the German National People's party (*Flucht in den Mythos: Die Deutschnationale Volkspartei und die Niederlage von 1918*), on the historian Hans Delbrück (*Hans Delbrück als Kritiker der Wilhelminischen Epoche*), and on Gustav Stresemann (*Gustav Stresemann: eine politische Biographie zur Geschichte der Weimarer Republik*).

Index

JUN 1986

German Nationalism and the European Response, 1890–1945,

designed by Bill Cason, was set in various sizes of Times Roman by Superior Type and printed offset on 60 lb. Glatfelter by Cushing-Malloy, Inc., with case binding by John H. Dekker & Sons.

CONNETQUOT PUBLIC LIBRARY

0621 9100 401 446 1

943.08
GER

German nationalism
and the European
response, 1890-
1945

DATE			

CONNETQUOT PUBLIC LIBRARY
760 OCEAN AVENUE
BOHEMIA, NEW YORK 11716

© THE BAKER & TAYLOR CO.